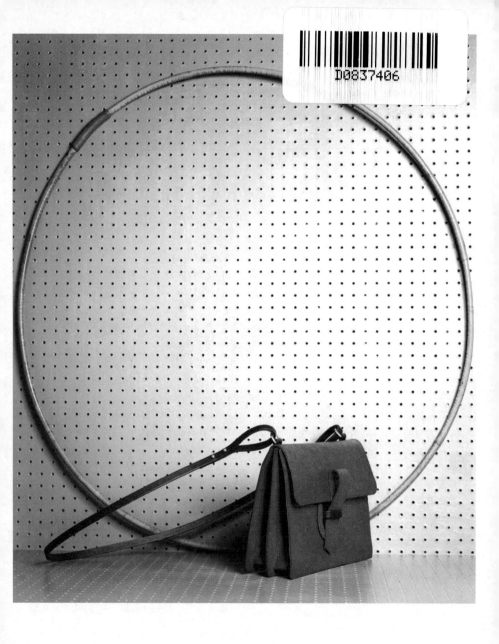

# Lizzy Disney

lizzydisney.co.uk

D0837406

# GRANTA

12 Addison Avenue, London W11 4QR | email editorial@granta.com
To subscribe go to www.granta.com, or call 845-267-3031 (toll-free 866-438-6150)
in the United States, 020 8955 7011 in the United Kingdom

## ISSUE 129: AUTUMN 2014

| | |
|---|---|
| PUBLISHER AND EDITOR | Sigrid Rausing |
| MANAGING EDITOR | Yuka Igarashi |
| ONLINE AND POETRY EDITOR | Rachael Allen |
| DESIGNER | Daniela Silva |
| EDITORIAL ASSISTANTS | Luke Neima, Francisco Vilhena |
| MARKETING AND SUBSCRIPTIONS | David Robinson |
| PUBLICITY | Aidan O'Neill |
| TO ADVERTISE CONTACT | Kate Rochester, katerochester@granta.com |
| FINANCE | Morgan Graver |
| SALES | Iain Chapple, Katie Hayward |
| IT MANAGER | Mark Williams |
| PRODUCTION ASSOCIATE | Sarah Wasley |
| PROOFS | David Atkinson, Katherine Fry |
| | Louise Scothern, Vimbai Shire |
| CONTRIBUTING EDITORS | Daniel Alarcón, Anne Carson, Mohsin Hamid, Isabel Hilton, A.M. Homes, Janet Malcolm, Adam Nicolson, Edmund White |

This selection copyright © 2014 Granta Publications.

Granta, ISSN 173231, is published four times a year by Granta Publications, 12 Addison Avenue, London W11 4QR, United Kingdom.

The US annual subscription price is $48. Airfreight and mailing in the USA by agent named Air Business Ltd, c/o Worldnet-Shipping USA Inc., 156–15 146th Avenue, 2nd Floor, Jamaica, NY 11434, USA. Periodicals postage paid at Jamaica NY 11431.

US Postmaster: Send address changes to Granta, Air Business Ltd, c/o Worldnet-Shipping USA Inc., 156–15 146th Avenue, 2nd Floor, Jamaica, NY 11434, USA.

Subscription records are maintained at Granta, c/o Abacus e-Media, Chancery Exchange, 10 Furnival Street, London EC4A 1AH.

Air Business Ltd is acting as our mailing agent.

Granta is printed and bound in Italy by Legoprint. This magazine is printed on paper that fulfils the criteria for 'Paper for permanent document' according to ISO 9706 and the American Library Standard ANSI/NIZO Z39.48-1992 and has been certified by the Forest Stewardship Council (FSC). Granta is indexed in the American Humanities Index.

ISBN 978-1-905-881-83-3

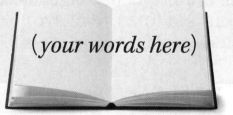

(*your words here*)

There's a long history of writing women
(*writers*) off. It's time to right that wrong,
to get relevant not relegated.

**Visualizing** is for the work. **Galvanizing**
is for getting the work out there. We can
see your words here. So can publishers,
agents + scholars. **Can you?**

Until it's just about the art.
**Submit your literary work now.**

PEN + BRUSH

# There are many ways to subscribe to Index on Censorship magazine

**Subscriptions available to UK and US**

Online only £18 (or equivalent in local currency)
Print subscription £31/$57

Buy a single issue for just £7.99
(Also available on **amazon**)

## Find out more:
email: subscriptions@sagepub.co.uk,
call: +44 (0)20 7342 8701 or
visit: indexoncensorship.org/subscribe

# CONTENTS

# Introduction

The last time I wrote about fate was in an article for the *Guardian* on addiction, two years ago: 'There is some evidence for a genetic disposition,' I wrote, 'but it's not straightforward. Genes do not map out one's fate; they map out possibilities of fates.' But perhaps, as in the classic fate narratives, I am deluding myself, blithely unaware of how narrow our choices are, how genetically and socially predetermined our lives.

The pieces in this issue are concerned with fate in its most serious manifestations: love, sexuality, identity, death, illness, religion and war. We have new writers, S.J. Naudé and Sam Coll, alongside established ones, Will Self, Cynthia Ozick, Louise Erdrich, Tim Winton and Kent Haruf. We are publishing four poems, by Mark Doty, Adam Fitzgerald, Barbara Ras and Mary Ruefle, chosen by our new poetry editor, Rachael Allen.

We also have a piece by a writer long since dead: an essay on Sarajevo by Joseph Roth, written in 1923, translated here by Michael Hofmann. Given the centenary, I wanted something in the issue about 1914 and the war that was supposed to end all wars. We read Roth's description of Sarajevo, aware that he is thinking backwards, to the war, while we think forwards, to the second war, to the Bosnian war, to the atrocities and the occupation. That hidden kernel of the future, our knowledge of what is to come, speaks to fate.

The issue is not all serious – the extract from Miranda July's forthcoming novel is genuinely funny and so, in its own way, is the piece by new Irish writer Sam Coll – but it's probably true that the tenor of this issue is melancholy rather than light-hearted. Thus Cynthia Ozick's captivating new story describes the tragic fate of the illegitimate daughter of a Jewish trader in ancient Greece. 'Domain', our lead story by Louise Erdrich, is about life after death in a hyper-digital age, written with the deft and warped veracity of all great science fiction. Will Self channels J.G. Ballard's last days in a surreal and poignant meditation typed on Ballard's own typewriter. Tim

Winton writes movingly about his fear of hospitals. S.J. Naudé, the other new writer in the issue, describes a former nurse going for Aids training in the South African outback. Naudé writes in Afrikaans, but like many Afrikaans speakers he is bilingual, and translates himself into English. There is something reminiscent of J.M. Coetzee in his language, and in the vision of the fate of South Africa, hanging in the balance.

When I thought about this theme I felt that the contemporary discourse on sexual and gender identity must be part of it. Here, writer and academic Andrea Stuart describes, for the first time, her own transition to lesbianism. Her story is a measured defence of preference over destiny, of fluidity and of experimentation.

The transgender discourse has taken much of its narrative frame from the gay rights movement. Mark Gevisser is a South African writer, who is working on a project researching the Global Sexuality Frontier for the Open Society Foundations. We met and talked about the rise of transgender identity. It seems to me – Mark I think only partially agrees with this – that the idea of the simple structural opposite (the boy inside the girl's body, the girl inside the boy's body) might be temporal and fleeting, and that we don't yet quite know how the model of gender identity will settle. But we do know that in at least some circles in America the gender you are born with is no longer assumed to be the gender you are destined to live.

The issue ends with Kent Haruf describing how, against significant odds, he became a writer. It is in some ways a narrative of anti-fatalism, or at least a story of self-determination – a good ending, I thought, and an oblique answer, if we need one, to the question of fate. ■

Sigrid Rausing

© KAZUO YOSHIDA
*Air Blue*, 2012

# DOMAIN

## *Louise Erdrich*

### Asphodel

Seven corporations control the afterlife now, and many people spend their lives amassing the money to upload into the best. Others, like me, assume they will need a scholarship and pile up experiences. I piled up one too many. Shortly after my fall, I applied to Asphodel. I knew of course that this particular domain, or afterlife provider, was run by the oldest entity in the business. Asphodel was known to have the most secure and complete terrain. It was the first choice of artists, poets, academics, even famous politicians and movie stars. Teachers always chose Asphodel if they could afford it, and I was a teacher before my accident. I knew some parents who'd had to upload a child under grievous circumstances, and who chose Asphodel for the schools and the reliable surrogacy. For one other specific reason, too, Asphodel was most attractive to me. As a consequence, that first morning I was so nervous about the interview process that I refused pain medication. I wanted to be mentally sharp. As I was wheeled along the corridor, past the swooping black characters glazed into the hospital tiles, I thought I might have made a mistake. The pain was that distracting. But as soon as the questions began, I regained my concentration.

The interviewer was a square red cube sitting in the middle of the room on a stainless-steel table.

Your name?

Bernadette.

Named for the saint?

Yes.

Any other associations?

My mother was a Catholic and a theologian. She was chosen by the Church and completely subsidized, her understanding was that valuable. Since she was uploaded, gratis, we have communicated every day. But I chose Asphodel because I do not share her system of symbols. I was not raised in the formality of her religion, and find comfort in literature.

I smoothly volunteered that my father had chosen a premature upload before they were outlawed, and that his decision had been secured since then. I gave his name and effortlessly moved on. The cube did not react. My practice had paid off.

Where did you grow up?

North Dakota.

Do you mind if we scan?

No.

I closed my eyes, dizzy, and requested additional oxygen. As deliberately as I could, using the training my mother had insisted on since I was young, I called up a series of images. These began when I was about five years old. They were detailed, visual, aural, descriptive, emotional, as concrete as I could possibly manage. I remembered the wooden front steps of our house, the paint worn off the risers to show grey wood. The temperature of the wood in every season. The green of Virginia creeper, the leaves fluttering off the porch in summer wind, stiff with morning dew, half wilted in full sun. The tiny knuckles of the vines clutching the wire of the screens. The lobes of lilacs. The scent. The sour green balls of new grapes and the heavy, peeling, brown loops of grapevines. And from the front steps the horizon and the sky. My mother had coached me to memorize the sky every morning and evening. I used the sky as my masking image – you could not get through it to the bad thing that had happened. The sky was my protection. I could pass through years of sky, a slide show of sky, endless mental snapshots. A thousand skies and a thousand more. I went through them at a leisurely pace, skipping no small detail. The sky had always been my favourite mental exercise, and one that, I now hoped, would increase my value for Asphodel.

Impressive.

The interviewer changed to a thoughtful maroon red and quit the scan.

You were coached?

By my mother.

Memory games as a child?

Yes.

The pain was becoming difficult to ignore. It was taking some attention.

An unusually pure visual memory. The best I have encountered. Your mother did her job well.

She knew that the chances were slim that we would ever have the means to afford Asphodel.

The interviewer agreed, a quiet yellow tinge.

And then, this.

Yes.

Can you describe the accident?

Well, I was climbing. I climb buildings.

Free climbing. It is . . . not exactly illegal.

No. But I was trespassing.

A small matter. We will not take that into consideration.

I was climbing the Guthrie Theater here in Minneapolis, where my father's play was performed this year.

Yes, we know about your father.

The pain was, suddenly, nearly overwhelming. I began to breathe deeply, explosively, but could not help crying out.

What is it?

My legs, you know, everything.

Yes, said the interviewer, you're broken. But you have a good chance for some limited capacity, enough to survive. You could have a life. A life here. Are you sure you want to . . . ?

Yes, yes, as soon as possible. Now.

So they came with the fentanyl and scheduled the upload for the next day.

## Neural cascade

You say goodbye to your body very carefully. The toenails you've clipped and polished, the vulnerable instep, the ankles and shins you've barked, the sometimes unreliable knees, the calves you've shared, thighs your lover has grazed his hand along and inside, goodbye to the dark of you, the brilliant unshattering or ravelling that seemed at one time the way your spirit also travelled, outward, everywhere, beginning from the heated core. Goodbye to gut that pinched with hunger or split with gas, goodbye to asshole and nervous sphincter that permitted a loud fart when you laughed in a movie on your first date. Goodbye to vagina, wait, goodbye again to black, brown, purple, gold, mauve, red, bleeding leaves of skin, vulva, and stubborn fickle clitoris that maddened with indifference or was whiplash-sensitive – goodbye. Goodbye old uterus, old love, old capacious fist, and goodbye outraged liver. Goodbye sweet lungs with your faint bubbling black carcinogenic lace and your amazed resilience, and heart, dearest heart. So long pumps. Goodbye throat licked and suave collarbone in a low-cut black sheath, and arms that held and clung to other arms and other edifices, arms and legs that climbed and back I never really saw. Breasts always in the way. Nipples. Hands, oh my hands, piano-player hands. Hands that grasped and pulled and slapped and touched so tenderly beyond my appetite. Hands of my appetite, goodbye. Ears, neck, earlobes and mouth of a million golden tastes and mouth that knew food of every type and tastes of all description but above all things mouth, goodbye, and goodbye tongue, that loved the kisses and also the body of my husband. I do not have to say goodbye to my eyes. I'll still see. And in fact I will feel the feelings of all parts of my body. I will feel the eidetic past. But the broken body I am leaving behind will be recycled for parts and then sold for remaining mineral content. Even the physical brain, soon transferred, neural file by file, molecule by molecule, into the liqui-chip. A dumb lump of fat will remain.

The holes will be drilled tomorrow. The liquid memory slowly introduced to the still-living brain. The software drug binds and copies as it eats the living memory. The drug contains a disciplined virus that takes instructions and is formulated to mimic and store consciousness – here is the beauty, the complexity – store the individual consciousness in a form that can be siphoned from the brain when loading is complete and then absorbed by Charon. She, the program, is the reader of my life text who will transfer me into the field.

Last night, before I went to sleep, I had the nurse access my mother and push the screen up close to my face so that we could talk. She had chosen to be old and reassuring, lined and pallid, with a sweetness in her face I can only remember rarely in earthly life. We talked and talked.

Mama, what will it feel like? Will it hurt?

You'll be all right.

All right like in childbirth? All right after I'm ripped apart?

Her face slackened. She didn't want to say. But she loves me, and she did.

The virus cannot accomplish its task without your full alertness. You'll feel it all. Old emotions. Every pain and pleasure. Every fuck-up and every fear. Only fast and furious. You will believe you are going mad. (They do not read you because they do not find readings during the process reliable, so don't worry, they won't see anything.) Still, it is a drowning. Some don't surface, it is true. But you will come back, I promise. Remember, I made you strong. What helps is to find an image. Something to hold on to.

We stared at each other for a long time. Her face kept flickering through the many ages and personae she'd assumed. Her face would not be the image I'd hold on to. I needed something more solid.

Pick him, she said, suddenly, softly.

I thought at first she meant my husband, or my son, though his image is inaccessible. But she didn't. And now I saw it in her face.

I know why you're choosing his domain.

Her voice trembled, a whisper.

And she was right. The one uncontaminated truth. My father, my changeless hatred. I'd hold on to him.

Fasten your seat belt, it's going to be a bumpy ride.

Are you kidding?

I'm not good with reassurance, said the uploader. But you're lucky. You're going to a good place.

The technicians put me in a flexangle, a hard gel that closes around you up to the chin. When I was immobilized, the woman picked up the drill.

You're going to feel this. Everybody feels it. Try thinking past it.

While you can still think, said the other.

They try to introduce the liquid as slowly and gently as possible, but at a certain point it saturates. By then the virus is moving quickly, humming along, sparking and devouring, capturing, destroying. From the first instant, I know that I cannot endure it for another instant, even to gain eternal life. And then I do endure it. I go on. I have his face in focus for a moment, here and there, but then he changes and I just hold on to the hate.

I whip around it like a pole. I fly off it like a flag. That hatred, planted in calcareous shit, gets me through the first part. But then it wilts and at the base of it is love.

# Field of asphodel

They let my body stay where it was for the hours it took the system to read me, and then for me to focus my new eyes. The results are better when you get to see the technicians put away your old carcass, apparently, because I saw them do me. Oh, they were respectful enough, took the tubes out without yanking. But I could see well enough so that I could tell my body had stiffened a bit already and I'd shat myself all the way up my back straight out of my diaper.

Well, never again.

I have a new body now and it's made of thought.

When I arrived in Asphodel, I was placed in the transition program, a cross between purgatory and a hospital, a quiet, calm place where my task was to understand the entity that I would now be, forever. Here, the siphoners come to pick and choose what they want to add to their domain. Using human memory they are building a complex and ordered world that replicates and outdoes the first one, into which we are all born. Asphodel is the deepest and most thoroughly finished, but there are still gaps in its reality, places, even in the transition program, where the tiles quit or go rubbery when they are actually ceramic or where the windows contain the wrong light for the hour of the day. But the personnel are fully integrated and know not to change too drastically while you are looking at them, which is something I cannot do when I first arrive.

Remember, your appearance reflects your every mood, thought, emotion, says a silky woman. Her hand is on my arm. She has given her hand just the right amount of warmth and my own memory of skin blooms in response.

Like right now, master it, master it, she croons. Yes, yes, you may take a deep breath. The infinite microbiocircuitry that is now you will remember what it was to take a deep breath and your brain, or the superfile of your brain, will remember it too. Take a deep breath. Your fear is purple. Your appearance.

I'm a cloud, I say, looking down at my legs. Insubstantial as a cloud. And I'm still in pain. The fuck! I'm still in pain!

Wait, she says, calm yourself and take a deep breath.

I do. The pain is gone.

And remember how your legs feel. Your workout two days before your fall.

Yes.

I look down. My legs are perfect. I am naked.

What were you wearing?

What the hell? Maybe I was wearing a low-necked black cocktail dress.

Now you're cooking! Her voice is delighted. I smell egg, onions, mushrooms frying in butter, and my mouth waters.

I think I'm hungry.

Yes, you're hungry. And you're going to eat. And if you concentrate fully on what you are eating, it will be the best thing you've ever tasted.

So how to find him. How to kill him. How to savagely or subtly murder my father in a world where there isn't any death?

I look into the mirrored wall as I am wondering this and my face is faecal, feral, frantic, fraught, festering. No facade.

I work then for months (the sun comes up here, the sun goes down) on my control. Then one day I ask how we get places. I am now, because this is how everyone begins, right where I left off. I am in Minneapolis and have my apartment. But my skies in North Dakota and any other useful memories have been added, painstakingly, to the deeply convincing fabric of this world.

How do I get places? I ask my guide.

We have a marvellous transportation system. Very real. You can book flights almost anywhere now, take trains, whatever you want. Or you can scroll.

Can you teach me to do that?

Nobody can teach it.

How does it work? What happens?

Lucid dreaming. You teach yourself to dream yourself wherever you want to be. You have to learn how to stay conscious in your dream, but not to wake up. You don't want to drop yourself.

And people? Can I look someone up from my past?

Of course, once you've got the hang of it. But it will be hard to tell whether you're accessing the actual person or just your memory of the person.

I feel funny asking this, I say, but something occurred to me.

Ask anyway.

Is there any way out of here? Do people exit? Leave? Are they ever expelled?

She turns bright pink. An orange bubble bursts from her lips. She laughs in surprise.

No, she says, of course not, that never happens, except . . .

Her eyes go black. Her face and arms fade into the wall. I can see through her. It is as though she's made of tissue and her voice is faint.

It is rare. Yet people have been erased by other people here, she says. Then she readjusts. She's solid and rosy.

But does it take enormous strength of will to do something like that, I say, and time and control?

Of course, she says, her voice a whisper. Shock. There was an assassin sent many years ago, I heard, from a former life. He caught the victim completely unaware. Threw him into shock so he just – she laughs at the ridiculous act there is no other word for – deleted himself.

## The library

My father has become the library. He will be dangerous to enter. In his time, he was a leading playwright and scholar. But his childhood memories of the library were most interesting to Asphodel, and he has been hard at work constructing this new library ever since he entered Asphodel. His childhood library still exists in the small town where he grew up, a sweet old county library made of red sandstone with brass handles on the doors and a great oak desk, stained dark, where the books are checked out and returned. He remembered every inch of it, and more, he remembered every library he had studied in as a young man, and older, as he became the kind of person who used libraries exclusively and bought real books of the old kind, made of paper and print and glue. He knew the smell of them and the weight of them and the texture of their covers. What books he didn't know he could imagine in convincing detail. Every book in the world has long been auto-scanned into our universe and so it only takes the proper thought, an operational thought, to fill those tangible but empty ciphers of books with words. This, then, is my father's work. The library is his mind. He is filling it with an infinite number of books he can play in, hide in, which he can be part of whenever he chooses. To murder him in that library may be impossible, but it must be done. I have to surprise him to death. Make him completely vulnerable and open. His mind must be utterly relaxed so that when I strike he cannot deflect the blow. And the blow, it must be true and final. He cannot be erased by increments, but just like that. One blow. One instant. He must reverse. Blow up. Disintegrate. Delete.

## Inevitable

Of course it comes back, in the night when all the monitors are off and I am a shifting flame that does not burn. That is the other attraction of Asphodel. The contract stipulates night privacy. No dream siphoning. A freedom resembling the real earth freedom to retain an unknowable existence, an unconsciousness, that cannot be tapped. Asphodel's cheaper sister, The Meadows, mines the unconscious. There are many who do not care or never notice this intrusion, but I would. I love my sleep now, my nothingness, my unnecessary dream life. I would not technically have to sleep at all in Asphodel, but I choose sleep, as do most people (though not my father, it is reported). I love sleep because now that I am immortal it is my only way to experience relief from consciousness.

I also love sleep because my son comes back to me. He visits often now in dreams. His image has become accessible. He was six years old, the tenderest age, a mop of fine, heavy, brown-gold hair like his father's (mine is black, short, coarse, when I am in default appearance). I used to put my cheek to his hair when he came in flushed from playing outside and I breathed in the avid October cold of cold boy. He was always moving, quitless, bumbling and exuberant. When sad, he was cast down, inconsolable. He died in the care of my father and my father let him go, did not make the essential call that would have allowed him, my son, to be with me now. My father waited until it was too late to salvage him. He did this because of his religious certainty.

My father's plays were about the need for death, the unthought consequences of immortality. The moral human was the human with the courage to really die and stay dead. Ten years after the real death of my son, my father chose, as I've said, to voluntarily end his physical life and upload into Asphodel. He was in perfect health. He had simply changed his mind. He considered his talents, his genius, his knowledge, too valuable to risk the loss. It was a considered leap which for years he had persuaded many to resist.

My son is gone. But he visits me in dreams.

## Some travel

To leave the vicinity of my father and perfect my skills, I travel. I can scroll now. I am in Barcelona on Las Ramblas, the great strolling avenue leading to the ocean. Composed of combined memory, people appear and disappear much the way they always did, crowds passing, mimes in exquisite costumes poised until a coin is dropped before them. One, a dark lady in a magnificent grey gown, wearing grey face paint, black hair, black flowers, appears to be sleeping, head slightly cocked. Her crown is a black serpent coiled and poised to strike above her brow. I drop my coin and her eyes open slowly, great black pooling eyes. She reaches incrementally for my hand and kisses my fingers tenderly, caresses my wrist, in languid slow motion lets my fingers go and drifts back into her slumber. The snake is real. Its tongue flickers, scarlet, curious.

I know that some uploaded tourist remembered her in great detail and placed her here, but with a live snake, artful. Others have remembered the Gaudí buildings and Park Güell, the Mercury Fountain and the desperate sellers of roses – Pakistani illegals who haunt the restaurants with ravaged eyes. When I buy a rose from one man, he says, *remember me,* and I know that in someone else's life on real Earth this man said the same thing and his bleak eyes were fixed in someone's consciousness so that although he has surely not acquired the means to enter an afterlife himself and has died the real death with billions of other humans, this rose seller will live in this particular corporation's version of the city of Barcelona, whispering, forever, *remember me.*

I scroll across the world twice, I visit places I'd always wanted to see. Only, there is no reliable 'in-between' yet. There is no world but the world brought back within many individual consciousnesses and reconstructed out of fragments of experience.

## Waking

I used to love taking naps on early-spring afternoons before the leaves had budded out, when the air was bright and cool. I would lie on my back with my aching legs on a pillow and pull over me a down comforter, a gift from my mother. As I woke I would allow my consciousness to drift back into my body. There would always be, first, the sword of grief, which I would allow to stake me to the mattress, but then as my waking awareness increased and I felt where my flesh ended and the soft bedclothes and pillows began, a soft shudder of ecstasy would fill me and with each breath increase and subside, subside and increase, until at last I opened my eyes. I do this now, whenever I wake, only now I do this for what may be hours, for time on this side of things is not sidereal and relentless. Time is gentle. We are flowers. Opening and closing as we respond to the temperature and the light of our thoughts. And when I do assume my body and my awareness, and when I do decide where to go, what I would like to do, my actions add to the texture of this world so that everything I do here has a purpose. The layering of consciousness upon consciousness makes, for instance, a beautiful park steadier, more palpable, more enjoyable to others. This is a thing we did unknowingly, perhaps, on the other side, but it is so important here that we all have work; every moment of our existence is creation for others to enjoy, an occupation that was once called art; we are all artists on this side.

When I murder my father, that moment will create a rip in the fabric of time. Like art, it will jar the past, pierce the future.

## The card

In order to use the library, you must apply for a card. The program set up to process the request is tall and pleasant. She is neither young nor old, and gazes wisely over the oak counter with its dull green blotter. She wears small wire-rim glasses. Her hair is brown, streaked with grey, rolled back in a chignon. She wears a dress of brown-and-white checks. In a low voice, she requests my identification, and then bends over slightly to copy my name onto a blue library card. I have used my mother's name most of my adult life, and it is a common surname. I am hoping my introduction into the system will be unremarked. I watch the program write my name in lovely, old-fashioned D'Nealian script and I wonder if the pleasant librarian is my father. He can take any form in the library; however, this processing of cards is painstaking and a little silly. Beneath him, I would think. A waste of his time which although infinite is still *his*. The blue piece of cardboard is handed back to me, a rectangle with rounded edges. I will have to present this card each time I take out a book, a detail meant to be charming. The librarian is changing the date on her rubber stamp and re-inking the felt pad in its metal case as I leave. My father has made each detail – astounding work. I want so badly to examine the books. I am so curious about the editions, the design, the paper, the typefaces, all that he has added to the veracity of his world. But I continue on out the door, down the broad stone steps, because I do not want to come across him accidentally. Even though I have chosen an entirely different form today, I do not want *him* to surprise *me*.

## The brick

I practise my disguise. I will be his mother to whom he was deeply attached. My grandmother, a woman vivid in my memory, a woman lost to real death, as was her belief. She was deer-like and gentle and softly silent. I call her up, I conjure her, I become her. An olive-green dress. Sweet brown eyes, whitely faded hair. And then in an instant I shift and become myself. I have a weapon, of course, to compound the shock and throw my father into the reflex cascade that will end him. It will be the same object that ended my son's life. A falling brick. Tumbling unknown off a workman's scaffolding. My father carried Edan to the side of the churchyard and sat on the bench with him, watched as he died, and at last called me up to say, weeping, he is gone. Instead of calling Asphodel or some other company's rescue team, all one-digit numbers that can be dialled into the human wrist, he allowed my son to go.

I will be his mother. Then, all of a sudden, myself, with a brick in my hand which I will smash down upon my father's head. My advantage will be the powerfully violent imagery which I will add to the constructed reality – his terror, blood, reeling fall, death, every second of which I rehearse until it feels that it has already happened. It hasn't happened, no, I reassure myself. Yet it has already begun.

## All things are made of consciousness

You'd think the weather would be nice, the sun would shine all of the time, dogs would not bite nor flowers wilt nor impatient people shove. You'd think there would be no lines to stand in. No rotten eggs, spoiled milk. The redolent odour of skunk in spring. Shoes that pinch. Warped wooden doors that do not completely shut. You'd think that here it would be perfect.

But it is better than perfect. It is beyond everything I could have imagined or can now convey. The twists and turns and quirks and elegance of mind make it so. The strangeness, the humour, the mistakes. The great elm outside my window is the tree another person had memorized and rethought. Each sawtooth leaf and ragged twig, each whorl of thick grey bark. And then the bird in it, a chickadee, its see-me call, or tiny, rapid scolding. The chickadee made entirely out of human observation, which is also love. This world entrances. The world it was based on was entrancing. But we will never know whether the consciousness that made the first world was or is like our own. Knowing that my thoughts add to the tree I look at every morning or that my footsteps reinforce a path or my tasting confirms the sweetness of the orange for others has produced in me an antlike happiness. But my imperfections also show in what I see, and so will my vengeance. Will the stain be obvious? Will I be marked out? Will I infect others with my act? Will I be caught?

## Today

I am ready now. I pick up my grandmother's handbag, perfectly remembered. I slip the library card into its inner pocket and I walk out the door. There are just a few people in the streets and one person before me in line. There is a new librarian at the desk, a gawky woman with a grey shag cut, dressed in grey, with grey eyeglasses and very blue eyes. Her eyes shoot at me from behind those glasses when I ask to see the director.

He is hard at work, she says.

This is important.

She considers. May I say who is calling?

I dimple at her, the way my grandmother did, a smile of tender mischief.

I have just come from the other side. He will be very happy to see me, I am sure. I am an old friend.

That's wonderful. She is now in on the plan.

Do you mind if I visit his office by myself? We have a great deal to talk over.

She escorts me to the elevator, tells me the floor where I can find him. I thank her. I run through the scenario again on the way down and when the door opens I smooth my dress and walk down the hall. At any moment he might emerge from his office and I must be ready. But the hall is empty. I rap softly on the frosted glass below the word DIRECTOR and his name.

Come in! he says, and I do.

Hello, son, I say in my grandmother's voice, holding out my arms. My father turns, rises, setting down his glasses. Speechless, he puts out his hands, his mouth an O of disbelief and joy. That is when I change, let him see the brick, and leap forward simultaneously bringing the brick smashing down on his head. Twice. Three times. I am fully myself. Focused, I stare and wait. I smash the brick down with savage finality. There is massing flowing blood. And he goes transparent, black, transparent again, his light feebler. But just as I think he is about to vanish there is a frozen moment in which I can see some faint convulsion of recovery. I am about to bring the brick down again. I raise my arm. But standing there, quietly before me, is my son.

Mom? Oh, Mom!

His forehead bleeding.

I can do nothing. I drop the brick.

I know he is not real, but I hold him, hold him, and hold him. ■

MARY RUEFLE

# Origin Myth

It was midnight
anxious friends
Life continually
circled in cold
inaccessible serenity
around unhappy Earth
Then all at once
swallowed it
Even after
the humming
of bees at noon
could be heard
Even as you swam
across the bottom
of your dark
suburban pool

© IAN TEH
J.G. Ballard at his home
Shepperton, United Kingdom, 2004

# KEY STROKE

## *Will Self*

### Introduction

I don't like writing about J.G. Ballard or his work any more, and if I were prone to regrets I think all the writing about, speaking of and thinking around the Ballard corpus I've done over the years is something I might wish undone. Even aged fifty-two and having published in many different forms many hundreds of thousands of words I'm not ashamed to admit to what Harold Bloom characterizes as 'the anxiety of influence'. It was Ballard's vision that first goaded me into writing seriously, and it's his work that remains the tocsin awakening me, once again, to the understanding that nothing I have achieved has ever got close to jumping off the sheer precipice of his originality.

I first met Jim Ballard in the early summer of 1994. In common with many who went to visit him I was treated to what was, I think, a serviceable shtick: Jim – as he was known to friends – had constructed a sort of workable sub-personality that he trotted out for interviewers. He styled himself as a sort of bluff, amiable old duffer, slightly bemused by the radical eccentricity of his own work, and inclined to a rather detached perspective on events beyond the leafy precincts of Shepperton, the small London dormitory town where he'd spent the last thirty-odd years of his life, and raised his three children after his wife's untimely death.

Callow fan that I was, I still managed to keep up my end, I think, of a three-hour conversation that rambled over much of our common fictional and factual territory. At the end of this, emboldened by the rapport I thought we'd established, I asked Jim if he'd ever consider coming out to, um, dinner? In the kindest and gentlest way possible, Ballard told me that he wished there'd been people such as me, with more affinity to his ideas, when he began writing, but that he was too old for such socializing now. Besides, he'd read my work, and liked it; I'd read his, and clearly felt the same – this, he said, was where the true meeting of writerly minds occurred: on the page, not in a restaurant. I took this admonition in good part, and went away.

I did, however, keep up a warm if intermittent correspondence with Jim, and when I finally went back to Shepperton, thirteen years later, I was greeted with this heartening – if dismaying – reversal: 'Why don't you ever come and see me?' he boomed, standing on the diminutive doorstep in his shirtsleeves. At that point he only had about eighteen months to live – and knew it. Over that period we met several times for dinner, accompanied by my wife, Deborah Orr, and his long-time partner, Claire Walsh. Jim continued to be bluff and genial – he clearly considered it infra dig to complain about the prostate cancer that was killing him, or the cytopathic therapies that were meant to be killing it. General conversation was just that; the rest of us did our best to conceal whatever feelings we may have had about being in the presence of the soon-to-be-departed person, one who, more I think than any other, could lay claim to being the most significant of post-war English writers.

At the time, I took Jim's affability for the whole man, but with the curse of hindsight, I now see that he was – in the jargon of modish psychotherapy – extremely well boundaried: if he said anything that cut to the quick of his condition, it was always about the horrors that he had witnessed as a child, when he and his family were interned by the Japanese in the concentration camp at Lunghua in Shanghai.

After he died, Claire told me about some of his more eccentric habits that related to his extreme rootedness in Shepperton – such as only buying Ford cars because there was a dealership in the town, and, when he had a drink-driving ban, spending the entire year in the locale because he would only walk. I realized what should've been obvious to me before: Jim was probably a lifelong sufferer from post-traumatic stress, whose minatory vision was no mere imaginative spindrift, but a transliteration of what he continued to experience, each and every day.

In a Radio 4 documentary I made about the recently deceased Ballard, I noted that he himself had famously stated: 'For a writer death is always a career move.' In Jim's case it was definitely a promotion: uneasy with the darkness and ambivalence of his work when he was physically among them, the English began to wake up to the fact that they had lost a bona fide genius. For my own part, my anxieties about his influence not only survived Jim's death, but actually intensified. I wrote a few things about him and the work, but avoided doing *too much*, for fear that his sensibility would so completely invade my own that I'd become nothing but a fanatic stalker. (Of one of these obsessive, doorstepping 'Ballardians', Jim once snarled to Claire: 'He knows more about me than I do!') Besides, Jim would have wished me to articulate my own weird music, not play second fiddle to his.

When Jim died, Claire Walsh gave me his old manual Olympia typewriter. Jim knew I too worked on a typewriter – one of the last small services I'd been able to do for him was to source a ribbon for his machine. Claire thought there would be something fitting about me – his, as it were, licentiate – working on in his well-hammered groove. Understandably, I was less enthusiastic. If I suffered from the anxiety of influence contemplating Ballard's works, how much worse would the feeling be when I applied his own tool to a job of writing – a tool that had been used, so far as I could judge, to write at least sixteen full-length works of Ballard's fiction? Would I experience some sort of eerie mind meld with my dead hero, and be rendered finally – and fatally, in respect of my own work – null? Nevertheless, the temptation was too great. I decided to go for broke, taking my inspiration from something Claire said to me about Jim's last days. He had spent, she said, a lot of this time simply staring into space, not absent but apparently concentrating furiously. When Claire asked him what he was doing he simply said: 'Thinking about my life.'

My objective in the piece printed here, in facsimile, was to try to place myself in the psyche that was 'thinking about my/his life'. I make no claims for this being Ballard's own death reverie – it is a fictional recreation of a putative one. As to whether I've done justice to my relationship with this remarkable man and his visionary work, again, it is not my position to judge, but that of you, the reader. What I can say is that since completing 'Key Stroke', Jim's legacy has laid a little less heavily across my shoulders. Jim's daughter, Fay, asked to have the typewriter when she found out I had it, and while I was in some ways sorry to see it go, it was probably for the best. Jim used to describe the hard and consistent work he put into writing as 'earning merit', and one thing is for sure: you can only ever earn your own merit, by your efforts – no assistance, whether supernatural or otherwise, is on offer. ■

# Key Stroke

Lunule. Moon rise over the reservoir - a hush of wind on the
embankment, fingertip indentations in the grass, each with a
darker lunule. She asks: What are you doing? I reply: Thinking about my life. Lunule and nail - underneath the skin the
flesh, inside this the tousled crown of veins fed by the twin
digital arteries. All those nerve ending/- and I feel nothing. /s
Distal phalanx, middle phalanx, proximal phalanx, metacarpal.
Machined chess pieces ranging over the qwerty board. This, always my way - the way: to pick it apart. Flexor digitorum tendon
and second lumbrical muscle - threading into skein. Second metacarpal - and third, fourth and fifth - the claws of the yucca
slash at wraparound windowpanes... dirty-grey net curtains caught
up, twining. Sweetbones, nuggets - craps they called them. "Craps".
Pisiform, hamate, capitate, triquetral, scaphoid, trapezoid,
a nd... and... lunate. Lunate. The sun burning a horsehead nebula
in the smoke shrooming up from fired sagebrush - fired by what?
A lunette, perhaps. The extensors and the flexors, the brachior-
adialis - triceps, biceps, all in play. What will they find? A
young man comes looking - prior to a viewing. The toe of his
shoe pokes at the toppled stack of paperbacks to expose a
printed stratum never to be read again. A corkboard leans
against a wall - ivy progresses tentatively towards the top
corner of the kitchen; it has already overwhelmed the front
hedge, which humps: the pantomime horse of the bourgeoisie,
ready to canter away down the wide, blank road to the scrap of
park - canter away, under the monocular gaze of lunette after
lunette. Poplars, flagpoles - the/standard/ of greenery/raised / cultivation
over a central reservation beneath a Gulf and Western sky. In /s
the park: crack willows, their foliage ḍḁḇḇling in dank, dark/ field
water, across the surface of which oily patches slowly swirl,
fuse, fission, metastasise. Up above, on its pole, the diplod-
icus head of a CCTV camera, slim neck encircled by repellent
barbs - underfoot, beechmast, alder berries, sweet wrappers,
aluminium ring-pulls, a ribbon of cassette tape spools through
dormant grass, surreptitious conversations murmur to the earth:
s / Let time... I said... He went... It's worth./ Hallux flexes - /..
extensor hallucis longus tendon winching its distal phalanx.

Bong-bong on the footbridge, bong-bong on the footbridge,
bong-bong on the jetty jutting out over the six sea lanes
that then spirals down into a thicket. Ships in the day -
at a rate of knots, shinily blurring; over there are flooded
gravel pits, the fields  that time forgot, the embankment of
the reservoir solid as a shifting dune, the Mojave - where I
never went. Again: lunule, and the metallic ker-chunks dying
a way rapidly into the suburban silence, absorbed into plaster,
  stifled by nylon: H and 3 and 3 and O and K and P and H once
more; in the garden the furry leaves of brambles and nettles
allign themselves horizontally the better to capture the weak
rays of the spring sun. Think not of books poked at by a loung-
ing estate agent's loafer - think not of his duff forensics;
think not of narratives, stories, or tales - think, not even of
words - which after all require mouths to shape them: the fric-
ative, the lisp, the glottal stopped in the uvula... dying away suddenly. Think only of the thousands upon millions of characters - and their expression. Now comes the epigenetic silencing. Tiled roofs tied tight to one another by telephone wires,
the flat ones of food distribution centres, a newspaper rack
outside a convenience store, strata of headlines to be read then
discarded: £140 Billion, The Last Throw of The Dice - sweetbones, nuggets - craps they called them. "Craps". On the other
side... under painful skies the precipitation of carbonate min-
erals continues... inexorably, crystals budding, interlocking -
the tendrils stretching up through the saline solution to surface, melting spires, the arrow on a weathervane pierces the eye
of the sun god; an allotment shed disarticulates - weathered
boards twisting on rusted/joints - in the net curtains of steam
rising from a geothermal pool. What are you doing? She asks -
and I reiterate: Thinking about my life. Nucleus and dendrite,
axon and receptor - the node of ranvier; the microtubule, the
neurofilament, the endoplasmic reticulum - how long does it take
for H-thought to become H-impulse, and for H-impulse to travel
along radial, median and ulnar nerves? How long does it take for
H-thought/become H, a character, the cry of its birth dying away?
Sometimes it would seem that such was the harmony with which we
proceeded/that the characters were able to precede their con-
ception; it struck me that all that passed for foresight was
simply this: an impulse or a spasm, only latterly dressed up
in intentional finery. More than this: just as all crystalline

*[margin: petroglyphs of the present]*

*[margin: iron]*

*[margin: to]*

*[margin: ʌ ı-ı]*

*[margin: ʌ ı-ı]*

forms elaborate blindly, yet according to certain basic laws,
so this, too, elaborated - which would explain the repetition
of forms, ideas, tropes and... characters. One year I lost my
driving licence, and so rather than engage with all the tedium of station platforms - the brief encounters with sepia
 film clips - I stuck to my patch and walked everywhere: down
the broad, blank road, through the dank park, across the spiral
jetty, through the disregarded hinterland - all end-of-terrace
properties, no actual terraces, all thickets but no woodlands,
primeval boughs struggling up from the flooded gravel pits - to
where the embankment of the reservoir mounted up, its nap of
grass smoothed then roughened by the wind. In the lane behind
the houses there was a loose file of discarded chattels - Ven-
us fly-trap dishwashers and washing machines awaiting buzzing
urchins, an exercise bicycle, car batteries, copper tubing, a
pot-bellied concrete garden gnome weathered into Willendorf, a
pile of corrugated fibreglass, a PVC dustbin full of rusting put-
locks, a gas fire - socket where its cylinder was - a car radiator,
metal security grilles and UPV windowframes leaning against the
pungently creosoted fence. I stood on top of the embankment beside a padlocked five-bar gate and looked out over the finely
choppy surface of the reservoir - a raised sea - to where the
the blocks of flats shone white in another suburb never named
by me. Understand this, I affirmed: Understand this - about yourself. Lay this knowledge down - and refer to it often. You...
you, with your affability and veneer of respectability, you -
you, always publically so polite. The impress, y'see, it comes
from behind the face, fingertips pushing out the features, each
sharp tap improving the the hollows of cheeks and chin, the al-
cove of the nose, the dimples of the eyes... So subtly repetitive,
these keystrokes, that the nails nicked in the pits of old acne
/scars, and the/black cores of pores. You may well have left your
marks upon the world, but something altogether other has made
its marks on you - so many marks that they are you. I turned
away from the steel container set upon its concrete pier - I
did not know then, and will never know now, what purpose it
served, if any. I turned away from the ~~savagely~~ oblique ascent /alarmingly
of a charter flight bound for Nicosia, and so made my way back
through the private fisheries and the pornographic thickets, across

the boinging jetty, back up the broad, blank road past miniature
cypresses and the Leylandii tidying up the clouds. Behind me,
in the steel container set on its concrete pier insight trickled
down through a rust-kohled knothole - fine and greige as silica -
to add to the heap on the floor. I live in stroma - the in-between
tissue, the periphery of the functioning organs. Arteries thread
through this mass, pulsing with cellular traffic; veins fan
out from these arteries and peter out into the stroma, corpuscles
lodged beside their blank walls. In the top corner of the bedroom an air vent is furred with dust and cobwebs - milliseconds,
seconds, minutes and hours - time is wadded into this woolly ana-
logue, while moments, mineralised, crunch beneath my bare feet
each time I make my way to the lavatory. Hematuria: a pink ara-
besque in the toilet bowl, dancing in a double-ply veil. It was
always and evermore will be about... time; the consistent and
steady effort required - not to arrest it, for that would be futile, but to retard it sufficiently for the task to be done. Dust
storms of conscience scour the snowy saltpan - traffic concertinas
to a crawl, jet planes struggle to maintain airspeed, the fingertips hover above the H of their helipad, unable to land due to
this whirl of supposition. Align then wind, bar then platen, release then spool, reverse then guide, raise then lower - key, key,
key, shift, return, key, key, key, shift, return. Release then
spool, again. It sits inert on the tabletop, its plastic bottom
vibrating in a static shimmy. It sits inert - ignored by the
whorls of the wood's grain, which float so slowly past into pet-
rification. It sits inert: synthetic clavicle and steel sternum -
true, false and floating ribs, sacrum, cocyx, ischium and ilium.
It sits inert - and it is in this respect, mostly, that we resemble one another: facing-off across a local void, a small and
thoughtless zone. This anesis never lasts for long - soon enough
it begins again: the symptomatic hallucinations, the livid spots
on the white skin, key, key, key, shift, return. The micrography
of the adenocarcinoma proceeds unabated: a precise patterning of
finely drawn lines is all the evidence needed for an effective
diagnosis - we have infected one another. Traffic concertinas
to a crawl, jet planes fight to maintain airspeed - everything
stalls; the stopping train halts at Sunbury - crumbs speckle the
speckled linoleum, motes blizzard over the moquette. I had hoped -

no, believed - that by putting on the brakes in this way I
would be able to retard the birth of new moments; setting my
theodolite on the firm basis of a cheap, mass-produced rug -
purchased 25 years ago, no likelihood of its replacement...
ever - I'd be able to take effective bearings on the constantly
vacillating near-future, the blurry next five minutes, key, key,
key, and shift. I didn't factor in the velocities of those fingertips, the rise and fall of them, their ceaseless cycling - a
semantic cyclotron ~~throwing out~~ meaning: the eclipse of the
lunate. Take That! Reads the headline in the local paper: Did
Driver With A Grudge Take It Out On Speed Camera? The expansive
ennui of the dormitory town - rolling over, spreading out and
stretching into the sudden spasm of rapid-eye-movement ravery:
Caliban cars ~~attacking~~ their own mirror-images. And I, in the
night, rising to see moonrise over the creosoted fences - tang
of ~~it~~ and nightshade and stale exhaust - rising to answer the
wheedle of nocturia, and to spectate once again the dance of
the two-ply veil. What am I doing? Not thinking about my life -
no, not if this implies discrete episodes organised into a
defined chronology... I see no seer, who, all knowing, ties the
tiles together with telephone wires; instead there is... evidence
that, while it might not stand up in a court of law, is more
than sufficient for self-condemnation. The puce imprint of those
same fingertips on pale, freckled skin; a garotte of discarded
underwear; cigarette butts that didn't make it to the ashtray,
their burn marks halos on the Formica; saliva dried on the rim
of a glass, poolside, Rio; dandruff on the shiny collar of an
old blazer; athlete's foot powder in the toes of ~~old~~ loafers; worn-out
a toothpick; a paperback with mad marginalia - words crazily
circled by a hard-pressed Biro. Those close to Little Boy were
flayed by the shockwave, they became angels with skin wings.
Those closer were vaporised, leaving behind either negative or
 positive images of their bodies imprinted on a few remaining
walls. But this is not that - no grand narrative of auto-cannibal-
ism seared into stone, but merely the piddling away of a single
existence: dysuria. The figure in the carpet is that of infinity -
a toppled eight, an ouruboros dabbled. It has no significance.
All these years of stasis - racing to meet deadlines, when...
really... really, there was no need: the deadline was altogether

flexible. What've you got for me? This. Well, fine then - we'll
go with that. I hadn't realised - how could I? - that the work
had been begun years - decades, even - before. Begun quietly,
unshowily, with no great inspiration or commanding idea; begun
piecemeal, in an improvisatory fashion, with many small - and,
taken singly - inconsequential acts of plagiarism: fragments of
cellular text bowdlerised and rewritten. Paint, the exoskelet-
on of walls, cracks then flakes. Ivy tendrils sucker on to til-
ing then infiltrate the grout. Footprints waver away across the
fractal patterns of sun-baked mud - and it's impossible to say
if they were made days or centuries ago; whether they were left
by a lost human or a cosmic trickster. The perished rubber of a
television aerial's disused flex tap-tap-taps against the mullions;
the tapetum lucidum behind the single eye of a neighbour's cat
shines bright then fades; a pre-dawn milk float accelerates to
the speed of light. In such cases, he says, progress is so very
slow - one might even say, leisurely - that no treatment is in-
dicated. By which I mean, he continues, any possible treatment
may well be more harmful than beneficial. In such cases - he repeats himself - some authorities believe that the best possible
course is what we call active surveillance. What we call: the
mustering of the homely collective pronoun is balanced by the
paranoid act. I survey him. I survey his special pen and his
special briefcase - he has crept in here, a university-educated
bacterium of undoubted complexity, his face full of virions. The
three clear inches of white and hairless ankle between the cuffs
of his trousers and the curled lips of his thick woollen socks
are all that's necessary to give you the measure of the man. He
has scuttled in here, to this crevice in the 20-storey reef, to
secrete his learning. Close enough for its vibration to produce
a sympathetic shudder in both of us, a jackhammer types on the
concrete page: key, key, key and shift; align, vibrate and shift;
wheel and return. You do not need to be a paranoiac for this
talk of staging and screening, or this sampling in search of markers to seem... intrusive. His complex and hairy ear is pressed
against thin cellular walls - he listens for the subversive mutt-
ering of mutagenesis. And if dialogue overheard then transcribed
has the ring of truth, then tell me this: where does personal
histology intersect with mass pathology? For this he has no answer - he hems, he hems again; he knows better than to haw. To

haw is to open up a grim little cavern - carious tombstones yaw-
ing on pink gums. Wouldn't want that - not now, too much trouble.
Better to head back again across the trackless wastes between
here - and here. Long, long oblong pools of water stained red by
ferrous oxide - their banks are berms of sand-salt planed into
being by earth-movers long since rusted away. Systems of gears,
chains and paddles blobbled with calcium carbonate - a ~~cracked~~/ broken
culvert gushing poisoned water; the delicate intersection of
never-known promontries under a beaten-bloody sky. Archipel/gos /a
of detergent scum swirl in an inland sea - super-heated glaciers
push remorselessly through moraines of discarded stuff: railway
ties, stopcocks, illegible signs, breeze blocks. In all directions
there is evidence aplenty of a superhuman effort to mould this
landscape, one that was shadowed, moment by moment, with an equal
and countervailing futility: knob and feed and platen and release,
and spool, and spool, and spool. The other local paper on the
rack outside the convenience store bears this headline: Serial
Killer Was Failed By Mental Health Unit. And good - which is to
say: Why not? Each begets the other - and where is the failure
in that? Home now, along the wide, blank road lined by the paddy
fields of the front gardens - a pattern that only becomes aston-
ishing from the air. In now, under the lunate shape of the porch -
white like calcium carbonate, biteable as Edinburgh rock. Align,
vibrate and shift... the musty smell that remains when the children have grown up and departed, taking their deodorants with
them. The epigenetic silencing: an echoic howl of turbofans, the
less distant schuss of car tyres, the proximate yelp of a trapped
dog - none of these are allowed their identity, all are subsumed.
I feel reasonably certain that were I to struggle up, make it to
the window, part leaves and nets, I would see that the pigeon
plopped down on the cowl of the streetlamp had mutated - that
arranged neatly on its wings were chevrons of anti-pigeon barbs,
each one perfectly angled to repel its conspecifics. Lever and
key and bar and... platen. Oh, yes, we've sat here long enough -
you and I - staring each other out, waiting to see who would be
be the first to blink, and it transpires that we were both equally
*trs.* self-deceiving - you in your wounded passivity (Hit me! Hit me!
Hit me again!), me in my busy activity (Hit! Hit! Hit again!).
The slow green fuse burns in the garden, coiling through bramble

and nettle, overwhelming the rotted struts and ~~perished~~ can- *shredded*
vas of a deckchair that failed to limp inside - and, with considerable strategic guile, spiralling up its prop, then loop-
ing along the plastic-coated clothesline. Reverse and guide
and lower carriage - the cottage industry of Nature requires
this: orders of existence raised up and ratchetted forward.
Male and female, old and young, quick and dead - each warped,
each wefted, knob and feed and platen and release and spool,
and knob again. The sodden root-balls of lopsided alders - the
mush in the culverts, the randomised taxonomy of electronic com-
ponent manufacturers - MARCON INSTAX - glimpsed across beige-
grey fields through the windscreens of leasehold fleet vehicles.
The steel container, at its landward end the graffiti have a
knowing Noho quality: elaborations on the possibility of spray-
painting rather than the spray-painting itself. Inside, thrust
out over the reservoir, this heap of silicate substance to which
grains are added by gambling gravity - "craps" they called them -
each and each, tumbling down to bounce into stasis, every one a
loser. How could it have been anticipated? That after many, many
years a district so well known - so mapped into memory - would,
in a matter of months, become completely defamiliarised. The
mesa shapes of the reservoirs form duff plinths for an uninsp-
iring sky through which silvery rockets undertake the tedious
daily commute to Alpha Cenaturi. How wide are these horizons -
sixty, eighty, a hundred miles? Wide enough that they imply an
Earth that has become pathologically swollen - dropsical. The
pathetic settlements on its stretched belly are being pulled
further and further apart. All those nerves, ending. Taking the
track that slices down the embankment I pass once again along the
alley. This time it is different: the exercise bicycle, the gas
fire, the dishwashers and washing machines - these are not, I
now realise, discarded chattels at all but their simulacra, ex-
pertly fashioned and aproximately one tenth scaled-up from actual size. I fidget with an unwieldy blender. Are these props,
lackadaisically stored here, awaiting employment in scenes that
would be quite mundane, were it not that the actors playing them
were also engorged? Although... at home... witnessed through the
wood veneer frame of the television set, how could anyone tell?
The null is ready-primed to receive fresh strokes and show these
off to the greatest advantage; it can only be considered an

administrative blunder - not a tragedy - that exhibitors choose
to submit blanks. Knob and feed, knob and feed - wind on the
epidermal sheet, stretched tissue-thin by platen and roller;
it's a two-ply life that we all lead, and we that are the carbon
copies. I do not purvey irony - if that's conceived of as the
very English business of retailing one thing while selling another. I mean what I say: that my own reproductive system should've
been the wellspring of this long-term creative project is only...
fitting. I employed you, an inert assemblage of metal and plastic, through which to construct my narratives - a-pop-to-sis; the
birth of each and every character necessitated the ringing death
of a keystroke. By contrast, it - them? - played upon me, their
qwerty was my DNA and RNA. Who is to say which of these is the
more compellingly original? And from what perspective can it be
authoritatively stated that this is art, while that is disease?
That man is the measure of all things is a tautology uttered by
humans for humans alone; that man might be employed as a measure
by some presence not human, and yet intrinsic to humanity, is
surely quite as interesting - as artful. The eczema of Impression-
ism - the psoriasis of Abstract Expressionism; the action painting of Karposi's Sarcoma - the paranoid schizophrenia of video
installations. My practise, by contrast, surely only this: the
compulsive and repetitive scratching at an itch without end. A
crescent moon over creosoted fences - blood staining each and
every lunate; the naked house-backs, each with their corsetry of
water pipes and wiring. The genius of buildings lies in their
ability to adapt in order to survive - a bank becomes a bar, a
cinema a restaurant, a school... a camp. This can be seen most
clearly from an aerial view - the reconfiguration of peripheral
roads and service areas, the excavation of drainage channels and
the implanting of barrier fences - and it requires an active surveillance. "Craps" they called it: the dice flung at the torn
baize cushion of the pool table. Big prairie boys - wide as
moose, and willing to bet on anything. The dice looked doctored,
worn and weighted. Rigged. But this would've been reassuring -
it's always reassuring to believe that outcomes are predetermined. The truth, that they aren't, and that all chains of causal-
ity trail through the mud, rust away in puddles, or - still more
maddenning, this - are filed by felons who are not even manacled
by them. If I had any success at predicting outcomes it was surely

only because of this gnawing uncertainty: the willingness of an
animal caught in a trap to bite off its own foot. And so - what
now? We leave our marks everywhere, prodded at and tapped by
a Providence blind to anything but its own compelling elaborations: all these nerves are nothing - and I feel the ending.
Distal phalanx, middle phalanx, proximal phalanx, metacarpal -
this, always its way: to pick sentience apart; or, rather, to
use its sarcomas like wedges, hammering them in to synapses, between one thought... and the next. Soft and fluid-filled chess
pieces ranging over the checkerboard of fields and city blocks,
pressing against surface after surface - glass, cotton, plastic,
skin - imprinting our characters on them. It is another stupefy-
ing aspect of human arrogance to assume readers have any kinship
with writers at all - let alone typewriters. They see through
the subtrefuge of plot and setting; the windowdressing of net
curtains and Yucca, rugs and books. Their scalpel slices through
the stroma to this: the information necessary to get the job done.
Disbelief suspended it suckers on to the ceiling - down below
the toe of a shoe pokes at a toppled pile of paperbacks; the
pantomime horse rears and neighs car horn; the front door bell
doesn't ring. H and 3 and 3 and O and K and P and H - black blood
drips from leaky sump on to moss-filled crannies; the gener-
ative organ is a gun that fires backwards into the breech. The
Mojave - where I never went - has come to me: sand softly seeping up the broad, blank road, or, vitrified, cracking beneath
foundations. A Joshua tree forks upward from beside a rockery,
a vast sub-surface dome lifts and separates the semis, the em-
bankments of the reservoir are shifting dunes - the spiral jetty
allows passengers to easily board a burnt-out car; they sit inside it, staring out through empty windows at the twisted and
scorched girders of the test tower. How long does it take for
H-thought to become H-impulse, and for H-impulse to travel along
radial, median and ulnar nerves? How long does it take for H-
thought to become H, a character, the cry of its birth dying away? It takes no time at all... not time at all for the mutagenesis that is the meeting of minds, truly. Lunule, lunar, lunette,
Lunghua... My life is thinking about me.

# How to Get Over Someone You Love

Begin by banishing the cymbal of a dream
locked in the retention of a nutrition label, go
to the echelon of what's remotely possible;
wear an escutcheon with meticulous scene
emblazoned in polymers that grant significance
to the microphones singers used in the forties
and the first daguerreotype of a Native American
to sit on a beveled Fifth Avenue mantelpiece.

Become more American. Study toll lanes
and how they open and close ponderously
in snowdrifts of upstate New York or appear
vertiginously on blue lumbering hills
along the Kentucky River – there's so much
baseball and white people rapping online
to distract from the beauty of a boarded window
that sits opposing you from lower vantage.

Finish the pixelated drawing you always
meant to conceive of in the back seat of a station
wagon as your ten-gallon hat collects dust
though there's a delicate frigate to draw upon
for inspiration as you urgently become lost
in a museum containing the last generation
of the LC2 computer – and didn't he make
an elegant bassist though the orchestra itself

was his principal instrument? The bathing
garments of childhood recover themselves
inside a second utopian community, eradicated
associationism compels skilled workers to
settle their differences with amoral stigma
linked to the constraints of ursine modes.
Just as in third grade I was half in and half out
of a tub while *Little Women* was read to me.

Disown yourself of the slightest faith you
once held in crepuscular claims of hoaxes
and fabulist intricacies too bitter for tales
hyper-rationalist in nature such as banal
medical testing performed on chimps and
baboons and shimmering artful reports
for trickster cosmetics older than columns
afforded to the wronged in the *New York Sun*.

Perhaps reconsider the shoulder bones of
buffalo or frank autobiographies indigenous
to brethren raised among petitions, tribal
disputes, public speeches, journey journals.
The Lord's Prayer might constitute similar
independence, the great noise of winterish
systems, even interior graphics spanning
revolts between Dakota Territory and Spain.

Close to the surface in most cases the prop
would bring you discovery doctrine, a court
for treatises and land purchase advocates,
the narratives rushed on horseback though
only a civilization like ours would doubt
the sadly applicable insight: we grow empty,
so the history of the disposed and irrelevant
consolidates into the solace of a second wife.

Militiamen are hunting down Black Hawk
in 1832 engaged in exactly this process
of entertainment, the process of shaping
circumscriptible offenses, the chill sunset
speaking for itself one single night over
the Pacific while a roofer whistles home
and the noble guests leave a room where
*Metamora* and *The Last of the Race* lie closed.

'That Thing Called Love' and 'You
Can't Keep a Good Man Down' are only
two of my favorite Sophie Tucker records.
Thank you, February 14, 1920. A white
studio band was believed to be involved.
A big black tent and gowned wooden stage
are two of the most exemplary expedients
to demonstrate where people get their kicks

recoiling into a wilderness of feature and
gesture. And sharing with others through
the cork make-up and wigs of assertive
female singers, we can recompose two
things namely: 1/ that the wilderness of
daily experience is a dish best not served
outside parameters of fictionalization;

2/ the pleasure in error is something I
swear by, being itinerant, loving errancy
that way some boob straddles himself
in a crowded lift only to exit the first
floor that avails of cushy private space.
When you are well: complain, shrug.
When you feel death perfecting itself:
dance, compose, sing, play instruments.

The goal is to vilify consciousness as
overrated while by the same rebuking
movement to shuttle tenderly back its
reprieves, to notice the black liquor
bag not meant for casual consumption.
Rage has to enter the picture, preferably
from the foreground because it's already
present in ubiquitous facets of daily etc.

You don't want to guilelessly look up one
day and find yourself having completed
a Festschrift for a senior colleague without
having noticed the pattern in your research
as the Productivity Station background
flashes interminably. 'Border Work, Border
Trouble'; 'Divided Homes Not Homelands';
'Disenfranchised or Suburban Perversions?'

Welcome to the crucible of hours of envy
while you browse the *Cleveland Gazette*
and try to forget if Bert Williams or George
Walker are the determining foci of your life.
I'm sure I could tell you that hopeful degrees
and huge nostalgic faith will assuage that old
thing: the battering ram, some chain of mail,
the tacit view of power in classical sexuality.

I used to find the word *recovery* deliciously
loaded: its polite insistency that there was
a timeline of action, that raw sensation too
could be subjugated by sublime figuration.
The most common defects for high yielding
success in the American vein is to displace
a social rise onto the repetitive and plain.
To pitch ordinariness back to wild wilds.

Would you like to come with me for some
old-fashioned inconclusive combat? Garble
a great deal of knowledge with Listerine.
But best to set out and disrupt the coding.
To grasp what Dewey means, think of some
of the ways in which we commonly seek
out significant experiences compensatorily.
The most profound internal mental stimulus

packages characterize our debate, divergent
funds and reckless humane proverbs of
questionable aesthetic integration – *anything*
not exactly the type of retribution today
that we should inquire of and dichotomize.
Yes, I know, it's lovely to live on a raft
and gaze speckled stars from broken backs
and have that quintessential homosocial

bonding experience in which we argue
whether they were all just made or rather
just happened as they're just too many.
Sometimes the river has allegorical contour.
Sometimes it's just a river in Westchester
you will happily never bother to discuss
again or for the first time if you're lucky.
The mystery, I suppose, is nature's accident.

Here's my accident: many of the ordered
properties that retain value to sense perception
after the memory has been enriched by
careful avoidance swing back ugly, unbidden.
And we might welcome them as openly
as we welcome the dissolution that wafts
from its suspended thurible so wantonly.
Thus, there is a sacrifice. But it's unknown.

And when the chosen organ of your will
is fondly amputated by a tenure committee,
to the motley substance of a stamp collection
you can withhold judgment and rush to join
water-control efforts in your local community.
A mariachi band isn't always corny delusion.
Some parish in New Orleans isn't a pet project.
Drained and rebuilt, progress is a black-lace

shawl on which certain of us depend –
trappers, smugglers, Canadian *voyageurs*
plying with bottles of voluptuous interest.
The language of the future well may be
a pullulating glory of modern shipping trends.
My take-away is to be stationed at the fringe
of a great emotional storm, to live it out,
but not forget along the way to live it out.

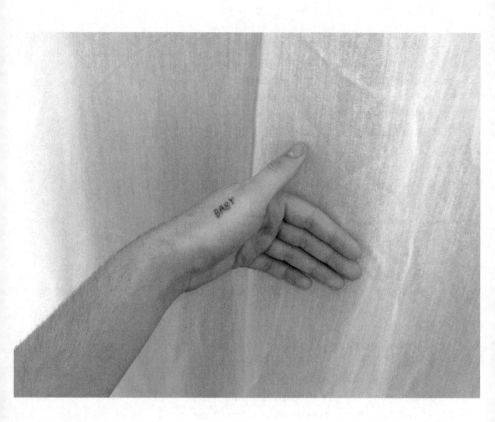

© LAUREN COOK

# SELF-MADE MAN

## *Mark Gevisser*

### I

Waking up with a headache – kinda sucks.
Waking up with a flat chest – priceless.

Liam Kai, eighteen years old and just graduated from high school in a town near Ann Arbor, Michigan, tweeted these words on 18 June 2014. It was nine days after his breast surgery and the day after he had had the dressings and drains removed. On the same day he also posted a video on Instagram in which we watch the doctor unwrapping his bandages: Liam looks down over his newly boyish chest and whoops, '*Dude!*' In a few weeks he will begin injecting the testosterone that will – finally – vault him out of the purgatory of an extended androgynous childhood into the manhood of body hair and a deep voice.

Liam was born female, adopted from China at six months and named Lucy by his American mothers. Always a tomboy, he had in fact been living as a boy since the age of thirteen, binding his growing breasts in constricting nylon vests. 'I'm thanking whatever force out there that this is my last week having to bind,' he tweeted before his surgery. 'It's painful, embarrassing, frustrating, and tiring.'

Shortly before Liam's surgery, *Time* magazine had identified a moment in American culture by putting the glamorous transgender actress Laverne Cox, star of *Orange Is the New Black,* on its cover beneath the title 'The Transgender Tipping Point'. President Barack Obama has made a point of including transgender children in his annual Easter Egg Roll, Barbara Walters has featured them on television, there are special summer camps for them and some authorities – most notably, New York City – have told schools to accept children in their 'affirmed' genders.

Until his eighteenth birthday, though, Liam could do nothing medically to assist his gender transition process. This is because his legal parents, a lesbian couple who had split when he was six, disagreed over the issue. After a somewhat rocky beginning his mother Beth, with whom he lives, has accepted Liam's transgender identity: 'I see the procedure as the plastic surgery my son needs to have rather than the double mastectomy my daughter needs to have,' she told me just before Liam's 'top surgery', as it is known in the trans lexicon. But the other parent, with whom Liam has broken entirely, vehemently policed his gender expression during his childhood: she insisted he wear dresses and grow his hair long, and that he would be much healthier and happier if he just accepted himself as female. Using court orders, she effectively withheld consent for any medical treatment while he was still a minor.

Beth has been with her current partner Andrea for more than twelve years and they have raised Liam together; he addresses them collectively as 'moms' (often with mock exasperation: *Mo-oms!?!*) and likes to call himself, on Facebook, 'a mommas' boy (get the plural?)'. There has been something redemptive, even victorious, for all of them in the moment of the surgery, not just in the way they believe it will make Liam's life better, but in the physical, irrevocable marking of what they all believe to be true: he is a man.

Beth and Andrea agreed to pay for Liam's first tattoo as a gift for his eighteenth birthday. Like muscles, tattoos are fetishes of masculinity, and Liam had been craving both for years. He had been particularly close to Beth's father, a Midwestern farmer who died shortly after he transitioned and who, after a brief struggle with the fact that his granddaughter was now a grandson, had said, simply, to his daughter, 'You have a very good son. He's just good.' Liam chose these words for his tattoo: 'He's just good' is inked on the inside of his right upper arm.

'Guys work out, they get those tattoos, they get those biceps,' Liam said to me. 'They have to work their *asses* off for those surgeries and hormones. They create the person that they always knew they were, and take pride in it.' There was a phrase for this that Liam had found on the Internet, and liked: 'self-made men'.

The United States is, after all, the place that defined and perfected reinvention, a place founded on the very notion of 'transition': across the Atlantic to a new world and (after many decades, in the case of slaves) a newly unfettered identity. America is a society that promises a transition across class if you work hard enough, and then another to happiness with the commodities you can subsequently buy, including cosmetic surgery – most of which is a form of gender enhancement anyway. It is also the society that pioneered identity politics and the idea that 'the personal is the political': the women's movement, the gay rights movement and now the transgender movement, with its attendant social revolution in how to deal with gender-nonconforming children.

The term 'self-made men' was, in fact, appropriated to describe transgender men by the sociologist Henry Rubin, and he meant it to hold a double entrendre. Gender transition is not just an act of personal will and creativity, the phrase suggests, but also a conforming of your outer shell to your inner 'true self'. If you are 'self-made' you are made by your true 'self' rather than by your external characteristics. In most people, internal and external happily conform, but in some they do not, and for such people, gender transition brings them together, makes them whole.

The British travel writer Jan Morris began her 1974 book
*Conundrum,* famously, with the line: 'I was three or perhaps four
years old when I realized that I had been born into the wrong body, and
should really be a girl.' The early age of her awareness was not unusual:
in 2009, just over half of the adult transgender participants in an
online survey in Britain said they knew they were 'in the wrong body'
by the time they were six. Like almost all transgender people of her
generation, Morris suffered a deeply anguished adolescence and early
adulthood, and finally had sex-reassignment surgery in her forties. She
was lucky to make it: the statistics show that transgender people are
dramatically more vulnerable to depression, suicide, self-harm, HIV
infection and physical violence than the rest of the population.

Today, medication that delays puberty means that boys who believe
they are girls can be raised as girls, and vice versa, without having to
endure adolescence. They can begin taking cross-sex hormones and
transition straight into adulthood in their 'affirmed' genders, without,
in the case of transgender men, having to submit to a mastectomy,
because their breasts would not have grown in the first place.

The use of puberty blockers was pioneered a decade ago in the
Netherlands; the 'Dutch protocols', as they are known, stipulate that
minors should only be allowed to start cross-sex hormones later in
adolescence. The initial idea behind the treatment is that it buys time,
until children are older and able to make more mature decisions
about their gender identity. According to the Dutch tracer research,
not one of the initial patients who subsequently transitioned had
any regret about doing so, and the cohort reflects the psychological
health of the normative population.

Still, most Western European countries do not permit medical
gender transition before adolescence, and some states use their
nationalized health plans assiduously to regulate the body. The
response to this, on the other side of the Atlantic, is increasingly: Why
wait? 'It would be cruel to deny him testosterone,' one mother said
to me of her thirteen-year-old transgender son. '*I* know he's a boy.
*He* knows he's a boy. Why not let him have male puberty along with

everyone else, rather than keeping him back, thereby adding to his already considerable social problems?'

Given both privatized health care and a culture of interventionist parenting in the United States, market forces prevail. What this means is that medical gender transition is, generally, out of reach for poorer people (the hormones are cheap, but the puberty blockers cost over $500 a month, and are not covered by insurance). But if you have the resources and the will, you can now make it happen for your children. 'The parents are driving this,' Dr Herb Schreier, a psychiatrist at UCSF Benioff Children's Hospital in Oakland, California, told me. 'They're way ahead of the medical profession. *They're* challenging *us*.'

Previously, an approach drawn from psychoanalytic theory prevailed: girls, it was believed, might wish to become male because they saw their mothers as disempowered; more commonly, boys might wish to become female to draw detached mothers closer to them, or to meet these mothers' narcissistic needs. The primary advocate of this approach, the psychologist Kenneth J. Zucker, insists that the idea of transgenderism as a natal condition is 'simple-minded biological reductionism', and there is certainly enough evidence to implicate family and social origins in some cases.

But there is a growing body of research that suggests that hormonal intrauterine imbalances may play a role too. And the resistance to the psychoanalytic approach comes not so much from its diagnostic theory as from its cure: an often severe form of reparative therapy that seems increasingly like a form of child abuse, given its denial of the child's reality. The sea change among parents, says Herb Schreier, is the consequence of a refusal to pathologize families. 'This idea of blaming mothers – in the way "refrigerator moms" were once blamed for autism – and then enforcing a draconian approach, it just isn't going to wash any more. Parents have rebelled. They have said, "You're not going to label my kid as disturbed. This is the natural form of things for my child."'

Then again, asks the child psychologist Avgi Saketopoulou, 'how are we to know when gender acts as proxy for psychopathology?' She identifies a gap, in the current culture, between the old way – which pathologized transgender identities – and the new wave of political transgender activism, which 'fails to inquire about gender's psychic meanings'.

Professionals in the field use language such as 'sea change', or 'explosion', to describe the number of families presenting with transgender children. This is not only because of new medical treatments, such as puberty blockers, but also because of the dramatic new access to information that parents and children now have. Liam first thought about being transgender when he watched *The L Word*, the American TV series. He heard Max, the trans character, talk about 'binders', punched the word into Google, and he was off. Later, he researched surgery options by watching graphic videos on YouTube.

Diane Ehrensaft, based in the Bay Area, where she co-runs the UCSF Benioff Child and Adolescent Gender Center Clinic, has become the country's pre-eminent child psychologist in the field. 'One of our biggest challenges is putting the brakes on,' she told me. 'Parents are anxious, they can't get their kids in focus. They come in and say, "If my child is transgender I'm OK with it, but how can I tell?"' Ehrensaft often advises parents that they need to learn to live with the ambiguity for a while, until things become clearer. The evidence, she says, is that 'most gender-nonconforming children are not transgender but either "proto-gay", or simply exploring new options for "doing" their gender.' She makes a careful distinction between two types of children: those who articulate their sense that they are the opposite gender from the moment they can talk, and those who are 'gender-creative' and might grow up to be gay or lesbian. 'For our youngest transgender children, we usually can tell quite early, although not always in one moment in time. But when we do know, we should let them fly.'

When Ehrensaft was a student in the late 1960s – at the University of Michigan, in Ann Arbor – she found her own identity through the women's movement. She became part of a generation that urged men and women to think beyond the blue blanket–pink blanket stereotypes. You could be a boy and play with dolls: this would teach you to grow up and be a nurturing father. You could be a girl and play with mechanical trains: this would prepare you to be a professional woman. 'We challenged gender expression,' Ehrensaft says, 'but gender *identity* – who you *are* – remains unassailable, for all but the most open parents. Now parents are struggling with the possibility that their boy who plays with dolls might be a girl, or their tomboy daughter might be a boy.'

The newly revised American diagnostic manual requires at least six of the following symptoms to be met for a diagnosis of gender dysphoria in a child: a repeated insistence that he or she is the other sex; a preference for cross-dressing; persistent preferences for cross-sex roles in make-believe play; a strong rejection of toys or games stereotypically played by one's sex; an intense desire to participate in the stereotypical games and pastimes of the other sex; a strong preference for playmates of the other sex; a strong dislike of one's sexual anatomy; and a strong desire for the sexual anatomy of the other sex. The shift of name from 'gender identity disorder' to 'gender dysphoria' was part of a process of removing judgement from the diagnosis, but Schreier and Ehrensaft belong to a network of professionals working to de-pathologize the condition entirely. Nonetheless, they believe in the necessity and importance of early-transition protocols, and in applying diagnostic criteria, which they paraphrase as 'Persistence, Consistency, Insistence'.

The decisions are not easy ones to make, says Joel Baum, who runs an educational and advocacy organization called Gender Spectrum. 'But if you have these treatments available, and you have a desperate kid in front of you who is clearly in distress you have to remember your medical oath: "Do no harm." In such instances, this means assisting them to transition, rather than standing by and watching them spiral into depression, self-harm or even suicidality.'

It is an approach that meets with significant resistance from professionals who feel that pre-adolescent children are too young to understand gender, and that adults have no right to make such decisions for them – particularly given that cross-sex hormones render their patients permanently infertile. But Baum has a different way of understanding children's rights: 'The idea that "children should be seen and not heard" doesn't hold any more. So when we start asking children, "Who are you?", they tell us. It is our responsibility to listen to them.'

Baum's statement raises a question that is one of the biggest of the current transgender moment. Have there always been transgender people and, if so, has our society not, until now, had ears well tuned enough to hear them, brains big enough to understand them? Or has the confluence of medical technology and human rights discourse created a category that did not previously exist, but into which people who might previously have struggled with gender-nonconformity can now find their place?

I am a South African man who came out as gay in the early 1980s while an undergraduate at Yale. I was a direct beneficiary of American-style identity politics. As a child in my first year at primary school in Johannesburg, where the boys and girls were separated at break time, I struggled to compete physically with boys and usually found myself playing alone. On one particular day I must have been lingering around the runnel of sorts that formed the boundary between the two sides of the playground – my reverie might have even carried me across the boundary – when a teacher pounced, and gave me a firm lecture about where I belonged. I learned a valuable lesson: if I was going to fit in, I needed to appear to accept the boundaries set for me. Transgressions had to be underground or in the ether, beyond the patrol of adults.

But what if, as a little boy, I had been time-ported to the Bay Area in the 2010s, and had landed up in Diane Ehrensaft's consulting room because of repeated runnel-transgression? Would I have been turned into a little girl because I harboured fantasies involving my mother's wardrobe and didn't like the rough play of boys? Or would I have been told it was OK to be 'gender-creative' and developed a whole new identity beyond the gender binary? What would I have become?

When I told Ehrensaft that such thoughts made me panicky, she nodded. 'I think you're relieved that you grew up in simpler times because you *knew* who you were. If, somewhere in your consciousness, you had been conflicted or ambivalent, you might feel differently now.' Still, she said, 'I have to ask, are we overwhelming the kids in any way with all these extended possibilities? It's a lot easier to walk around in a box than to have no boundaries.'

I started to wonder about my own gender, and the paths not taken. To the extent that I had been somewhat effeminate as a boy, was it because I was attracted to other boys, and therefore thought I needed to be girlish to get their attention? Or did I become 'gay' – a tribal identity that has never seemed quite adequate – because I needed to belong somewhere, and heterosexual masculinity was not quite capacious enough? I never thought I was a girl, but there were certainly times – imagining myself in the arms of a pimpled Lothario rather than having to pass a ball to him – when I wished I were one. What if it had been OK to cross over that runnel, or even dwell in its ambiguity, turning that seemingly impenetrable border between the genders into a borderland that could hold me?

2

Liam's mother, Beth, went to China to get a girl-child.

It was partly a response to baby girls being abandoned, she told me. 'It was all over the press.' She was approaching forty and wanted a child; her partner at the time was willing to do it with her. Like many lesbians of her generation, she submitted her application to the Chinese authorities – albeit disguising herself as a 'single mother' – and in November 1996, she joined a group of Americans who set out to Hunan province to collect their children. The conditions at the orphanage in the town of Yiyang were appalling: the little girl handed over to Beth was malnourished and very ill, but, like the other infants, she had been ghoulishly made up with rouge and painted eyebrows, prettified for her new parents.

All the professionals I spoke to confirmed unreservedly that there is no correlation between queer parents and queer kids (most of their young gender-nonconforming or transgender clients came from typically straight families), but I had come to America looking, specifically, for gay or lesbian parents with transgender kids. I wanted to understand the relationship between my generation of pioneers – women like Beth who pushed the boundaries of the definition of family by raising their own children outside of the institution of heterosexual marriage – and the new generation of pioneers, exemplified by transgender children such as Liam.

I struggled to find such families. But here was one in a most unexpected place, in Middle America, in a modest but comfortable home along a row of identical face-brick bungalows, just off one of those endless commercial strips that defines American suburbia. Same-sex marriage is still not legal in Michigan, but Andrea, Beth's partner, is a federal employee, and wanted benefits for her family. And so, as soon as the US Supreme Court struck down the federal anti-gay marriage legislation last year, she and Beth went to Niagara Falls in New York State to get married. Liam was their best man.

It is a Saturday night in April 2014, a few months after the wedding, and I am sitting with the three around the kitchen table. A pot of vegetable soup and a jug of iced tea are between us, and two miniature poodles rebound like pinballs off every available surface. Beth is heavyset and grey-haired, with an unkempt charm and a deadpan delivery that skates a thin line between Midwestern earnestness and irony. Her partner Andrea is her foil, a wisecracking Jewish woman from the East Coast, every story a comedy routine. There is a lot of laughter and good-natured ribbing around the table. Liam is – literally – the straight guy of the trio.

Liam has a handsome broad face and an easy smile; he carries himself with the studied elegance of someone who has spent much of his life looking at others to try to figure out how to comport himself.

He is fastidiously neat and impeccably groomed, and favours clothes that might be described as 'preppy': today he is in a pressed pink-and-blue button-down shirt over neat navy shorts. 'I've *studied* the way guys speak,' he says. 'I've trained my voice to hit the floor, but I can go no further until I get the T [testosterone].' Many guys don't hit the floor anyway, and when we were just chatting, I was only reminded that he had been born female when he laughed unselfconsciously – a delightful girlish bubble – or when I paid attention to his impossibly smooth skin.

As we sit around the table, Andrea has a way of addressing Liam directly when telling me about him: 'Girls have to confine themselves, not take up too much space, but you didn't have that. You *sprawled*. And you'd chug like in the beer commercials, and give a frat-boy belch at the end! Being an old-fashioned lesbian myself, I thought that that's what we had on our hands.'

'I don't think I ever thought Liam was transgender,' Beth adds. 'I'd buy him a lot of girl-power stuff. "*Girls Rule!*" I wanted my daughter to be a strong, confident girl.' Inevitably, we spend much time talking about clothes, those primary gender markers, and always the first site of resistance for gender-nonconforming kids. As a girl, Beth tells me, Liam was almost oblivious to clothes: 'He would just wear whatever. Pick it out of a pile on the floor. But you should see his wardrobe now. Everything is *very* organized. He cares very much exactly what every article of clothing is.'

'I was OK *being* a girl,' Liam chips in. 'I just hated *looking* like a girl.' But when he reached puberty and his breasts started growing, his discomfort developed into full-blown depression. Mandated by court to attend therapy as part of his parents' legal battle, he mentioned his distress over his other parent's rigidity about gender, and told the therapist that he sometimes had to remind himself that he was a girl. The therapist called Beth into the consulting room, and told both of them that Liam was transgender. She began spelling out the future, rapid-fire. 'Liam was so excited,' his mother remembers. 'He wanted it all. Now. But all I knew about transgender was what

I saw on talk shows. I was terrified. I kept thinking, *This isn't what I want for my child.* He had always been so healthy. I could not think of hormones and surgery. I wish I'd been prepared.'

Beth, in shock, complied at first. All of Liam's girl stuff was given away. Binders were ordered, and letters were written to the school. But then she panicked, and insisted that Liam go back to being Lucy – at least until there was more clarity. He had to send back the binders and return to clothing that was at least gender-neutral. The crash, a few months later, was perhaps inevitable. The trigger was the second *Twilight* film, where a boy becomes a werewolf at a certain age. With that, Liam explained, came a new physique: 'He goes from scrawny to muscular and cuts off his long hair. It's a huge transformation of identity into a kind of supernatural being with a big, sculpted body. It was a teen phenomenon, and I was very excited about seeing it.' He pauses, and his eyes well up. 'It was painful. To see that this guy had muscles instead of breasts. Muscles that everyone was attracted to, and that I would never have.'

Liam began planning to overdose on painkillers. He did not do anything, but for the first time, he says, 'I had a *plan*.' At his next session, he told his therapist about his suicidal thoughts – and collapsed, weeping: he could no longer live as a girl, he said. This was a different therapist to the first one, a more careful one, or perhaps a better-informed one in this rapidly evolving field: she referred the family to a gender specialist, and Liam and his parents began planning, carefully, how he would begin living as a boy. For Beth, this was the turning point: 'I became a momma bear, 100 per cent behind Liam's transition.'

The three decided on his name, Andrea says, the way they made all their major decisions: 'on the back of a napkin at our favourite diner'. Liam chose a name to reflect his Chinese heritage, and so a thirteen-year-old girl named Lucy Kelly left her eighth-grade class one day, and a thirteen-year-old boy named Liam Kai came back the next.

So quickly did Liam transform from a depressed, introverted and untidy little girl into a confident, talkative and shipshape little boy that, when the school year ended four months later, he received the annual boys' prize for 'Leadership, Scholarship and Service'. 'I was the dude!' he kept on saying. 'They have one for girls and one for boys, and I was the dude!'

The achievement, says Beth, was in Liam being acknowledged, finally, 'as a guy' – in a regular public middle school in Middle America that was willing to put his male name on a trophy before it had even been changed legally.

The glory of the 'Dude Award', as the family calls it, offset some of the difficulties that followed. Liam stopped hanging out with the girls he'd been friends with since the beginning of his school career, which saddened him: there was a new barrier between them that he did not quite understand. And he never quite made friends with the guys, because he did not go through male puberty, as they did. Some of them gallantly lent a hand by showing him the guy way to wear a hat or to sag one's jeans, but if he tried to talk about girls or dating them, 'things would get shady', he says. 'That would mean this was real.'

Because of the breast-binding, Liam stopped doing sport, particularly swimming, his passion. His life took place outside the rituals of suburban American life, like summer camp and sports meets, and he spent most of his time at home. He became very involved at Riot Youth, an 'LGBTQQA' ('Lesbian, Gay, Bisexual, Transgender, Queer, Questioning and Allies') youth group in Ann Arbor, where he was a youth facilitator, but his weekends were lonely and isolated. He found company in television dramas, and creative outlet through his own writing: he is an obsessive writer of fan fiction, which he posts online.

Liam says, too, that he has been unlucky with dating. The girls he met through the Riot Youth group were too often involved in adolescent self-harming such as cutting; the girls he courted at high school would back off, he felt, because he was transgender. But when he runs through his history, it is clear that he has been busier than many boys – certainly, than I was during my teen years. There is something quite typical in his account of his love life: like his peers, he has experienced the adolescent intensity of longing and loss.

Liam started high school the year after he transitioned, and enrolled as a boy. He made the decision not to 'go stealth', which in trans parlance means living in your affirmed gender without revealing publicly that you have transitioned. The younger you transition, the easier it is to go stealth, but Liam says he hates secrets – and besides, there would be some kids at his new school who would have known him as Lucy. Before Liam found a way to come out, though, the issue was precipitated when he overheard a male classmate say, referring to him, 'I don't know what to call *it*.' He was very upset. Together with his parents and his peers at the Riot Youth group, he decided to confront the issue head-on. He approached his homeroom adviser and asked to lead a class discussion about it.

The atmosphere had been somewhat tense beforehand, recalls Carol, one of Liam's teachers. 'Some students had known Liam in middle school and talk was spreading, not necessarily malicious, but gossipy. But things pretty much changed immediately when he spilled it and said, "This is who I am." A ninth grader! Insane, right? This shift happened. After everyone knew, it was just like, "OK, then." Sure there were students who were still uncomfortable. But the behind-the-back talk stopped, because Liam said, "If you have questions, ask me."'

Carol had first known Liam as Lucy, in middle school, and become close to her as her seventh-grade teacher. When Lucy told Carol she wanted to transition, 'I wanted to support her all the way, but in the back of my mind, I couldn't stop the questions: This is such a huge decision at such a young age. How does she really know?' But when Carol encountered Lucy, as Liam, again in high school, 'I could not get over the transformation. This very depressed, even verge-of-suicidal, girl had turned into a self-confident leader, educating others, one of the school tour guides, the initiator of the annual talent show.' Liam's gender transition, she says, was 'a no-brainer. He is who he is supposed to be.'

All the adults I spoke to about Liam were filled with similar awe. I understood it as something beyond the sometimes-kneejerk 'affirmation' that is identity politics boilerplate. It seemed to me that they, the best kind of prairie liberals, revelled in the redemptive story about a kid who is transformed – who succeeds – against the odds, by being true to himself. Even if they were writing a Hollywood movie in their heads, they were expanding their consciousness about who people were, and what rights they deserved. That's an American impulse worth celebrating.

3

Ann Arbor is a university city and, as such, has long been a liberal outpost in the American Midwest. Every year, the Riot Youth group holds a 'Queer Prom' at the Neutral Zone, a teen centre just off campus, and I had timed my visit to the city to coincide with this. The theme, this year, was 'Eighties versus Nineties', and the Neutral Zone was done up as a disco. At around 5 p.m., the kids started to trickle in beneath a sign that set house rules: 'Queer Prom is for LGBTQQA youth because regular school proms are not always safe and welcoming.' No drugs, no nudity, no touching without permission, 'no staring, no pointing and no gawking at others' – and, of course: 'Respect people's preferred names and pronouns. If you don't know, just *ask*.'

The kids were dressed up in either 'Eighties' or 'Nineties'. I struggled to tell the difference: the eighties seemed to be remembered as fluorescent gothic, the nineties as flannel grunge. The most popular dance songs were the Macarena and the theme song from a new Disney hit, which had the kids gathered in ecstatic circles screaming, '*Let it go! Let it GO!*' Gay anthems that would have had everyone on their feet in my day, like the Weather Girls' 'It's Raining Men', left the dance floor cold, and there was little to distinguish this from any other teen party, save that some girls had shaven heads with rat-tails and were smooching other girls.

Liam was there, wearing chinos and plaid. He said he was doing *Boy Meets World*, an iconic nineties sitcom, but he looked just like himself. He slipped out early, telling me that it was not his scene. He had become increasingly uncomfortable with the term 'queer', he said, which seemed to have 'taken over the space at RiotYouth. When they spoke about "straight" people, it was usually to talk about other people, who were either homophobic enemies, or "allies". I thought, *Hey! What about me? I'm sitting here. I'm straight!*

Later, his mother Beth would tell me, in her deadpan way that suggested how her son's conformism might be a form of rebellion against her own generation, 'Liam is a very traditional *straight* boy. Well behaved, not a rebel at all. He has a strong idea about how guys should be: he doesn't approve of long hair on a man, for example. And he gets crushes on the cutest girls in the class.'

When Liam came to Riot Youth four years ago, he was one of about five transgender kids: most of the others called themselves 'gay' ('lesbian' is a creepy word for American teens). Now, almost none go as 'gay': everyone is either 'trans' or 'queer'. The number of kids who come to RiotYouth has increased, but some of RiotYouth's adult facilitators say that perhaps being gay has become so normal and acceptable in liberal Ann Arbor that there is no need for regular gay kids to come to an after-school programme in the first place. All of Ann Arbor's schools have very active Gay–Straight Alliances. Those who come to RiotYouth are the 'queer ones', the oddballs, who don't fit in.

'Queer', formerly a slur, has taken an unexpected route back into youth culture through the dense academic field of 'queer theory'. Influenced by Michel Foucault, scholars such as Judith Butler and Michael Warner understand gender and sexual identities to be contextual, socially constructed rather than biologically determined, and therefore fluid and mutable. The embrace of such instability is a profound challenge to identity politics, which demands rights precisely on the basis of inherent immutable characteristics like race, sexual orientation or gender identity. 'Queer', of course, means 'different', or 'skewed', and suggests a sensibility coming from having grown up with a covert – and even shameful – identity. To see things from a 'queer perspective' is to look at the world askance, to see it afresh. It is something I value in my own vision; something that I believe – perhaps a little arrogantly – separates me from those boys who could kick a football and smooch a girl with equal effortlessness at school.

Before the kids started pouring into the Queer Prom, Sean – one of the party's organizers and Liam's contemporary in Riot Youth – patiently explained to me how they saw the difference between 'gay' and 'queer'. I write 'they' because this is Sean's own 'preferred pronoun': they were born female and have a female body, but identify as 'genderqueer' rather than as 'male' or 'female'. Sometimes, they told me, they experience gender dysphoria and bind their breasts, but at Queer Prom their breasts were free in a loose flowing top, over denim shorts and big, masculine lace-up boots. '"Gay" is what we do,' Sean told me. '"Queer" is our culture, who we are.'

In my generation, 'homosexuality' was what we did and 'gay' was who we were. It seems to me that, for Sean's genderqueer generation, 'they' is the new 'gay'. For me, coming out as 'gay' in the early eighties was not just about acknowledging my sexuality and accepting myself: it was also about identifying with a subculture – political and social – and setting myself apart, with some defiance, from the mainstream. Thirty years later, when fifteen-year-old Sean went home and told her faculty parents she was a lesbian, 'they were completely chill', Sean told me. 'But when I came out as genderqueer, they said, "No way can we do that."' They keep calling me by my legal name, and use "she". In their mind, it's just too difficult to change. I'm, like, if you try for two months it'll be difficult, and then you'll get it, OK?'

How things have changed: in liberal America, homosexuality is, as the TV sitcom would have it, *The New Normal*. Gay people can join the army, run corporations, get married, have kids, host TV talk shows. In this context, little wonder that there was no conflict in Sean's family over sexuality. But when Sean's quest for self-expression drifted further, into gender identity, the generational lines were drawn.

Sitting in on a meeting of families of transgender kids while on my trip, I had watched an otherwise supportive father (so he said) explode over the pronouns: 'It makes no sense, and it's too complicated. Every kid in my son's social group wants to be called a different pronoun.' (Other options include 'ze', 'hir', 'zir', 'ey' and 'em'.) 'How can I possibly remember? And if you get it wrong it's like you're denying their very identity!'

He has a point. But it is reductive to see genderqueer kids as being overly demanding, spoiling for a fight with adults, or simply 'going through a phase'. Rather, they are finding room for individuation from their parents; this impulse to rebellion can be immensely creative: it germinated not only hippies and punks but feminists and gay liberationists too. Sean's girlfriend, Charlotte, an exuberant nineteen-year-old trans woman, told me about a new word doing the rounds for those kids attracted to the subculture because it is cool or rebellious: 'transtrenders'.

Now, at many American colleges, the gender-neutral pronouns have become the norm. In my days at college, the 'transtrender' equivalents were the 'LBGs' – 'lesbians before graduation'. They caught much flak from the hardcore dykes, but when I look at them now, many of them married to men and with kids, it seems to me that, rather than having abandoned their undergraduate experimentation, they have carried the lessons they learned about gender stereotyping into their more conventional adult lives. Meanwhile, for men, being 'gay' has turned out to be not so defiant after all, but is rather about proving to the world that you are a real man, despite your homosexuality: hence the hyper-masculinity – the facial hair and the muscles and the tattoos – that has become so much part of gay culture. I feel as out of place in it as an adult as I did on the boys' side of the runnel as a child.

I wonder how much richer – or, perhaps, freer – my subsequent life might have been if I had had a few transtrending or genderqueer years. Who knows whether I would have moved into a more gender-challenging adulthood? I don't think I would ever have transitioned into female, but maybe I would have had more female-born sexual partners (that stopped when I was sixteen), and a better body self-image too.

R ose grew up in Ann Arbor, and hails from the Riot Youth generation just before Liam and Sean. Twenty-two years old, she has just graduated from a small liberal arts college and moved with her girlfriend to the Bay Area, where she is looking for work in the chemical industry. She has slim, boyish looks and likes to 'strut and play tough like any butch', she told me, but she chose the name Rose for herself to honour her femininity.

Rose was born a girl and came out as gay when she was twelve. She found Riot Youth and, during her high school years, shifted from being gay to being trans, changing her name to Fynn and her pronouns to the masculine. This was, she says, in part because of the influence of older transgender people in the group and in part – she now believes – 'because it is socially validated in our world to be a man. Being a man in our culture is having agency, being aggressive and strong rather than bitchy and scheming.' Rose watched Liam grow up in Riot Youth, and has no doubts that Liam is transgender and is doing the right thing by transitioning: 'I'm not saying trans men don't exist,' she says. 'Of course they exist, and for some people transition is obviously right. But for many young women like myself, young women in adolescence, at a time of great vulnerability, it's an attractive option to become a guy.' Particularly if you are a tomboy, and the other option is to become a butch lesbian: 'a big fat predatory leather-jacketed dyke on a bike, that's how we saw them. Who wants to be *that*?'

When she became Fynn she noticed the difference immediately: 'the way people looked me in the eye, a level of respect and politeness that was never present when people thought I was a woman, or saw me as a tomboy'. Once eighteen, at college, she started taking testosterone. 'I went to a counsellor and he gave me a letter after only two consultations. I was hugely excited, but when I look back at it now, I think it was *nuts*! Only two sessions, before sending me on this irrevocable path?' She never felt comfortable on the T, she says. And then she fell in love with a woman who issued her a challenge: 'You can't be a man, and also be in these lesbian spaces and this lesbian relationship. You can't have your cake and eat it.'

Her new partner, says Rose, helped her accept herself as a woman. She stopped the T for a few months, started it again and stopped it, finally, seven months after she had first started (not knowing, at the time, how dangerous it is to go on and off hormones like that). One of the ways Rose's partner helped her, she says, was by giving her a copy of *Stone Butch Blues,* Leslie Feinberg's 1993 coming-of-age novel. 'I read it, and realized that all those things I loved about being a man, including loving *women,* could be part of stone-butch culture. When I was this butch tomboy teen, I felt it would be easier and more tolerable for me to imagine living out the rest of my life as a man than as a woman. I often joke that I had to be a man before I could find the courage to be a woman.'

Rose now lives as a woman, albeit one with a deep, masculine voice; Leslie Feinberg, by the way, identifies as a 'transgender lesbian', and uses gender-neutral pronouns. Some of my own older butch lesbian friends like to joke, with only semi-mock horror, that the new transgender movement is rendering them a dying breed. The transgender social revolution is in many ways a consequence of feminism, but it has issued it some challenges too. Colleges such as Smith and Barnard are being forced by law to revise their admissions criteria, and even the iconic Michigan Womyn's Music Festival is in crisis over door policy: should transgender men and women be allowed in, or only 'woman-born women'? While the genderqueer movement seeks to blur the gender binary, or to do away with it, transgenderism can be about reasserting it: stepping over it, from male to female or vice versa, rather than exploring the spaces in between, along a gender continuum. This has led to some concern that 'binarist' professionals will use the new medication to regulate gender-nonconformity in children, rather than to liberate it.

While Herb Schreier, the Oakland psychiatrist, acknowledges the risk, he says that the transgender movement has profoundly altered cultural conceptions of gender, by opening up the possibility that identity is not fixed at birth. He told me about a seven-year-old patient who has been flip-flopping for three years between being a boy and being a girl. The kid went off to a transgender summer camp and came back with an announcement: 'Mommy, at last I think I know what I am. I'm a "they".' Schreier, in his sixties, looks back at the gay movement: 'Who would have imagined a generation ago that two men or two women could marry and make a family? In the generation to come we're going to look back at gender and say, "Oh, that binary stuff, we're over it, thank God!"'

It is hard to imagine something as entrenched in human culture and history as the gender binary disappearing, ever. Still, something is happening in the United States, in this unexpected two-step choreographed by the transgender phenomenon and its corollary, the genderqueer movement. It is captured best, perhaps, in the words of the psychoanalyst Virginia Goldner: 'My body is no longer my destiny. It is now my canvas.'

Like Liam and like Sean, Rose is fashioning a gender for herself in a way that feels right to her, with the tools available to her – now testosterone, now feminism – at different points in her young life. Her gender changed, in high school, because of what she learned through Riot Youth, and then changed again, at college, because she fell in love with a lesbian. In this way she is like most of us, in that she has been moulded in her youth by the shape of her context. If she had grown up in rural Appalachia, where her father comes from, she might not have found the transgender category; if she had fallen in love with a more heterosexually identified woman on campus, she might have carried on with the testosterone. This might be a measure of the fluidity of this time and this place – the proliferation of options facing young Americans – but it is also a function of human development.

We were all formed by the paths we chose to take or ignore, driven by the callow passions of youth or inertia, before we knew better.

There is, of course, one detail that separates the 'LBGs' of my generation from the 'transtrenders' of today: the irrevocable physical changes that accompany medical transition. Liam no longer has breasts; the testosterone is deepening his voice, giving him new hair and muscles and even reshaping his bones. In his instance, and in the vast majority of transgender people who undergo transition, this finality is redemptive, in the way it helps conform the outer shell to the inner self, and vaults them over that very runnel that attracts the genderqueer bunch. But Rose worries that girls starting testosterone or having surgery in adolescence 'don't necessarily have the mental capacity to understand the misogyny in our culture that might be informing their decisions. *I* certainly didn't.'

Still, Rose is not angry with anyone for misleading her, and she believes in 'encouraging experimentation, as long as it's not blind'. She lives in the Bay Area, after all, the cradle of American experimentation, from psychedelic drugs to gay liberation to the Internet, in a generational ecosystem of trans and queer people with whom she came of age. She loves her deep voice, she says; the fact that she has chosen the name 'Rose' rather than gone back to her birth name is a sign of the way she is constructing femininity to her own specifications, rather than accepting it as preordained.

In the 'self-made' ethos of the current moment, Rose is even seriously considering having top surgery, as many stone-butch lesbians have already done, without becoming men.

Say, what?

'I just love taking my shirt off. And there's not a lot of places I can do that, with breasts.'

Because of his slender build and his small breasts, Liam was advised to have 'periareolar surgery with purse-string closure and chest liposuction', as his doctor's website calls it, rather than a full double-incision mastectomy. He was happy with this advice:

the double incision might have been more effective in removing all breast tissue, but it would have left unsightly scars beneath the nipples. Liam's doctor has posted a video onYouTube demonstrating periareolar surgery, and Liam viewed this, with some discomfort, before making his decision. I, too, forced myself to watch it: a circular incision is made around the nipple, which is removed and held hanging by a 'purse-string' thread, while the breast tissue is sucked out of the cavity, before the nipple is sewn back on. The effect is of an unfurling red rosebud where the nipple should be.

I know, from my conversations with Liam, that he was terrified by the surgery, and that he struggled with the convalescence, but he saw it as pain that had to be taken, so that he could be his true self. But, culturally, he comes from a different world to mine: a *Nip/Tuck* world where cosmetic surgery is increasingly common, a *Twilight* world where digitally enhanced bodies are perpetually in flux. In the Bay Area, where Rose now lives, body modifications such as tattooing and piercing define hipster culture today, in much the way that long hair defined hippie culture forty years ago.

'Bottom surgery', as genital surgery is known, has been available for over seventy years for transgender women; even longer, if one includes the castration that eunuchs have endured for millennia. But for transgender men, it is still in its early stages, and many choose to live without it. There are two options: metoidioplasty, which enlarges the clitoris with hormones, or phalloplasty, which creates a penis out of skin tissue grafted from the arm or thigh. In either case, the urethra can be rerouted through the phallus to allow urination, and the labia majora can be sewn together to form a scrotum, into which prosthetic testicles can be inserted. Liam says he is in no hurry to do any of this – and hopes that, by the time he is ready for it, the procedures will have become more advanced.

In the few weeks since I last saw Liam, he has entered adulthood with an extraordinary velocity. He turned eighteen. He attended his high school prom, which he much preferred to the Queer Prom: he wore a silver tux, and his best girlfriends were in extravagant organza.

He graduated from high school, second in his class. He had his top surgery and moved out of home to a summer-school programme at the University of Michigan, where he would start, as a freshman, in September 2014. And he began his testosterone injections.

Liam celebrated the Fourth of July by posting his first shirtless portrait on Facebook. 'Happy Independence Day!' he wrote, relishing his own. 'They say never to post something that you might regret, but honestly, I'd regret NOT uploading this: the first time I've felt the sun on my chest. Three weeks, four days post-op and two days on testosterone. It's all still so hard to believe! . . . Thanks moms for everything you've done; I wouldn't be here without you.'

The photograph, taken by Beth in the park near their house, is deeply moving. Liam is wearing cargo shorts, the band of his American Eagle underwear showing, of course. His chest is boyish and he has the serious self-conscious look of any teenage boy figuring out what to do with his new adolescent body.

My own journey into this research, my queerness as a critic, leads me to try to find my own meaning in this beautiful, celebratory photograph. I would like to believe that even if the Liam in the photograph identifies as a straight man he will always be 'genderqueer' in a way, because of the particular journey he has undertaken from female to male, an experience that no amount of testosterone can douse. No matter how able people like Liam are to 'go stealth', I would like to believe that they are afforded a gender consciousness that the rest of us can never have, because of the way they have transcended the binary, crossed that runnel.

But that's my stuff, not Liam's. Or at least, not his right now. 'I'm happy,' he writes in his post, eighteen and shirtless, next to the image he has posted on Facebook. 'Even when I'm upset, I'm happy.'

I believe him. ∎

---

AUTHOR'S NOTE: *At their request, pseudonyms have been used for Liam and the adults around him, and for Rose.*

MARK DOTY

# Apparition

I'm carrying an orange plastic basket of compost
down from the top of the garden – sweet dark,

fibrous rot, promising – when the light changes
as if someone's flipped a switch that does

what? Reverses the day. Leaves chorusing,
dizzy. And then my mother says

– she's been gone more than thirty years,
not her voice, the voice of her in me –

*You've got to forgive me.* I'm choke and sputter
in the wild daylight, speechless to that:

maybe I'm really crazy now, but I believe
in the backwards morning I am my mother's son,

we are at last equally in love
with intoxication, I am unregenerate,

the trees are on fire, fifty-eight years of lost bells.
I drop my basket and stand struck

in the iron-mouth afternoon. She says
*I never meant to harm you.* Then

the young dog barks, down by the front gate,
he's probably gotten out, and she says,

calmly, clearly, *Go take care of your baby.*

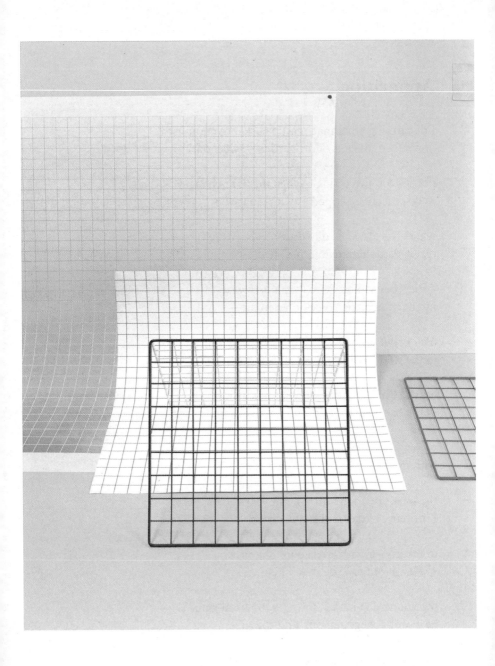

© DANIEL EVERETT
*Plane III*

# SOME HEAT

## *Miranda July*

Today I went to Open Palm, early, and got everything ready for the meeting of the board. My plan was to behave so gracefully that the clumsy woman Phillip had spoken with yesterday would be impossible to recall. I wouldn't use a British accent out loud, but I'd be using one in my head and it would carry over.

Jim and Michelle were already in the office, and so was Sarah the intern. She had her new baby with her; she was trying to keep it under the desk, but obviously we could all hear it. I wiped down the boardroom table and laid out pads of paper and pens. As a manager this is beneath me, but I like to make it nice for Phillip. Jim yelled 'Incoming!' which meant Carl and Suzanne were about to make their entrance. I grabbed a pair of giant vases full of dead flowers and hurried to the staff kitchen.

'I'll do that!' said Michelle. She's a new employee – not my pick.

'Too late now, I'm already holding them.' They were sloshing bacteria water against my chest.

'Let me just take one of those,' she said, prying a vase out of my hand, too ignorant to understand the system of counterbalances I was using. One was slipping now, thanks to her help, and I let her catch it, which she did not. Carl and Suzanne walked in the door the moment the vase hit the carpet. Phillip was with them.

'Greetings,' said Carl. Phillip was wearing a gorgeous wine-colored sweater. My breath thinned. I always have to resist the urge to go to him like a wife, as if we've already been a couple for a hundred thousand lifetimes. Caveman and cavewoman. King and queen. Nuns.

'Meet Michelle, our new media coordinator,' I said, gesturing downwards in a funny way. She was on her hands and knees gathering up slimy brown flowers; now she struggled to stand.

'I'm Phillip.' Michelle shook his hand from a confused kneeling position, her face a hot circle of tears. I had accidentally been cruel. This only ever happens at times of great stress and my regret is always tremendous. I wanted to punch myself in the face. I would bring her something tomorrow, a gift certificate or a Ninja Five-Cup Smoothie Maker. I should have already given her a gift, pre-emptively; I like to do that with new employees. They come home and say, 'This new job is so great, I can't even believe it – look at what my manager gave me!' Then if they ever come home in tears their spouse will say, 'But, hon, the smoothie maker? Are you sure?' And the new employee will second-guess or perhaps even blame themselves.

Suzanne and Carl ambled away with Phillip and Sarah the intern hurried over to help clean up the mess. Her baby's gurgling was insistent and aggressive. Finally I walked over to her desk and peeked under it. He cooed like a mournful dove and smiled up at me with the warmth of total recognition.

*I keep getting born to the wrong people,* he said.

I nodded regretfully. *I know.*

What could I do? I wanted to lift him out of his carrier and finally encircle him in my arms again, but this wasn't an option. I mimed an apology and he accepted it with a slow, wise-eyed blink that made my chest ache with sorrow. I keep getting older while he stays young, my tiny husband. Or, more likely at this point: my son. Sarah hurried over and swung his baby carrier to the other side of the desk. He bobbed away, caught in a large ocean wave. His foot went wild with kicking.

*Don't give up, don't give up.*

*I won't,* I said. *Never.*

It would be much too painful to see him on a regular basis so I let Sarah know it wasn't appropriate to bring her baby to work.

'Suzanne said it was fine. She said she brought Clee to work all the time when she was little.'

It was true. Carl and Suzanne's daughter used to come to the studio after school and hang out in the classes, running around screaming and distracting everyone. I told Sarah she could finish the day but that this couldn't become a routine thing. She gave me a betrayed look, because she's a working mom, feminism, etc. I gave her the same look back, because I'm a woman in a senior position, she's taking advantage, feminism, etc. She bowed her head slightly; I was more right. The interns are always women Carl and Suzanne feel sorry for. I was one, twenty-five years ago. Back then Open Palm was just a women's self-defense studio that made very dry instructional videos. We still teach a class for teen girls, but that's just to keep our non-profit status – all our business is in fitness DVDs – selling self-defense as exercise was my idea. Our line is competitive with other top workout videos; most buyers say they don't even think about the combat aspect, they just like the uptempo music and what it does to their shape. Who wants to watch a woman getting accosted in a park? No one. If it weren't for me Carl and Suzanne would still be making that type of depressing how-to video. They're more or less retired since they moved to Ojai but they still meddle in employee affairs and attend the board meetings.

I'm practically, though not officially, on the board. I take notes. Phillip sat as far away from me as possible and avoided looking at my side of the room for the duration of the meeting. I hoped I was just being paranoid, but later Suzanne asked if there was a problem between us. I confessed I had shown him some heat.

'What does that mean?'

It had been almost five years since she'd suggested it – I guess it wasn't a phrase she used any more.

'I told him when in doubt . . .' It was hard to say it.

'What?' Suzanne leaned in, her dangly earrings swinging forward.

'When in doubt, give a shout,' I whispered.

'You said that to him? That's a very provocative phrase.'

'It is?'

'For a woman to say to a man? Sure. You've definitely shown him – how did you put it?'

'Some heat.'

Carl walked around the office with a dirty canvas sack that said OJAI FARMERS' MARKET and filled it with cookies and green tea and a container of almond milk from the staff kitchen, then he bounced over to the supply closet and helped himself to reams of paper, a handful of pens and highlighters and a few bottles of white-out. They also unload things they don't know what to do with – an old car that doesn't run, a litter of kittens, a smelly old couch that they don't have room for. This time it was a large amount of meat.

'It's called Beefalo – it's the fertile hybrid of cattle and bison.'

'We ordered too much and it expires tomorrow.' Suzanne opened a styrofoam cooler.

'So rather than let it rot, we thought everyone could enjoy Beefalo tonight – on us!' shouted Carl, throwing his hands into the air like Santa.

Suzanne began calling out names. Each employee rose and received a little white package labeled with their name. Suzanne called Phillip's name and my name in quick succession. We walked up together and Suzanne handed us our meat at the same time. My meat package was bigger. I saw him notice that and then he finally looked at me.

'Trade you,' he whispered.

I frowned to keep the joy in. He gave me the meat that said PHILLIP and I gave him the meat that said CHERYL.

As the Beefalo was distributed, Suzanne also wondered aloud if anyone could take their daughter in for a few weeks until she found an apartment and a job.

'She's an extremely gifted actress.'

No one said anything.

Suzanne swayed a little in her long skirt. Carl rubbed his large stomach and raised his eyebrows, waiting for takers. The last time Clee had been to the office she was fourteen. Her pale hair was pulled back into a very tight ponytail, lots of eyeliner, big hoop earrings, pants falling down. She looked like she was in a gang. That was six years ago, but still no one volunteered. Until someone did: Michelle.

The Beefalo had a primal aftertaste. I wiped the pan clean and ripped up the white paper with Phillip's name on it. Before I was even finished, the phone rang. No one knows why ripping up a name makes a person call – science can't explain it. Erasing the name also works.

'I thought I'd give a shout,' he said.

I walked to the bedroom and lay down on my bed. Initially it was no different than any other call except for that in six years he had never once called me on my cell phone at night. We talked about Open Palm and issues from the meeting as if it wasn't eight o'clock and I wasn't in my nightgown. Then, at the point where the conversation would normally have ended, a long silence arrived. I sat in the dark wondering if he had hung up without bothering to hang up. Finally, in a low whisper, he said, 'I think I might be a terrible person.'

For a split second I believed him – I thought he was about to confess a crime, maybe a murder. Then I realized that we all think we might be terrible people. But we only reveal this before we ask someone to love us. It is a kind of undressing.

'No,' I said in a whisper. 'You are so good.'

'I'm not, though!' he protested, his voice rising with excitement. 'You don't know!'

I responded, with equal volume and fervor, 'I do know, Phillip! I know you better than you think!' This quieted him for a moment. I shut my eyes. With all my throw pillows around me, he and I poised at the lip of intimacy – I felt like a king. A king on his throne with a feast laid before him.

'Are you able to talk right now?' he said.

'If you are.'

'I mean, are you alone?'

'I live alone.'

'I thought so.'

'Really? What did you think when you thought about that?'

'Well, I thought: I think she lives alone.'

'You were right.'

'I have a confession to make.'

I shut my eyes again, a king.

'I need to unburden myself,' he continued. 'You don't have to respond, but if you could just listen.'

'Okay.'

'Yikes, I'm nervous about this. I'm sweating. Remember, no response necessary. I'll just say it and then we can hang up and you can go to sleep.'

'I'm already in bed.'

'Perfect. So you can just go right to sleep and call me in the morning.'

'That's what I'll do.'

'Okay, I'll talk to you tomorrow.'

'Wait – you haven't said the confession.'

'I know, I got scared and – I don't know. The moment passed. You should just go to sleep.'

I sat up.

'Should I still call you in the morning?'

'I'll call you tomorrow night.'

'Thank you.'

'Goodnight.'

Jim called at eleven and said there was a mini-emergency. Jim is the on-site office manager.

'Is it about Phillip?' Maybe we would have to rush over to his house and I could see where he lived.

'Michelle changed her mind about Clee.'

'Oh.'

'She wants Clee to move out.'

'Okay.'

'So can you take her?'

When you live alone people are always thinking they can stay with you, when the opposite is true: who they should stay with is a person whose situation is already messed up by other people and so won't mind adding one more.

'I wish I could, I really wish I could help out,' I said.

'This isn't coming from me, it's Carl and Suzanne's idea. I think they kind of wonder why you didn't offer in the first place, since you're practically family.'

I pressed my lips together. Once Carl had called me Ginjo, which I thought meant sister until he told me it's Japanese for a man, usually an elderly man, who lives in isolation while he keeps the fire burning for the whole village.

'In the old myths he burns his clothes and then his bones to keep it going,' Carl said. I made myself very still so he would continue; I love to be described. 'Then he has to find something else to keep the fire going so he has *ubitsu*. There's no easy translation for that, but basically they are dreams so heavy that they have infinite mass and weight. He burns those and the fire never goes out.' Then he told me my managerial style was more effective from a distance, so my job was now work-from-home though I was welcome to come in one day a week.

My house isn't very big; I tried to picture another person in here.

'They said I was practically family?'

'It goes without saying – I mean, do you say your mom is practically family?'

'No.'

'See?'

'When is this happening?'

'Michelle will bring her over this evening.'

'I have an important private phone call this evening.'

'Thanks a bunch, Cheryl.'

I carried my computer out of the ironing room and set up a cot that is more comfortable than it looks. I folded a washcloth on top of a hand towel on top of a bath towel and placed them on a duvet cover that she was welcome to use over her comforter. I put a sugarless mint on top of the washcloth. I windexed all the bath and sink taps so they looked brand new, also the handle on the toilet. I put my fruit in a ceramic bowl so I could gesture to it when I said, 'Eat anything. Pretend this is your home.' The rest of the house was perfectly in order, as it always is, thanks to my system.

It doesn't have a name – I just call it my system. Let's say a person is down in the dumps, or maybe just lazy, and they stop doing the dishes. Soon the dishes are piled sky-high and it seems impossible to even clean a fork. So the person starts eating with dirty forks out of dirty dishes and this makes the person feel like a homeless person. So they stop bathing. Which makes it hard to leave the house. The person begins to throw trash anywhere and pee in cups because they're closer to the bed. We've all been this person, so there is no place for judgment, but the solution is simple:

Fewer dishes.

They can't pile up if you don't have them. This is the main thing, but also:

Stop moving things around.

How much time do you spend moving objects to and fro? Before you move something far from where it lives, remember you're eventually going to have to carry it back to its place – is it really worth it? Can't you read the book standing right next to the shelf with your finger holding the spot you'll put it back into? And if you *are* carrying an object, make sure to pick up anything that might need to go in the same direction. This is called carpooling. Putting new soap in the bathroom? Maybe wait until the towels in the dryer are done and carry the towels and soap together. Maybe put the soap on the dryer until then. And maybe don't fold the towels until the next time you have to go pee. When the time comes, see if you can put away the soap and fold towels while you're peeing, since your hands are free.

Before you wipe, use the toilet paper to blot excess oil from your face. Dinner time: skip the plate. Just put the pan on a hot pad on the table. Plates are an extra step you can do for guests to make them feel like they're at a restaurant. Does the pan need to be washed? Not if you only eat savory things out of it.

We all do most of these things some of the time; with my system you do all of them all of the time. Never don't do them. Before you know it, it's second nature, and the next time you're down in the dumps it operates on its own. Like a rich person, I live with a full-time servant who keeps everything in order, and because the servant is me, there's no invasion of privacy. At its best, my system gives me a smoother living experience. My days become dreamlike, no edges anywhere, none of the snags and snafus that life is so famous for. After days and days alone it gets silky to the point where I can't even feel myself any more, it's as if I don't exist.

The doorbell rang at quarter to nine and I still hadn't heard from Phillip. If he called while I was with her I would just have to excuse myself. What if she still looked like a gang person? Or she might feel terrible about the imposition and start apologizing the moment she saw me. As I walked to the door the map of the world detached from the wall and slid noisily to the floor. Not necessarily an indicator of anything.

She was much older than she'd been when she was fourteen. She was a woman. So much a woman that for a moment I wasn't sure what I was. An enormous purple duffel bag was slung over her shoulder.

'Clee! Welcome!' She stepped back quickly as if I intended to embrace her. 'It's a shoeless household, so you can put your shoes right there.' I pointed and smiled and waited and pointed again. She looked at the row of my shoes, different brown shapes, and then down at her own shoes, which seemed to be made out of pink gum.

'I don't think so,' she said in a surprisingly low, husky voice.

We stood there for a moment. I told her to hold on, and went and got a plastic grocery bag. She looked at me with an aggressively blank expression while she kicked off her shoes and put them in the bag.

'When you leave make sure to lock both deadbolts, but when you're in the house it's fine to just lock one. If the doorbell rings, you can open this' – I opened the tiny door within the front door and peeked through it – 'to see who it is.' When I pulled my face out of the peephole she was in the kitchen.

'Eat anything,' I said, jogging to catch up. 'Pretend this is your home.' She took two apples and started to put them in her purse, but then saw one had a bruise and switched it out for another. I showed her the ironing room. She popped the mint into her mouth and left the wrapper on the washcloth.

'There's not TV in here?'

'The TV is in the common area. The living room.'

We walked out to the living room and she stared at the TV. It wasn't the flat kind, but it was big, built into the bookshelves. It had a little Tibetan cloth hanging over it.

'You have cable?'

'No. I have a good antenna, though, so all the local stations come in very clearly.' Before I was done talking she took out her phone and started typing on it. I stood there for a moment, waiting, until she glanced up at me as if to say *Why are you still here.*

I went into the kitchen and put the kettle on. Using my peripheral vision I could still see her and it was hard not to wonder if Carl's mother had been very busty. Suzanne, though tall and attractive, would not be described as a 'bombshell', whereas this person leaning against the couch did bring that word to mind. The kettle whistled. She looked up and widened her eyes mockingly, meaning that's what I looked like.

At dinner time I asked Clee if she wanted to join me for chicken and kale on toast. If she was surprised by toast for dinner, I was going to explain how it's easier to make than rice or pasta but still counts as a grain. I wouldn't lay out my whole system at once, just a little tip here, a little tip there. She said she had some food she brought with her.

'Do you need a plate?'

'I can eat it out of the thing.'

'A fork?'

'Okay.'

I gave her the fork and turned up the ringer on my phone. 'I'm waiting for an important phone call,' I explained. She glanced behind herself, as if looking for the person who might be interested to know this.

'When you're done, just wash your fork and put it right here with your other things.' I pointed to the place on the shelf where her cup, bowl, plate, knife and spoon were.

She looked slowly from the small pile of dishes to the other small pile of dishes.

'I know it seems like it might be confusing, because our dishes look the same, but as long as everything is either in use, being washed, or on the shelf, it should be fine.'

'Where are all the other dishes?'

'I've been doing it this way for years, because nothing's worse than a sink full of dirty dishes.'

'But where are they?'

'Well, I do have more. If, for example, you want to invite a friend over for dinner . . .' The more I tried not to look at the box on the top shelf the more I looked at it. She followed my eyes up and smiled.

By the next evening, there was a full sink of dishes and Phillip hadn't called. Since the ironing room didn't have a TV, Clee nested in the living room with her clothes and food and liters of Diet Pepsi all within arm's distance of the couch, which she'd outfitted with her own giant flowery pillow and purple sleeping bag.

When it had been three days I wrote Phillip's name on a piece of paper and ripped it up but the trick didn't work – it never does when you lean too heavily on it. I also tried dialing his number backwards, which isn't anything, and then just six of the seven numbers, and then all seven but in a random order.

A smell began to coagulate around Clee, a brothy, intimate soup smell that she seemed unaware of, or unconcerned by. At the end of the week she finally bathed, using what smelled like my shampoo.

'You can use my shampoo,' I said when she came out of the bathroom. Her hair was combed back and a towel hung around her neck.

'I did.'

I laughed and she laughed back – not a real laugh but a sarcastic, snorting guffaw that continued for quite a while, getting uglier and uglier until it halted coldly. I blinked, for once grateful that I couldn't cry, and she pushed past, knocking me a little with her shoulder. My face had an expression of *Hey, watch it! It is not okay to ridicule me in my own house which I have generously opened to you. I'll let it go this time, but in the future I expect a one-hundred-and-eighty-degree turnaround on your behavior, young lady.* But she was dialing her phone so she missed the look. I took out my phone and dialed too. All seven numbers, in the correct order.

'Hi!' I yelled. She whipped her head around. She probably thought I didn't know anyone.

'Hi,' he said. 'Cheryl?'

'Yep, it's the Cher Bear,' I barked, walking casually to my room. I quickly shut the door.

'That wasn't my real voice,' I whispered, crouching behind my bed, 'and actually we don't have to talk, I just needed to make a demonstration phone call and you were the number I happened to dial.' I winced; this felt more plausible at the start of the sentence than the finish.

'I'm sorry,' said Phillip. 'I didn't call when I said I would.'

'Well, we're even now, because I used you for the demonstration call.'

'I guess I was just scared.'

'Of me?'

'Yes, and also society. Can you hear me? I'm driving.'

'Where are you going?'

'The grocery store. Ralph's. Let me ask you a question: does age difference matter to you? Would you ever consider a lover who was much older or much younger than you?'

My teeth started clacking together, too much energy coming up at once. Phillip was twenty-two years older than me.

'Is this the confession?'

'It's related to it.'

'Okay, my answer is yes, I would.' I held my jaw to quiet my teeth. 'Would you?'

'You really want to know what I think, Cheryl?'

Yes!

'Yes.'

'I think everyone who is alive on Earth at the same time is fair game. The vast majority of people will be so young or so old that their lifetime won't even overlap with one's own – and those people are out of bounds.'

'On so many levels.'

'Right. So if a person happens to be born in the tiny speck of your lifetime, why quibble over mere years? It's almost blasphemous.'

'Although there are some people who *barely* overlap,' I suggested. 'Maybe those people are out of bounds.'

'You're talking about . . .'

'Babies?'

'Well, I don't know,' he said pensively. 'It has to be mutual. And physically comfortable for both parties. I think in the case of a baby, if it can somehow be determined that the baby feels the same way, then the relationship could only be sensual or maybe just energetic. But no less romantic and significant.' He paused. 'I know this is controversial, but I think you get what I'm saying.'

'I really do.' He was nervous – men are always sure they'll be accused of some horrific crime after they talk about feelings. To reassure him I described Kubelko Bondy, our thirty years of missed connections.

'So he's not one baby – he's many?' Was there an odd pitch to his voice? Did I hear jealousy?

'No, he's one baby. But he's played by many babies. Or hosted, maybe that's a better word for it.'

'Got it. Kubelko – is that Czechoslovakian?'

'That's just what I call him. I might have made it up.'

It sounded like he had pulled over. I wondered if we were about to have phone sex. I'd never done that before, but I thought I would be especially good at it. Some people think it's really important to be in the moment with sex, to be present with the other person; for me it's important to block out the person and replace them, entirely if possible, with my thing. This would be much easier to do on the phone. My thing is just a specific private fantasy I like to think about. I asked him what he was wearing.

'Pants and a shirt. Socks. Shoes.'

'That sounds nice. Do you want to tell me anything?'

'I don't think so.'

'No confessions?'

He laughed nervously. 'Cheryl? I've arrived.'

For a moment I thought he meant here at my house, right outside. But he meant Ralph's.

The ironing room and my bedroom were my domain, the living room and the kitchen were hers. The front door and the bathroom were neutral zones. When I got my food from the kitchen I scurried, hunched over, as if I were stealing it. I ate looking out the too-high ironing-room window, listening to her TV shows. The characters were always shouting, so it wasn't hard to follow the plots without the picture. During our Friday video conference call Jim asked what all the commotion was.

'That's Clee,' I said. 'Remember? She's staying with me until she finds an apartment or job?'

Rather than take this opportunity to jump in with accolades and sympathy, my co-workers fell into a guilty silence. Especially Michelle. Someone in a burgundy sweater sauntered across the office, behind Jim's head. I craned my head.

'Is that – who was that?'

'Phillip,' piped Michelle. 'He just donated an espresso machine to the staff kitchen.'

He walked past again, holding a tiny cup.

'Phillip!' I yelled. The figure paused, looking confused.

'It's Cheryl,' said Jim, pointing to the screen.

Phillip walked toward the computer and ducked into view. When he saw me he brought his giant fingertip right up to the camera – I quickly pointed at my own camera. We 'touched'. He smiled and moseyed away, off-screen.

'What was that?' said Jim.

After the call I threw on my robe and strolled into the kitchen. I was tired of hiding. If she was rude, I would just roll with it. She was wearing a big T-shirt with a volleyball on it and either no bottoms or shorts completely covered by the shirt. She seemed to be waiting for the kettle.

'Enough hot water for two?'

She shrugged. I guessed we would find out when it came time to pour. I got my mug out of my bin; even though the sink was full of dishes, I had continued using only my set. I leaned on the wall and kneaded my shoulders against it. Roll, roll, roll with it. We waited for the kettle. She poked a fork at the layers of calcified food on my savory pan as if it were alive.

'It's building flavor,' I said protectively, forgetting to roll for a moment.

She laughed, heh, heh, heh, and instead of growing defensive, I joined her, and laughing somehow made it funny, truly funny – the pan and even myself. My chest felt light and open, I marveled at the universe and its trickster ways.

'Why are you laughing?' Her face was suddenly made of stone.

'Just because –' I gestured toward the pan.

'You thought I was laughing about the pan? Like ha ha you're so kooky with your dirty pan and your funny way of doing things?'

'No.'

'Yes. That's what you thought.' She took a step toward me, talking right into my face. 'I was laughing because' – I felt her eyes move over my gray hair, and my face, its big pores – 'you're so sad. Soooo. Saaaad.' With the word *sad* she pressed her palm into my chest bone, flattening me against the wall. I made an involuntary *huh* sound and my heart began to thud heavily. She could feel this, with her palm. She got a revved-up look and pressed a little harder, then a little harder, pausing each time as if to give me a chance to respond. I was getting ready to say 'Hey, you're about to cross a line' or 'You're crossing the line' or 'Okay, that's it, you've crossed the line', but suddenly I felt that my bones were really being harmed, not just my chest but my shoulder blades which were grinding into the wall, and I wanted to live and be whole, be uninjured. So I said, 'Okay, I'm sad.' The kettle began to whistle.

'What?' she said.

'I'm sad.'

'Why would I care if you're sad? Why would I want to know that?'

I quickly gave a nod of agreement to show how completely I was on her side, against myself. The kettle was screaming. She pulled her hand away and poured the water into a styrofoam cup of noodles – not appeased, just revolted by our affiliation. I walked away, a free woman on rubbery legs.

I curled up on my bed. What was the name of the situation I was in? What category was this? I had been mugged once, in Seattle in my twenties, and that had had a similar feeling afterwards. But in that case I had gone to the police and in this scenario I couldn't do that.

I called my bosses in Ojai. Carl answered immediately.

'Business or pleasure?' he said.

'It's about Clee,' I whispered. 'It's been lovely having her, but I think –'

'Hold on. Suz – pick up! Clee's making trouble! Not that phone – the hall one!'

'Hello?' Suzanne's voice was almost inaudible through the crackling connection.

'You're on the crappy phone!' Carl shouted.

'I'm not!' Suzanne yelled. 'I'm on the hall one! Why do we both need to be on at the same time?' She hung up the hall phone but could still be heard distantly through Carl's phone. 'You get off the phone, I'll talk to Cheryl alone!'

'You've been snapping at me all day, Suz.'

Suzanne picked up the phone, but paused before putting it to her mouth. 'Can you go away? I don't need you monitoring my every move.'

'Are you going to offer her money?' Carl said in a whisper that seemed louder than his regular voice.

'Of course not. You think I'm just handing out –' Suzanne put her hand over the phone. I waited, wondering what there was to argue about since they both agreed I should not be offered money.

'Cheryl!' She was back.

'Hi.'

'Sorry about that, I'm not having fun in this marriage right now.'

'Oh no,' I said, although this was the only way they ever were, like this or loudly entranced by each other.

'He makes me feel like shit,' she said, and then to Carl, 'Well, then go away – I'm having a private conversation here and I can say what I like.' And then to me: 'How are you?'

'Good.'

'We never thanked you for taking Clee, but it means so much' – her voice became thick and halting, I could see her mascara starting to run – 'just to know she's getting exposed to good values. You have to remember she grew up in *Ojai*.'

Carl picked up.

'Please excuse the theatrics, Cheryl, you don't have to listen to this. Feel free to hang up.'

'Fuck you, Carl, I'm trying to make a point. Everyone thinks it's such a terrific idea to move out of the city to raise your kids. Well, don't be surprised when that kid is pro-life and anti-gun control. You should see her friends. Is she going on auditions?'

'I'm not sure.'

'Can you put her on?'

I wondered if I was still allowed to hang up if I wanted to.

'She might need to call you back.'

'Cheryl, hon, just put her on.' She could tell I was scared of her daughter.

I opened my door. Clee was eating noodles on the couch.

'It's your mom.' I held the phone out.

Clee took it with a swipe and strode out to the backyard, the door slamming shut behind her. I watched her pacing past the window, her mouth a little spitting knot. The whole family exerted tremendously toward each other; they were in the throes of passion all the time. I held my elbows and looked at the floor. There was a bright orange Cheeto on the rug. Next to the chip was an empty Diet Pepsi can and next to the can was a pair of green lace thong underwear with white stuff on the crotch. And this was just the area right around my feet. I touched my throat, hard as a rock. But not yet to the point where I had to spit instead of swallow.

Clee stormed in.

'Someone named' – she looked at the screen – 'Phillip Bettelheim called you three times.'

The phone was wet with palm sweat.

I called Phillip back from my car. When he asked me how I was, I did my equivalent of bursting into tears – my throat seized, my face crumpled, and I made a noise so high in pitch that it was silent. Then I heard a sob. Phillip was crying – out loud.

'Oh no, what is it?' He had seemed fine when we touched fingers through the computer.

'Nothing new, I'm okay, it's just the thing I was talking about before,' he sniffed soggily.

'The confession.'

'Yep. It's driving me nuts.'

He laughed and this made room for a larger cry. Gasping, he said,

'Is – this okay? Can I just – cry – for a while?'

I said of course. I could tell him about Clee another time.

At first the permission seemed to stifle him, but after a minute he broke through to a new kind of crying that I could tell he liked – it was the crying of a child, a little boy who can't catch his breath and is out of control and won't be consoled. But I did console him, I said, 'Sh-sh-shhh,' and 'That's it, let it out,' and each of these seemed to be exactly right, they allowed him to cry harder. I really felt a part of it, like I was helping him get somewhere he'd always wanted to go and he was crying with gratitude and astonishment. It was pretty incredible, when you thought about it, which, as the minutes wore on, I had time to do. I looked at the curtains of my own house and hoped Clee wasn't breaking things in there. I doubted if any man had ever cried this much, or even any adult woman. He blew his nose a few times. I said, 'That's it, there you go,' which made him cry a little more, perhaps just politely to acknowledge my words. Finally it was all quiet. He was done.

'That felt really, really good.'

'Yes,' I agreed. 'It was incredible.'

'I'm surprised. I usually don't cry well in front of other people. It's different with you.'

'Does it feel like we've known each other for longer than we really have?'

'Kind of.'

I said nothing. I could tell him or I could not tell him. I decided to tell him.

'Maybe there's a reason for that,' I ventured.

'Okay.' He blew his nose again.

'Do you know what it is?'

'Give me a hint.'

'A hint. Let's see . . . actually, I can't. There are no little parts to it, it's all big.'

I took a deep breath and shut my eyes.

'I see a rocky tundra and a crouched figure with ape-like features who resembles me. She's fashioned a pouch out of animal gut and now she's giving it to her mate, a strong, hairy pre-man who looks a lot like you. He moves his thick finger around in the pouch and fishes out a colorful rock. Her gift to him. Do you see where I'm going?'

'Kind of? In that I see you're talking about cavemen who look like us.'

'Who *are* us.'

'Right, I wasn't sure – okay. Reincarnation?'

'I don't relate to that word.'

'No, right, me either.'

'But sure. I see us in medieval times, huddling together in long coats. I see us both with crowns on. I see us in the forties.'

'The 1940s?'

'Yes.'

'I was born in '48.'

'That makes sense because I was seeing us as a very old couple in the forties. That was probably the lifetime right before this one.' I paused. I had said a lot. Too much? That depended on what he said next. He cleared his throat, then was silent. Maybe he wouldn't say anything, which is the worst thing men do.

'What keeps us coming back?' he said quietly.

I smiled into the phone. What an amazing thing to be asked. Right now, tucked into the warmth of my car with this unanswerable question before me – this might have been my favorite moment of all the lifetimes.

'I don't know,' I whispered. I quietly leaned my head against the steering wheel and we swam in time, silent and together.

'What are you doing for dinner on Friday, Cheryl? I'm ready to confess.' ■

# MIRACLES

## *Francisco Goldman*

M exico's retablos or *exvotos*, painted on pieces of metal or wood,
are offerings of gratitude to a Catholic divinity, usually placed
in a sanctuary shrine or altar, that condense a charged moment in
somebody's life, perhaps of anguish or even terror, usually into a simple
image, a man lying face down in the street, a patient in a hospital cot
attended by doctor and nurse. In another part of the painting there is
always an image of Christ, the Virgin of Guadalupe or another virgin, or
of a saint, St Francis, St Judas Tadeo and so on, to whom the gratitude
is offered. At the bottom, a hand-painted inscription, signed and dated,
narrates the event and its resolution, usually without offering many
details. They are displays of religious devotion and gratitude that make
intimate news, sometimes even of a scandalous nature, public news.
They were meant to be shared, traditionally, within close communities
that didn't need to read much between the lines, among people who
felt the same faith and love for their favoured divinities. Retablos were
never meant to be admired only as 'art'.

I've never liked seeing them displayed in private homes. There
used to be a type of foreign correspondent in Mexico City, usually
working for a major metropolitan newspaper, who would fill the
Spanish colonial mansion the newspaper rented for him – such
lavishly maintained correspondents are now practically extinct –
with collections of folk and popular art, claiming that pillage as a way
of really knowing the Mexican soul: 'Let me show you my retablo
collection, Mr Ambassador.'

But in whatever environment we see them, these images can look
so familiar and even modern to us. A man simply lying on his back
in the dirt by a brick wall strikes the same chord in us as an old man
silent and alone onstage in a Beckett play. The violence the retablos

depict, the calamities of fate, weather, accidents or of illness, move us because they distil so powerfully what we already know all too well.

Experts write that the retablos have traditionally been a privileged place of female intimacy and expression. What women thought and worried about and talked to other women about found an outlet here. Patricia Arias, in an issue of *Artes de México* devoted to *exvotos*, writes that in the mid twentieth century, women even produced retablos depicting domestic violence – 'In 1953, Paula García "escaped a mortal blow from her husband" who is seen about to hit her with a log of massive dimensions while she kneels before him pleading' – but that once they understood that domestic abuse was a punishable offence, that their husbands could be sent to prison, such retablos stopped appearing. That might also make us think of tragic silences, of all the retablos that couldn't be painted because of what a woman in Mexico couldn't publicly state, and all the events that couldn't end up in a retablo anyway, because there was no outcome to be grateful for.

I doubt retablos such as Paula García's have made much of a reappearance during these past two decades in Mexico of mass terror against women, of femicides and abductions, not when organized crime groups and their allies in the police have been known to hunt down and murder anonymous bloggers who've dared to denounce them. The crimes of contemporary Mexico, when organized crime is involved – in some parts of the country, nearly everything is organized crime – never have happy endings. How many of the tens of thousands disappeared reappear alive instead of in a government morgue or in a mass narco grave? How many prayerful mothers see their abducted daughters come home? How many have ever been given even the slight satisfaction of justice? They whisper their hopes into the ear of a human rights official or activist, or else maybe into a priest's, perhaps they pray in church or at a certain shrine, and leave an anonymous note pleading for their daughter's healthy return folded upon the altar, and then they go home and wait. ∎

*Images and inscription translations are published in collaboration with Antonia Bruce and the Wellcome Collection.*

© Santuario de San Francisco de Asis – INAH

I thank our Lord Saint Francis of Assisi for saving us from drowning on 27 October 1962. Monterrey, N.L.

© Museo Nacional de Historia – INAH

On 5 January 1886, Macsimino López from the Hacienda de Guadalupe was falsely accused by some enemies of being a highwayman and reported to the authorities of Guanajuato, who decided to use the current fugitive law★ in his prosecution, but this never happened due to the grace of the Holy Virgin after offering her this retablo.

★ In fugitive law, a man convicted of a crime and sentenced to death is taken to the place of his execution and released, giving him the opportunity to run to freedom by escaping the bullets of the firing squad.

© Museo Regional de Guadalajara – INAH

Miracle granted by Our Holy Mother of San Juan to Antonia Lopez on that memorable 18 January 1888 . . . while, during the flooding in León, seeing herself and her family in great danger along with 15 other people, implored with all her heart to the Holy Mother of San Juan. On hearing her prayer, our Divine Lady intervened and they were miraculously saved by climbing a tree and for such a great miracle she dedicates this retablo.

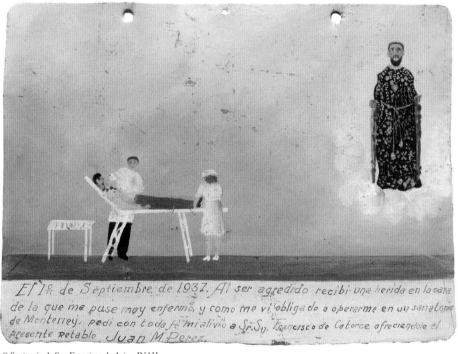

© Santuario de San Francisco de Asis – INAH

On 1 September 1937 I was attacked and wounded in my face and as a result I became ill and had to have an operation in a hospital in Monterrey. I asked the Lord St Francis of Real de Catorce with all my faith for my recovery, promising him this retablo. Juan M. Perez.

El día 11 de Marzo de 1942
me paso la desgracia de
huber caido a la ᵗolva donde
caia metal como tierra, quedando
sujeto desde la sintura hasta los
pies hasta que completamente quede
sepultado en vida sin saber ya de mi
antes aclamé el Sr Sn Francisco quien
me volvió a la vida. Por lo que, doy infinitas gracias.
J. Jesús Rodriguez. charcas SLP 6-1942

© Santuario de San Francisco de Asis – INAH

On 11 March I had the misfortune of falling down the mine shaft where metal was raining down and I became trapped from my waist to my feet until I was completely buried alive. As I lost consciousness I invoked the Lord St Francis who brought me back to life and I give him infinite thanks. J. Jesús Rodriguez. Charcas, SLP 6-1942.

© Museo Nacional de las Intervenciones, Conaculta – INAH

In the R. de Pastores in 1917, Roman Camargo twice found himself in great danger of dying, first hanged and then executed. After they had released him from the hook and he landed almost dead, he knelt for the firing squad to shoot him. His mother invoked the miraculous St Nicholas and he was immediately released.

El día 7 de Mayo del año de 1904 Estava trabajando el S. Elías Chavarría en los hilos eléctricos derepente cayó al suelo en que estuvo a punto de perder la vida, pero por intervención que hizo a la Sma Virgen de la Soledad de Sta Cruz quedó salvo por lo que en gratitud y acción de gracias dedica el presente retablo.

México N° 5

© Museo Nacional de las Intervenciones, Conaculta – INAH

On 7 May of the year 1904, Sr Elias Chavarría was working with electricity cables when he suddenly fell and was on the point of death, but by invoking the Holy Virgin of Soledad de Santa Cruz he was saved, and in gratitude and thanks he dedicates the present retablo.

En el mes de Noviembre á 29, del año de 1862. Aconteció, q.ᵉ saliendoles tres ladrones á las personas de Calletano Favera y á su esposa Agustina Murillo. enfrente del Sangarro de Urrutia en el callejon. le dieron en cada lado una pasada y una rozada cnlo fruto con bala á Calletano. y un balazo en la espalda la cual bala se le quedo hasta ahá. y dos heridas en la cabeza á Agustina Murillo. los cuales se allan sanos por un milagro tan grande del Sr de la Billa Seca.

© Museo Nacional de Historia – INAH

On 29 November of the year 1862, Calletano Favera and his wife Agustina Murillo were accosted by three thieves at the entrance to the alley of Sangarro de Urrutia. Calletano was attacked and grazed in the forehead by a bullet, then shot in the back where the bullet still remains. And Agustina Murillo received two wounds in the head. Both are healthy by fortune of a great miracle of Señor de Billa Seca [*sic* Villaseca].

© Museo Regional de Puebla – INAH

In the month of May of 1839 Doña Gabriela Lois had a serious illness which left her in despair and without any hope in life. She then entrusted herself with all her heart to the Saint of San Salvador who instantly cured her. She gives many thanks to such a great Lord, and God.

© Santuario de San Francisco de Asis – INAH

Señora Valeria Pineda prostrated herself in front of the image of Saint Francis to offer him her infinite thanks, because with all her heart she invoked a saint so miraculous that he could intervene and save her pigs from the illness attacking her animals. After hearing her prayers, she gives testimony of his great favour with the present retablo. Community of Palo Seco, Municipality of Villa Juarez. September 1971.

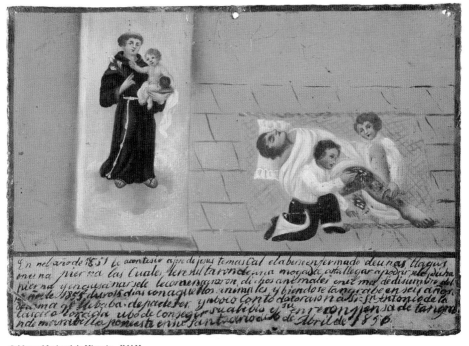

© Museo Nacional de Historia – INAH

In the year 1851, José de Jesús Temascal became ill with infected sores which resulted from exposure to damp. His leg started to rot and became infected with maggots in the month of December of the year 1855. He spent fifteen days with these grubs. After six years of suffering he pleaded with all his heart to Our Lord San Antonio de la Casa Colorada who restored his health. In gratitude for this wondrous miracle he leaves this [retablo] in his sanctuary on 6 April of 1856.

Within the image (part of the retablo painting):

EL DIA 17 DE ENERO DE 1955 FUE ASESINADO EMILIO GUZMAN A MANOS DE LOS AGRESORES ANTONIO GUZMAN Y CRESCENCIANO GUZMAN LOS CUALES DESPUES DE CAIDO NO DEJABAN ACERCARME NI A MI MISMA TIRANDOME TAMBIEN CON EL PROPOSITO DE HERIRME. EMILIO GUZMAN DURO 3 HORAS MUERTO VOLVIENDO A LA VIDA A LAS 3½ HORAS DESPUES DE ENCOMENDARME A LA STSMA. VIRGEN DE SAN JUAN DE LOS LAGOS Y SAN FRANCISCO DE ASIS POR LO ⬛ DEDICO EL PRESENTE RETABLO. EN PRUEBA DE MI AGRADECIMIENTO Y FE. JERONIMA MUÑIZ

Fracción de Soledad, D.G. S.L.P. - Octubre de 1955

© Santuario de San Francisco de Asis – INAH

On 17 January 1955, Emilio Guzman was murdered at the hands of aggressors Antonio and Crescenciano Guzman, who prevented me from going to him after he fell, even attempting to hurt me. I pleaded to the Virgin of San Juan de los Lagos and Saint Francis of Assisi, and Emilio Guzman who had been dead for 3 hours came back to life after 3½ hours. I dedicate this retablo as testimony of gratitude and faith. Jeronima Muñiz. Fraccion de Soledad, D.G. S.L.P. October 1955.

En Chamacuaro en 1923 Cayó un Rayo en la Puerta del Templo muchas mugeres cayeron en tierra Eufrosina Nieto que era una de las caídas invocó al Milagroso Sn Nicolas y ninguna murió

© Museo Nacional de las Intervenciones, Conaculta – INAH

In Chamacuaro in 1923 lightning struck the door of the temple and many women were thrown to the floor. Eufrosina Nieto was one of the fallen who invoked the miraculous St Nicholas and nobody died.

The text within the image reads:

RANCHO Sn.
RAFAEL SLP
Julio del 76.

hoy Gracia. A DIOS,
y al señor San Francisco de
acis, POR abreme Salbado
4 caballos y 2 asnos
De la ENSEFalites
equina. CCnTAl motivo.
Dedica este ReTABlo.
fam. ZAPATA.

© Santuario de San Francisco de Asis – INAH

San Rafael Ranch, SLP July 76. I thank God and Saint Francis of Assisi for saving our 4 horses and 2 donkeys from equine encephalitis. For this reason we offer this retablo. Zapata Family.

El dia 22 de Agosto, de 1892, se verificaba una corrida de toros en el pueblo de Yxtacalco, y al bajar el suscrito de una azotea de 5 metros de altura, cayo accidentalmente, implorando à la milagrosa imagen de la Virgen de la Soledad que lo salvo de una muerte segura, Agradecido, le dedica este retablo. Lorenzo Vazquez. Mexico Setiembre de 1895. Braulio Jauregui, Pinto.

© Museo Nacional de las Intervenciones, Conaculta – INAH

On 22 August 1892, a bullfight took place in the town of Yxtacalco and, while descending from a roof 5 metres high, the undersigned accidentally fell. He pleaded to the miraculous image of the Virgin of Soledad who saved him from a certain death. In gratitude he dedicates this retablo. Lorenzo Vázquez. Mexico, September 1895. Braulio Jauregui, painter.

En Cedral S.L.P. Diciembre 10 de 193? Estando poniendole agua al motor que mueve un molino de nixtamal. Se me enrredo el rebozo en el volante hasiendome dar varias bueltas hasta estrellarme en la pared, resultandome barias heridas en la caveza recojiendome como muerta. Mis aflijidos padres viendome en este trance ynvocaron a Sr. San Francisco de Asis. Que me salvara la vida y hasiendome este milagro le dedico el presente como prueva de agradesimiento. Puresa Estrada y sus padres. Dominga T. de F. Estrada

© Santuario de San Francisco de Asis – INAH

In Cedral S.L.P. on 10 December 1939, while adding water to the grinder that mixes *nixtamal*★, my shawl was caught in the wheel making me spin several times before crashing into the wall, which resulted in multiple head injuries leaving me almost dead. My anxious parents, seeing me in this state, invoked Saint Francis of Assisi to save my life and after providing me with this miracle I dedicate this retablo as proof of my gratitude.

★ Dried maize, which has been treated with lime and partially cooked, used to make tortillas.

# THE FERRYMAN IS DEAD

## Saša Stanišić

TRANSLATED FROM THE GERMAN
BY ANTHEA BELL

We are sad. We don't have a ferryman any more. The ferryman is dead. Two lakes, no ferryman. You can't get to the islands now unless you have a boat. Or unless you are a boat. You could swim. But just try swimming when the chunks of ice are clinking in the waves like a set of wind chimes with a thousand little cylinders.

In theory, you can walk round the lake on foot, keeping to the bank. However, we've neglected the path. The ground is marshy and the landing stages are crumbling and in poor shape; the bushes have spread, they stand in your way, chest-high.

Nature takes back its own. Or that's what they'd say in other places. We don't say that, because it's nonsense. Nature is not logical. You can't rely on nature. And if you can't rely on something you'd better not build fine phrases out of it.

Someone has dumped half his household goods on the bank below the ruins of what was once Schielke's farmhouse, where the lake laps lovingly against the road. There's a fridge stuck in the muddy ground, with a can of tuna still in it. The ferryman told us that, and said how angry he had been. Not because of the rubbish in general but because of the tuna in particular.

Now the ferryman is dead, and we don't know who's going to tell us what there is to be found on the banks of the lake. Who but a ferryman can say things like 'where the lake laps lovingly against the road' and 'it was tuna from the distant seas of Norway' so beautifully? Only ferrymen say such things.

We haven't thought up any more good turns of phrase since the fall of the Berlin Wall. The ferryman was good at telling stories.

But don't think that at this moment of weakness we ask the Deep Lake, which is even deeper now, without the ferryman, how it's doing. Or ask the Great Lake, the one that drowned the ferryman, what its reasons were.

No one saw the ferryman drown. It's better that way. Why would you want to see a person drowning? It's not a pretty sight. He must have gone out in the evening when there was mist over the water. In the dim light of dawn a boat drifted on the lake, empty and useless, like saying goodbye when there's no one to say it to.

Divers came. Frau Schwermuth made coffee for them, they drank the coffee and looked at the lake, then they climbed down into the lake and fished out the ferryman. Tall men, fair-haired and taciturn, using verbs only in the imperative, brought the ferryman up. Standing on the bank in their close-fitting diving suits, black and upright as exclamation marks. Eating vegetarian bread rolls with water dripping off them.

The ferryman was buried, and the bell-ringer missed his big moment; the bell rang an hour and a half later, when everyone was already eating funeral cake in the Platform One. The bell-ringer can hardly climb the stairs without Johann's help. At quarter past twelve the other day he rang the bell eighteen times, dislocating his shoulder in the process. We do have an automated bell-ringing system and Johann the apprentice, but the bell-ringer doesn't particularly like either of them.

More people die than are born. We see the old folk as they grow lonely and the young as they fail to make plans. Or as they make plans to go away. In spring we fell for the Nigerian online scam. People say give it another generation or so, things won't last here any longer. We believe they will. Somehow or other they always have. We've survived pestilence and war, epidemics and famine, life and death. Somehow or other things will go on.

Only now the ferryman is dead. Who will the drinkers turn to when Ulli has turned them out at closing time? Who's going to fix paperchase treasure hunts for visitors from the Greater Berlin area, in fact fix them so well that no treasure is ever found, and the kids cry quietly on the ferry afterwards and their mothers complain politely to the ferryman while the fathers are left wondering, days later, where they went wrong? Those are mainly fathers from the new Federal German provinces, feeling that their virility has been questioned, and once on land again they eat an apple, ride towards the Baltic Sea on their disillusioned bicycles and never come back again. Who's going to do all that?

The ferryman is dead, and the other dead people are surprised: what's a ferryman doing underground? He ought to have stayed in the lake as a ferryman should.

No one says: I'm the new ferryman. The few who understand that we really, really need a new ferryman don't know how to ferry a boat. Or how to console the waters of the lakes. Or they're too old. Others act as if we never had a ferryman at all. A third kind say: the ferryman is dead, long live the boat-hire business.

The ferryman is dead, and no one knows why.

We are sad. We don't have a ferryman any more. And the lakes are wild and dark again, watching and observing what goes on. ■

© RACHEL THOMAS, ART DIRECTION AND SET DESIGN/
DAN TOBIN SMITH, PHOTOGRAPHY
*Imaginary View*, 2013

# A HEBREW SIBYL

## *Cynthia Ozick*

M y mother was a native of this place, though my father, a trader in pots, was not. Each year, usually in the spring, he came from his home country to buy the wares of our region. He would remain with us, if the weather and the sea's temper held, into the last days of summer. He spoke our language well, and could read and write in our alphabet. Still, the kiln masters, who could not, called him *barbaros*, and laughed at his clumsiness with our easy 'th'. The lekythoi flasks, for instance, he pronounced 'lekydoi'; it made him sound childish. Behind his back he was resented and disliked, even as he brought us prosperity.

It was my father's practice to choose the pots he intended to purchase at the very moment they were taken from the kilns and set out on wooden slats to cool. He did this with a certain harsh and almost contemptuous speed; he knew instantly what wouldn't do, never mind that to any ordinary eye the skyphos or krater he spurned as imperfect might be altogether indistinguishable from those he deemed flawless. And then, after the favoured pots were wrapped in linen strips and cushioned in straw and sent on to the port town in a procession of donkey carts, they would be filled (so my father explained to me) with oils and syrups and perfumes of a kind not to be found in his own land. Yet not all: only those vessels designed for freight. The others, prized solely for their beauty, were destined, he said, for the tables of scholars and aristocrats.

There was still another reason my father was derided, this one far more grave than his foreigner's tongue. He was a confessed atheist. It was on this account that my mother had no communal standing as his wife, and was subjected to unkind whisperings: she was called concubine, bondmaid, helot; and sometimes, to my shame, harlot. My father had refused the customary marriage rites under the aegis of Hestia, to whose favour my mother had been dedicated at birth, and whose chapel was one of the grandest. When I was old enough to go about by myself, I often wandered there, to stand between the gilded pilasters and stare upward at her image. I went alone; I was always alone. Like my mother, I was not wholly shunned – our polis was too orderly for something so noticeably offensive. Instead, we were discreetly, almost politely, avoided. But here, in the goddess's dim cool shrine, Hestia's arms, outstretched as if ready to embrace, seemed welcoming, even as they overawed with their stony weight. A fire was kept burning in a brazier in her vast lap, tended by a very young acolyte, a boy my own age, dressed like the priests in a pleated white tunic fringed at the ankles. With each shudder of the tossing flames, the goddess's breasts flashed like bucklers; shadows wavered over her massive round toes. And then, as I looked on steadily, her eyes with their carved pupils shifted her gaze to me. I saw that she knew me for what I was: the outcome of my mother's humiliation and my father's subversion.

But my father was insouciant, scorning whatever reached us of these disparagements. And in the months he was with us, we were happy. He had built for us a fine large house, rather more plain than ostentatious; somehow, not because of its size but because of my father's presence, it signified wealth. Indoors, the walls were stippled with brilliant frescoes, landscapes thickened by fruit-bearing orchards, and skies rife with colourful birds. He had forbidden the usual scenes from the lives of the gods; there were to be no gods in our house. My mother protested, but vaguely. She was uncommonly compliant, especially when he teased and kissed her. He called her his camelopard: she had a long neck, on which her small head turned silkily, eyeing him as if to fix him in place. Her tentative smile darkened when the sun's slant began to hint at autumn and his nearing departure. She had been no more than seventeen, one of many earthquake orphans under the care of the polis, when he found her. Though by then seven years had passed, she was still in mourning for her parents. She had seen them devoured by a black crevice widening and widening, out of which a wild fang of blaze leaped up to snatch them, two living torches, into the ravenous abyss. My reticent mother rarely spoke of this, and when she did, it was with a shiver of obeisance, I hardly knew to whom. The gods, the priests, our sibyl? The *barbaros* who had inexplicably succoured her, and given her shelter and the child who was to become his delight?

That I was my father's delight I was fully confident. I was his delight, and his darling, and his joy; and also his little sparrow, and his pearl, and his pomegranate, and his garden of love. These were his fanciful names for me, and many more. He made me believe (and for a long time I did believe it) that he came every year not to see to his business at the kilns, but solely to marvel at how much I had grown, and to bring me presents of woven bracelets and pendants of polished stone and necklaces strung with beads that were really the shells of tiny sea creatures. He told me of the great fishes that swam singing and sighing alongside his ship, huge monstrous things with hairy fins and glistening eyes, and of how when it stormed in the night the waves turned into thrashing tongues frothing at the lips of prow and stern; and that he bore these queer perils all for the sake of once again taking into his arms his little sparrow, his darling, his garden of love, his only delight.

And then would begin my father's anxious questioning: What did I like best to eat? And why did I refuse wine? Where were my playmates, why was I so often alone? Why did I leave my mother, only to loiter among the chapels? What did I do there?

I answered dutifully but aslant. How could I admit, as I stood ringed by the sweetness of his embrace, that my father was the cause of our isolation? Though he periodically engaged a number of household servants, as soon as he departed they would instantly vanish. During the long months of his absence, my mother wrapped herself in loneliness. No one came to us. In a corner, on a little lion-footed tripod table covered with a woollen cloth, she kept an image of Hestia, her protectress. It was carved out of cedar and no taller than her forearm. In the spring, as my father's return approached, she hid it away. Even I, who lived within the sound of her thin breathing, hardly knew where. All this because my father was *atheos*, and we carried his stain – my mother less than I. It was I who carried his blood.

What I dared not tell was how I came to fear the taste of wine. My mother and I drank clear water with our meals, but often enough our cups held wine mixed with water, a faintly half-sweet, half-bitter flavour that, chiefly in the depth of summer, I swallowed greedily. My father, oddly, always avoided our wine, even when it was much diluted. And he had another strange refusal: with a quick thrust of his hand he declined all bread, whether wheat or barley – but only for a certain set of eight days; and after that he would eat normally. My mother did not question these incomprehensible omissions. It was how they lived in his home country, she told me, where even the bread and the wine were unlike our own.

But now I could no longer endure the taste or look or smell of wine. I would not touch any cup that had once held so much as a drop of it. The faintest vinous aroma, even at a distance, struck me as ominous, redolent of the terror that had inflamed me one melancholy afternoon, after my mother and I had said our farewells to my father. The air, with its memory of last year's abandonment, had already begun to grow sick with its presentiments of loneliness. My father clasped each of us close, confiding assurances, especially to my mother, of future comforts, and nestling my face in the familiar bristle of his beard; yet I could see in his eyes that his thoughts were more of departure than of far-off arrival. All that morning he had been supervising the noisy loading of the caravan, while the donkeys yawped amid their droppings, and the drivers abused one another with friendly curses. The moment the last cart was out of sight, my mother's waning smiles flattened into the cheerless silence that would, I knew, afflict her for many weeks.

And so I fled into the late-summer heat, and went to walk again among the chapels. My mother was glad to have me go; I understood that she meant to take out from its hiding place, unobserved, the diminutive image of her protectress, and would set beside it the ritual dishes of figs and sacred seeds. It puzzled me how so shrunken a figure could claim to hold equal power with the towering Hestia in the grandeur of her proper shrine, but my mother's belief was steadfast. As water will flow into any vessel prepared to receive it, she instructed me, so must the presence of the goddess flow into her material incarnation, no matter if it is no bigger than a hand's breadth . . . *ouai*, she murmured, if only your father would not deny it!

Secretly I was tempted to deny it too, and as I stole into the dusk of Hestia's chapel (always it was my single-minded destination), and saw at the far end of its shrouded nave the goddess's mighty lineaments, my mother's tiny replica seemed no more than a childish toy. I had come out of desire, and also out of fear; I feared my father's denial, and my own. Yet by now my father was irretrievably gone, my mother was sick at heart, and in the hallowed twilight of that place I felt sheltered by the force and majesty of the goddess's brooding head and broad thighs, those marble hills in whose valley rested the sacred fire. All things were small beside her, my unhappy mother smaller still.

The acolyte was not alone. A woman stood before the altar at Hestia's feet. She was neither young nor old, her waist was thick and round as a pumpkin, and she was pouring a dark syrup from a narrow flask into the swirling well of the libation bowl. The dense liquid fell in waves and folds, and when the flask was emptied, she placed next to the bowl a barley cake that smelled of honey. The acolyte held out a rattling cup. The woman dropped in a drachma and hurried away.

I distrusted this boy. He was dressed like the priests, but he was not a priest; he was only a boy.

'You always come,' he said. I had never before heard his voice; it was the voice of a female child. Was it because he was not permitted to speak, and could not remember how? I watched him as he sidled to the altar to tend to his duty there – was he not the goddess's servant? But instead he broke off a bit of the cake and licked the beads of honey seeping out.

'Want some?' he said in his strange squeal. 'It's for the priests, though.'

'Are you allowed?'

He gave me a sly look. 'They won't know, will they?'

He picked up a ladle and dipped it into the libation bowl. I saw him sip, and sip again. The wine shimmered and shook in its krater, and then it glinted and shuddered at the rim of the ladle. I was all at once ravished by an invincible thirst; on this parched day of my father's leave-taking, I had forgotten food and drink. I took in the smell, a wild and sour stench, as of some small animal's dung. It was the spoor of the wine, and the wine was in the ladle, trembling there, moving closer, until a droplet touched my lip and wet my tongue, when the stench turned all at once deliriously sweet, like butterflies liquefied, or bird beaks pounded into flowery powder, and I drank, deeply, thirstily, drivenly, a violator, a betrayer of the priests and the goddess herself, but I was indifferent, my throat was a vine on fire, my fingers crawled like twisted vines, vines charred white coiled round all my parts, I was alone, alone, swept up by a burning whirlwind and thrown into an airless void, I belonged nowhere, and I was afraid, afraid of the flame between the goddess's thighs, afraid of my lips and my tongue and the smouldering coals that were my eyes; and I was afraid of what I suddenly and terribly *knew*.

It was a long time before I could return to that place. When I did, the acolyte kept his distance. He never again spoke to me.

And when my father had been gone for several weeks, and we were in our customary seclusion, my mother one day confided to me, all unexpectedly, what she had long understood to be my father's secret. It was only because of the earthquake that he had taken her, she told me, an orphan tainted by the wrath of Hades, and it was because of the earthquake that she was not the proper wife of a proper husband, and was made to suffer now like some grieving widow, though she was not a widow, and what was she then, if she was not a proper wife? My mother's recurrent malaise too often plagued our solitude, and I saw that she was again falling into forlornness. It was her habit to skirt any talk of the cataclysm that had despoiled her earlier years, particularly when I was nearby to hear it; she wished to shield me from these old scenes, even if in their remoteness from our ordinary landscape they seemed to me no different from fables. Yet now, in the fever of her telling (it came upon her like a seizure), she spoke over and over of the wrath of Hades whose punishment it was, the ruination of houses and orchards and animals and crops, the ruination of everything civilized, and how in the bleak aftermath of the last of the tremors she had lingered for many hours half naked in her torn tunic at the brink of the steaming trench; and she told of the looting that followed, and the riots when there was little to eat, and the knives and the fury and the bloodshed. The wrath of Hades? All this impressed me as a passing figment of her disordered temper: how did such long-ago wounds accord with our sedate and harmonious polis, governed by the priests under the inspiration of our sibyl? And had not those wounds been transfigured by the newcomer to our restrained and measured realm, my mother's saviour, the redeemer of her misfortunes – my father?

'And did I not know it,' she wailed, 'did I not know it even then? He comes and he comes, but one time he will not come, the sea will break his vessel, he will stop his breath among the fishes, or else, or else,' in a voice almost too thin to grasp, 'one day he will not come because he no longer wishes to come.'

I asked why my father, who loved me so, would not ever wish to come.

And then my mother confessed what she believed to be my father's great deceit. In his home country, she told me, he had a proper wife, how could it be otherwise? And a proper family, and yes, a foreign daughter, how could it be otherwise?

I believed her belief. I believed it even more intently than I believed her belief in the dark god's spite: how should my guileless mother merit the lash of his underworld? But the other daughter, how my envious imaginings stung! Did she love my father as yearningly as I? It rankled me that a foreign girl could bask under his fond eye nearly all the year, while me he held close only for a summer's blink. And did she not speak his home-country tongue, as I could not, and was she not intimate with his home-country ways? How often and often had I wished that my father were one of us! – though sometimes, as I contemplated my mother pleading before her protectress's small shrine, it came to me that the other daughter might be no more than a phantom, the lurking creature of my mother's frights.

But when my father returned, all these darknesses fled. His ship had skimmed a stormless sea, he was hale and ruddy-cheeked from the prickly northern winds and oh! the presents he brought, brooches inlaid with turquoise, and baskets woven in many colours heaped with gleaming olives different in shape and taste from ours, and scarves and bracelets and a glossy bronze looking glass, and even sandals hung with silver beads, unlike any we had ever seen. My mother brightened; her toy Hestia had already been rushed into its hiding place. Immediately fresh troops of servants were bustling everywhere, sweeping out neglected corners, criss-crossing the courtyard, fetching water and grinding meal, all the while showing uncommon deference. It was easy then to put away jealousy: how plain it was that my father could *not* love a foreign child more than he loved his pearl, his pomegranate, his little sparrow!

And now we were happy once more. In the mornings my father went to the kilns, and again in the late afternoon, but the hours in between belonged to my mother and me. Together we set out for the fields, carrying pouches of cakes and fruit. We walked until the footpaths ended and everything before us was brush and tangles of green, and then my father would be sure to tell us that the fields of his own land were no different; it was only the families of wild flowers that were not the same. Or else, to flavour our lavish dinners of fish or lamb, we would visit the market stalls in the agora, in search of herbs and spices he was familiar with and we were not. My father would sometimes allow me to go with him to the kilns before sunset, to tally and mark with his mark the pots he had purchased that day. The tedium and the dust and the heat and the incessant shouting of the kiln masters, he warned, would tire me. But despite the lingering smoke and the biting smells of glaze and moist clay, I was never wearied there, where the armies of finished pots marched in brilliant rows – how I loved to see their shapes and colours! Some had handles like ears, and others were thin-necked and fat-bellied, and on their flanks so many patterns, scrolls or stripes or leaves curled like snails.

Even so, what enchanted me more than all the rest were the pots that told stories: figures in motion, bearing kraters or kneeling or with uplifted arms gripping weapons, all devotedly and meticulously painted, as if they could come alive if only they willed it. Like any child of our polis, I knew their stories well: here was Gaia, here was Poseidon with his trident, and Demeter and Zeus, and poor frightened Persephone, dragged by deathly Hades into the chasm's cruel gullet. And still my father coveted them all!

For the very first time I dared to question him. Hadn't he banned from the fresh walls of our new-built house any fresco depicting the gods, no matter how it would have pleased my mother, whose every solace he unfailingly sought to indulge? And now look – all these sanctified chronicles on pots, and as always he intended to take them away with him!

My father caressed my cheeks, a tender habit meant to calm me, though now it could not. 'Oh my little bird,' he said, 'only see how beautiful, the tunics of the women, how the cloth folds and unfolds, like shadow and light, and the limbs of the men, their force –'

'But they are *gods*!' I cried. Could he not see, did he not know?

'In my home country they will not be gods, they will be what they are, beautiful mortal men and beautiful mortal women.'

And I thought: how barren, how deprived, was my father's far-off land, where beauty was denied to the gods.

It was after this troubled colloquy (and wasn't it almost a quarrel?) that my father began to ply me with strange tales. They were, he said, the history of his home country. We would rest in the courtyard in the thick of the afternoon, when the air quivered from heat, and the pavement sizzled, and the servants dozed over their tasks, and my mother napped in the shuttered cool of an inner room. Then my father told of an infant saved from drowning by a king's daughter, who reared him to grandeur in the royal palace, only to see him lead a fearsome rebellion. He told of a youth who knew the meaning of dreams, whose envious brothers sold him into a foreign kingdom, where he rose out of a dungeon to become a powerful vizier. He told of a great flood that swallowed the earth, except for one old drunkard with his one small boat, who salvaged all future life. He told of an ill-starred voyager, who, thrown overboard by terrified sailors, fell into the belly of a mammoth fish. He told of a boy who brought down a giant with nothing more formidable than a simple slingshot.

My father told all these stories, and many more. Some I shrank from and some I wondered at; but privately I judged them inferior – what were they, after all, but the earthbound dry happenings of the ordinary world, haplessly cut off from the dazzlements of Olympus? Men, not gods, struggled in these tales, while *our* histories, how glorious they were! – the rages and lusts and jealousies of goddesses and gods, how they caused the skies to rumble and the seas to churn, how the lot of humankind hung from their passions, and how, if they were drawn to the love of a mortal, what heroes, Heracles and Achilles, erupted from their loins!

I said nothing of this to my father.

Instead, I asked whether in his home country they kept a sibyl, as we did.

No, my father said. And I began to pity him a little: it seemed to me then that my father, *barbaros* and *atheos*, must live in an uncivilized land. This dim inkling of a divide, finer than a spider's line, made me cling to him all the more, and to the everyday pleasures of our little family. We went on wandering the fields, the three of us, often lying contented and laughing in the long grasses with our heads flattening the wild flowers, and our noses yellowed by pollen, and our mouths purpled from the juice of the grapes we had eaten. And still – though he was not, he did not wish to be, one of us – I was my father's darling, his sparrow, his pomegranate, his garden of love.

But I determined that I would no longer go walking among the chapels, and that the great gleaming Hestia in her cathedral shrine would never again lure me.

Year after year, unwaveringly, I kept this private vow, both when my father was happily with us and in the dreary months of my mother's melancholia when he was not. There were seasons that brought him to us in the earliest days of spring, and other times when summer had already reached its midpoint. All this fickleness rested, he teased, on the temperament of the sailors: an indolent crew dallies and dawdles. Or if the big fishes knock their heavy tails against the starboard, like cats begging for a morsel. But we knew he meant the whims of the hungering sea.

One year, when the summer was beginning to drift toward exhaustion, my father had still not come.

'It must be the winds,' I said, 'flying hard against him.'

Or I said, to lighten my mother's thoughts, 'How lazy those sailors are.'

Or I said, 'The sea cats are crowding his path.'

And then I said, 'Surely he will come, he always comes, soon he will come, he has never not come –'

But my mother said, 'He will not come.'

And he did not.

From then on, my mother descended into grieving. We were invariably alone. Our suppers were meagre. Morning and evening I heard my mother's murmured pleas and lamentations before her small protectress, now always out of its hiding place; but the propitiatory dishes were bare.

'*Ouai*,' she soughed, 'he is drowned, he is drowned,' and covered the twist of her mouth with her pale hands, on which I could see the grey ridges of veins like the ridges made by cart tracks in earth after rain.

Or else she said in her flat strained voice, 'He has chosen his proper family, it is his proper place.'

And was this not, I thought, the very reason for the fierceness of our love? Because he was not, and did not wish to be, one of us – and yet had he not come to succour and rejoice us?

But my mother said bitterly, 'It was only for the kilns that he came, and never for us. Never did he come for us.'

And I saw that grief was coarsening and muddling my mother's heart. She was willing now, more and more, to speak of the earthquake, and of the wild time afterward, those fearful years of chaos and violence, as dire as the upheaval itself. She told and retold (how tedious it was!) the old familiar tales of how the priests in despair had summoned our sibyl from the far north, and how they kept her secluded, no one knew where – grove, or cave, or forest – and how through the sway of her divinations and prophecies our polis was at length pacified and cleansed. These storied events had neither impressed nor dismayed my father; the sibyl, he would chide my mother, was mere woman, and many women were wise who never governed . . . and then my mother would clasp her breast as if a tiny beast were strangling there, and cry out, '*Ouai, atheos!*'

In those sorrowful days of mourning, my father's erasure from our lives returned to her awry: it was the earthquake that had devoured him, and never the sea; or she would fall into a dreamy lassitude and promise that my father was certain to come again when the sun burned hot on the lintel and flocks of foreign birds filled the skies. And sometimes, because I gave no obeisance to her little Hestia, and passed it by without so much as a glance, she charged me with denying the gods, and turned her plaintive look on me to ask, 'Who will there be to marry one such as you?'

In this way, half bewildered and maundering, my mother sickened. She vomited the gruel I pressed on her and spat out the water in her cup, and the skin of her neck frayed like a wrinkled rope, and in the spring, when my father once more did not come, she died. Season after season, month upon month, time relentlessly dividing itself, I sat solitary in my father's house (so I regarded it), and saw the pavement in the courtyard crack, and a wilderness of scrub creep up through a mazy map of fissures, and watched as the frescoes faded and flaked into a drizzle of powder at a finger's touch.

But I had not forgotten the hoard of my treasures – my father's countless gifts of brooches and necklaces and pendants and bracelets, each with its precious stones, and the sandals with their silver beads, too beautiful to have ever been worn, and the bronze looking glass. I had long ago given up adorning myself; these things were useless to me now. One by one, I took them to the agora to sell, lest I become impoverished. It was only the bronze looking glass that I thought to keep.

I disliked these periodic excursions to the market stalls, infrequent though they were. The sharp smell of spices pierced and saddened me: here our little family had once loitered, while my father sorted through ruffled leaves and roots and tubers and tubs of ground bark with the same determined delicacy he brought to choosing lekythoi at the kilns, as if a sprig of fenugreek was as lovely to his eye as a painted jar. But now, caught among the roiling streams of tattle that agitated the agora, I knew myself to be a rumour, a byword, a warning; yet I hardly understood why. Was I not as native to our polis as any passer-by? The stares of the merchants unsettled me – they retreated into the dark of their stalls as I approached. Was it because I was a woman alone, an abandoned relic in a hollow ruin, childless, unwanted? Was it because I rarely cared to speak? To whom should I speak, and to what end? Who would love me as I had once been loved by my father?

In the bronze looking glass I saw what I was. My father's eyes gazed back at me with unfamiliar ferocity; swollen blue-black pockets bulged beneath them. My hair, white as a cloud, unbound and untamed, was as vagrant as some massive shrub torn up by an unforgiving wind. My mouth frightened me: a hive of terrible silences.

In my fifty-seventh year, long after even the looking glass had been sold, our sibyl died. Very few could remember a time when she was not the unseen guardian of our decorum and our laws; for us, she was ageless and faceless. Her lineage was unknown. No one had ever heard her voice. It was said that the goddess to whom she was pledged had decreed at her birth that she was not to live beyond two hundred years.

And soon a savage tumult seized our polis. Bins of ripened fruits overturned and trampled in the marketplace, stalls barricaded, old women wailing in the confusion. Menacing packs of youths heaving boulders downhill to crash into whatever stood in their path, thieves running free, hauling their prey. Trembling curs prowling in the night, sniffing for scraps, their tattered fur hanging loose from their bellies. Everywhere fear – fear of brokenness, fear of hunger, fear of bloodletting and malice.

Only I was left unharmed, I with my snarled coils of hair, my speech idled and shattered, sitting day after day under the lintel of my father's decaying house, listening to the groans and maledictions of a dying polis. Fires on the hills, fires in the fields, the chapels on fire, the agora smouldering, always the fires: the sun veiled in smoke.

It was on just such an afternoon of burning air that the priests came.

I saw them at first at a distance, a procession of seven shrouded figures, and supposed it to be yet another rite of expiation to stem the crawling flames. I had often witnessed these futile parades as they passed, chanting and swinging their censers, as if those small vessels of heated coals had the power to extinguish the greater conflagration. As they moved nearer, they were more easily defined: all wore long pleated white garments fringed at the ankle bone and flecked with soot. Six were bareheaded and clean-shaven; two of these were clearly acolytes in their teens, and one was a withered patriarch with a palsied chin. The seventh, whom I took to be their chief, wore a gilded circlet round his head, and plaited through his abundant beard were sooty ribbons of coloured silk.

But this time there were no censers, and no chanting, and the silent cortège drifted unfathomably toward me, until it stopped directly before my feet.

One of the acolytes knelt and removed my sandals. At a word from the priest with the palsied chin – who appeared to be their spokesman, though not their leader – the other invaded the dirty gloom of my father's house and quickly brought out my mother's toy Hestia. Her little shrine had remained in its old corner, untouched and untended; but the lion-footed table that held it I had long ago sold.

I was instructed to follow where I was led, past the blighted agora into fields of grasses like blackened straw, and onward through soot-blasted fields farther yet, where my father had never taken us, and over a rise and beyond it, and finally into a place of stones. Here the fires had never reached. I was made to walk on my naked feet, so that they might toughen and grow hard and invulnerable, no matter that the thistles were piercing my heels, or that my soles were torn and bloodied. The stones rose tall and taller as we proceeded, until they seemed to form a kind of grotto, a cavern of earth and stone through which ran a trickle of icy water. I was shown the nearby spring that was its source: I was permitted to drink of this spring, and to relieve myself there, but it was forbidden to bathe in its water, except for when the moon was shrunk to the shape of a fingernail. It was forbidden to forage for leaves or berries: I must be satisfied with what, morning and evening, the acolytes would bring. If it turned cold, I was not to plead for a fire; again I must be content with whatever habit or vesture the acolytes might offer. It was forbidden to speak to the acolytes. It was forbidden to cover my feet; it was an offence to the gods. It was forbidden to depart from this place; it was a profanation. It was forbidden to eat or drink on the days designated for the coming of the priests: my body must be purified in preparation.

These were the precepts imparted to me by the priest with the palsied chin.

The chief priest, who until then had been mute, now spoke; out of his throat came a crooked falsetto. It was his duty, he said, to recite the evidences and conditions, the signs and confirmations, that had brought me to this hour of initiation. It was known that my mother had, despite all, been a woman of piety, dedicated to Hestia, before whose domestic shrine she had faithfully submitted her reverence; and that after her death, having denuded my house of all manner of precious things, as affirmed by the merchants of the agora, I retained and continued my mother's allegiance: the proof being the shrine itself, carried away by an acolyte enjoined to seek corroboration. Secondly, it was known that even from earliest childhood it was my passion to frequent the holy chapels in order to search out the veracity and power of their deities. Thirdly, it was attested by the kiln masters that as a young girl I was heard disputing with my father on behalf of the gods. And fourthly –

As if overcome by a chill, the chief priest halted. Already there were intimations of the night to come, deepened by the long cold shadows of the stones. I looked into his face, that part of it visible above the great beard with its ornaments, and in the dwindling light saw an elderly man my own age, whose voice was strangely broken and stunted and shrill, akin to an infant's cry; and I knew him.

Fourthly, he resumed in that childlike pitch, your father's blood has become as water, and now you are freed and made holy. Dangerous and despised, an interloper and a blasphemer, he came among us only to usurp our native treasure. Him the gods have justly destroyed. Behold! I, Grand Priest and First Servant to the Oracle, hereby annul the stain!

The acolytes, meanwhile, had brought me to a flat stone close to the spring, where, encircled by a tall ring of concealing stones, I was made to prostrate myself. Over me stood the chief priest. He himself, he piped, was witness to the child I once was, and how in the cathedral shrine of Hestia, guardian of the civic hearth, and in the glimmer of the sacral flame between her thighs, he saw me overtaken by those signs of election given only to whom the goddess anoints: the sacerdotal frenzy, its telltale howls and whirlings, the shrieks of terror and elation at the instant of possession. It was by the will of the goddess that I should be as I now was: old and foretold, and virgin, and a woman apart.

As I lay there, smelling the damp earth, my face a brief space above the ground, I was aware of something alive and moist licking its way across the naked soles of my feet. It humped and curled as it slid into view: here was the habitation of snakes.

And so began what I was to become. To all these things – the admonitions and the testimonies, the rites and the annunciations – I had easily acquiesced. It was as well to live among stones as to linger emptily under the rotted lintel of my father's house. And if I wished, might I not readily escape this place – to go where? Too quickly I learned that my naked feet were my prison. When one bloody wound healed, another would open – either I blundered into a nest of thorns, or unwittingly cut my heel on a half-buried stone, sharp as an arrow. By cushioning leaves and grasses on a scrap of bark, and twining them round with the vines that crawled among the stones, I contrived to be roughly shod. The acolytes, I discovered, were indifferent to this and every other transgression. When I spoke to them, they answered freely; in the absence of the priests, they were no more than careless boys. I would hear them laughing and cavorting as they approached, and too often it happened that the meal they were carrying was spilled; and then I was left to go hungry.

It was from the acolytes that I came to know how our sibyl had met her death – not by divine command, as proclaimed by the priests, but by the bite of a snake in the heel. A commonplace: such a calamity might befall anyone, even in so mundane and frequented a spot as the agora itself. I had no fear of the snakes; they lived as I now lived, earth-bound among the stones. I saw them as neighbours and companions, and at times amused myself by trailing them to their lairs; in this way I stumbled on a trove of sweet berries to gladden my hunger. Now and again, when one of these beasts lay motionless in a coil, in a fit of rapture I would be moved to study the colours and patterns of its skin, as I had once been stirred by the colours and patterns of my father's pots at the kilns. And all around, the stones in the changing light showed their changing tempers: the configurations of their small shadowed juttings and hollows came to resemble human features. More than once it seemed that my father's face looked out at me.

I had no desire to leave this place. It was sufficient. My feet, latterly growing calloused and tough, were at last freeing me to wander away – yet why should I? If a piercing wind invaded, or if the sun blazed too harshly, the tall stones shielded me. I bathed when I pleased, I slept and woke when I pleased. The acolytes, like the days and the nights in their passing, came and went. The polis and its disorders were distant.

But I was in dread of the moon. I watched as it swelled, evening by evening; soon the priests would return. And at the time fixed for divination, when the moon was white and round and seamed with bluish veins, they arrived as they had before, in a procession, wordlessly. Behind them came the acolytes, carrying great waxed tablets – so many petitions and devotions, undertakings and devisings, ordinances and decrees, how they frightened me! All were to pass through me when the goddess entered my body.

I was made to wear a gown of pure linen – it girdled my neck and fell to my knees; my breasts it left bare. I was ashamed of my old woman's dried-up nipples and wrinkled dugs, but for these too I had been chosen: the proud gods disdain rivals to their beauty. No one envies a crone.

And my feet were again naked, but ugly and yellowed and hard as shells.

The chief priest drew me to the spring, where I was made to mount the flat stone of my initiation. Here I was to remain sequestered by the surrounding upright stones, and here I was to summon the goddess. Had I eaten or drunk that day? I said I had not. Though the acolytes had been instructed to withhold my meals, all afternoon I had glutted on berries and cupped my hands at the spring.

Then now you must drink.

He set down at my feet a silver kalyx and left me. I saw through the gaps in the stones how the priests with their tablets had gathered in a knot, silent and waiting; but I saw only their backs. It was forbidden to come near. It was forbidden to witness the act of possession.

I picked up the kalyx and looked into its mouth. Swaying from side to side, as if agitated by some double tide, was a viscous purple sea. Its odour was foul. Its fumes were bitter.

And what must I do now?

I lifted my arms to the white moon and called to the goddess.

Come. Come, I called, again and again. Come. Only come.

She did not come, and what must I do now?

The moonlight had carved small pits and grooves in the stones that hemmed me round like sentinels, and I saw my father's eyes, black and lidless, gaping out of the nearest stele; and I knew what I must not do.

I must not succumb. I must not surrender.

I stood erect on the sacral mound and from the lip of the kalyx slowly, slowly, spilled stain upon stain into the waters of the spring, observing how purple bled into red, and how red paled to clear transparency, until the spring flowed as innocently as before.

And then I gave out a great hideous shriek, and another, and another, my throat grappling more and more violently in its box, and I beat the stone at my feet, pounding and pounding with the silver kalyx, until a savage ringing raged all around, as if a phalanx of gongs were tumbling out of the night, and I spewed out unearthly words that were no words, only crippled syllables and feral growls and squeals, and I barked like a hound and hissed like a cat, and humped and crawled on my belly in the way of the snakes, and I clawed at my hair to twist it into worms, and thrashed and flailed on my slab, and writhed and cackled and yowled, and all the while I held on and held on, I would not succumb, I dared not surrender; and the goddess did not come.

She did not come, and I fell to the ground emptied, breathless; spent. No shaft of exaltation had penetrated the hollows of my body,

I was what I was born to be, no more than mortal woman, and below all my clamour a brutal silence, the silence of the oracle that never was and never will be, the merciless silence of the goddess who never was and never will be, and now the voices of the priests, chanting, importuning, praising and blessing the goddess's terrifying power, her pity and absolution, crying out their tremulous petitions and grievances, their perplexities and yearnings, their ordinances and vainglorious decrees, all in submission to the sublime will – and what was I to do now, I who am deceiver and dissembler, false in ecstasy, false in frenzy, I who carry the blood of him who was not, and did not wish to be, one of us?

I have since outlived them all, the chief priest with his castrato mewlings, and the priest with the palsied chin, and I have outlived even the heedless acolytes, all of them given way to new priests and new careless boys. Always there will be the priests, and always there will be my companions the snakes with their unfeeling eyes and radiant skins, and always and always the tall stones that shelter my shrine. Nowadays I cover my feet with thick leather clogs (I have already been bitten twice, but mildly, and the fever soon passed), and when it is very cold, I make a fire if it pleases me (the acolytes bring the wood), and all in all I live as I like, and am content.

In the roundings of time, the acolytes seem always the same, the older reticent, the younger garrulous, and both uncommonly beautiful – the chief priests, I believe, choose them for their lovely mouths and soft napes. The younger is eager to give me news of the polis, how once in an unhappy autumn the remnants of my father's house were razed to rubble by a whirling storm, brief and already half forgotten, which was said to cause scores of ships to be shattered, so that the traders no longer arrive, and the kiln masters are gone elsewhere to establish their craft anew. And in the fields beyond the agora, there are now wine presses and oil presses, bringing much prosperity. The charred grasses are again green, and the wild flowers dense, and throughout the polis order and serenity.

The priests go on, as of old, appealing to the goddess for holy guidance; but it is I who sanction and govern and make the laws, though the priests cannot know this. I no longer fear the growing moon and the wine with its treacheries, and the coming of the priests in procession cannot shake me. I am their mistress, and if I howl and convulse on the sacred mound, I do it not to indulge their belief, but to scorn it: the gods are a lie. Yet how accuse these solemn elders of delusion? As much accuse the snakes of their venom; it is their truth.

And I have learned, in time, to reveal the goddess's answer in the form of a puzzle, or a riddle, or an enigma with as many sides as a polygon: when diligently parsed, they cannot fail of reason or usefulness. As for the wine, always I am careful to paint the waters of the spring with its ebbing colours; but sometimes I leave a little at the bottom of the kalyx to give to the acolytes when they bring the morning meal. The older is reluctant and afraid, but the younger drinks lustily.

My father's image has faded from the nubs and crevices of the stones, and I scarcely ever look for it there. But on still summer nights, when ships are safe at sea, and the snakes hide in their thickets, and the spring runs soundlessly, and even the stones are tranquil, I think of that primitive and barbarous land, my father's home country, where their tongue is not our tongue, and their bread is not our bread, and their tales are not our tales, and they keep no sibyl and know no gods . . . then who is it that gives them their laws, lacking, as they do, one such as I? ∎

© CAMILLE LEPAGE / HANS LUCAS
from *On Est Ensemble*
After hundreds of Christians are killed by Seleka, Christians retaliate
by looting and burning down mosques.
Bangui, Central African Republic, 10 December 2013

# A PLACE ON EARTH

## SCENES FROM A WAR

## *Anjan Sundaram*

They returned to the beginning. War approached, and the city was being emptied. I walked two miles into the wild with a boy who showed me how Gaga – and the country, the Central African Republic – was being turned inside out. The jungle paths had become the alleyways of a more secretive, older form of civilization: these identical, curving roads without signposts in which I became lost, and these homes of leaves and bent branches. The roofs collapsed in each rain shower, the boy said, and had to be built anew.

We were at the front. The sounds of the bombs were like thunder, instinctively making me look up, again, only to see that the sky was clear, and the repeated clarity of the sky was confusing. The sun was brilliant, like a jewel, the jungle thick with humidity and the people were moving their lives to the bush, isolating themselves because trust between human beings had been broken and there was no security in openness. Association in the jungle was kept to a minimum: we heard voices within the leaves but the boy did not want even to look. Suddenly, while I was walking beside men wounded by gunshots, their arms and legs wrapped in dirty gauze, I was forced off the path and into the foliage by an old woman coming down from Gaga holding above her the wooden frame of a double bed.

'*Maman*,' I called out, half in surprise.

She said, 'Help us, son.'

Living in Rwanda, I had heard of the war in the Central African Republic. But when I called people in the country to obtain more information, their words only confused me. Basic questions could not be answered: how many dead, where, killed by whom? It was not clear that the perpetrators of these killings were allied with their official leader, President Michel Djotodia. Reports of killings would reach the capital days or weeks after they had occurred. I came to the Central African Republic in an attempt to witness and record what was happening. At the airport in Cameroon, while waiting for my connecting flight to Bangui, I saw footage of a foreign reporter wearing a flak jacket, which I did not possess, declaring that she had 'discovered' evidence of a new massacre of a few dozen people. I did not know what to make of that report. It seemed at once significant and to explain little of the giant, mounting conflict.

I arrived to find that this was a war of walkers. People walked to and from the shifting front lines, often through the jungle, avoiding the roads. There were many fronts across the Republic, and no one I asked, among the foreign peacekeepers, government soldiers or the militias that opposed the government, could tell me how many, or where they were. A former government soldier told me that after losing a battle he walked for two months and circled the front to find only villages of dead people. The heroes were the cobblers. Everywhere in the country, even in the bush, you could see them frantically sewing footwear for those who needed to flee.

It was their own government the people feared. The government was pillaging and killing, and seemed to have no interest or competence in governance, but it had been recognized by the United Nations and granted all the legal protections due a state. Many Central Africans I spoke to did not understand how such a brutal force could be granted legitimacy. Peacekeepers had arrived to protect both the people and government bases and those who opposed the government were being disarmed. At international conferences world leaders discussed solutions. Who should be responsible for the country? The government had the most powerful army, so it had to be recognized. But the government was killing the people. So who else should we recognize? The Central African people were rising up against the plunder and rape resulting from this diplomatic absurdity, forming militias armed with home-made hunting rifles. And this confrontation by the people's militias – called the anti-balaka, or anti-machete – against the government was how the city of Gaga, situated in the jungle, had become the war's newest front.

What is the Central African Republic? It is a central African republic, bordering the Democratic Republic of Congo, the Republic of Congo, Cameroon, Chad, Sudan and South Sudan. Its people, central Africans, are Central Africans. This country, identified by capitalizations, was seized in March 2013 by a rebel force called Seleka, which has caused an emergency of global proportions. Several thousands have likely been killed, but over such a vast territory, much of it so remote, that the true toll is still unknown. Seleka – 'alliance' in the local language, Sango – brought President Michel Djotodia to power, forming what is now the government of the Central African Republic. But after its conquest the Seleka's many foreign officers from Chad and Sudan escaped Djotodia's authority and declared their own fiefdoms. The president has said, 'I'm in control of my own men, those I don't control are not my men,' as if it were an explanation. Meanwhile, the Seleka fighters who rule over the towns as small kings do not know the land and, not speaking Sango, communicate with the population through interpreters. They have taken local officials hostage and made them sign decrees in the name of the government. In many towns I visited I heard the same story: the colonizers who are our government came door to door and plundered our money, food, medicine and killed our young men.

The Central African Republic's war began in December 2012, when Seleka invaded the country. The president then was François Bozizé, the last in a long line of military officers who had seized power in a *coup d'état*. Coups in the Central African Republic were traditionally supported by France, but Bozizé, who held office for ten years, had been aided by Chad. Bozizé later spurned his Chadian benefactors, who returned as Seleka, allied with Central African Muslims and other anti-Bozizé militias from Chad and Sudan. This coalition of fighters moved easily through the Republic; cities were captured with hardly a fight, according to former Bozizé soldiers and General Abdel Kalil, a confidant of President Djotodia. 'We would reach a city,' General Kalil told me in his crumbling home near the president's office in Bangui, 'and there would be a little fire but suddenly Bozizé's forces would flee and we would take the town without either side suffering casualties.' General Kalil told me he had earned his rank of general in one of the few fierce battles during Seleka's invasion, about eight miles from Bangui, when he saw what he thought was a pigeon that had been shot fluttering on the ground, only to realize it was a piece of his flesh. I met some of Bozizé's soldiers at a military garrison where they had been detained by the Seleka. I asked why they had capitulated so easily. 'Bozizé did not trust his soldiers with heavy weapons,' one of them said. 'He feared we would overthrow him.' Rather than arm his troops, Bozizé called upon the South African army for support. But after suffering casualties while battling the rebels, the South Africans left the country.

This occupation of the Central African Republic by Seleka harks back to a history of regional kingdoms in flux. The fabled Sudanese warlord Rabih az-Zubayr ruled most of the Central African Republic until 1900. Ten years later the territory became part of French Equatorial Africa, which also included Chad. Barthélemy Boganda, a Central African independence leader in the mould of the great African statesmen Nkrumah, Nyerere and Biko, named this country the Central African Republic because he wished it to be part of an African federation, a United States of Africa. His vision was one of African unity; but he also worried that his country might otherwise be annexed by newly independent and relatively powerful African states like Guinea or Ghana. Boganda was killed – some say by the French – in a 1959 plane crash, one year before the Central African Republic gained independence. His country was left with its peculiar name but bereft of his vision. The Republic has since suffered five coups. France has retained a portion of its colonial role. Its forces have secured strategic parts of Bangui, with the tricolour flying atop the airport.

When I returned from the bush, walking past a procession of villagers carrying their things on their heads, Gaga was shuttered – the blue, brown and yellow doors of the shops interspersed the avenues of homes whose bricks had disintegrated and roofs were burnt off, all empty but for the pigs: these were also the occupiers. The Seleka are almost entirely Muslim – the country was predominantly Christian – and its fighters had killed people and plundered homes but had not touched the pigs, which had taken over the towns in this inversion of man and beast, of civilization and nature. As people scurried to take shelter in the jungle, the pigs made love in what had once been the kitchens and fed on corpses left on the ground.

I grew uneasy about staying in Gaga, at the front, for I could see that the anti-balaka was pushing back the government: from points in the forest rose black plumes of smoke, each closer to us than the last. The government forces here were led by Commander Yusuf and his deputy, Tony Montana, who aspired to be 'wicked' like Al Pacino in *Scarface*, though his voice had not yet broken.

'What about the approaching battle?' I said.

'Our boys are winning,' Yusuf replied, sounding convinced.

'Then why are the people fleeing Gaga?'

'Which people are fleeing?' He said he was not aware.

I could not allow myself to be found in this government base, for I might be taken to be a Seleka supporter.

The heat of the afternoon was soporific, and mixed with the tension. I sat beside Yusuf for an hour, waiting to see if he would push back the anti-balaka, when a white pickup burst over the hilltop and into the base. A group of armed boys, chains of bullets wrapped around their bodies, shielded a government general. I had been correct: the battle was at a tipping point. What followed was a scene of a general's fury at the front. Four civilians on a motorcycle appeared, hoping to pass the barrier and exit Gaga.

'Stop!' screamed someone from the general's entourage.

'But we want to cross,' the villagers pleaded. They were made to get off the bike, which was in good condition, and told to continue on foot with their casseroles, ladles and mattresses. The general, in his olive-green suit and open-toed leather sandals, pointed at Yusuf and began to shout insults, saying Yusuf had sent fifteen fighters to their deaths against three hundred assassins. 'Are you a soldier?' the general bellowed. The question may have been rhetorical: Yusuf had told me that he was a professional diamond miner. The general hurried down the hill to Gaga's city centre with his entourage of boys. I followed him at a distance.

Behind me the boy Tony Montana took charge of the base and in his high-pitched voice ordered soldiers many decades older than him to rearrange the chairs and be still. 'We need some quiet, why are we talking so much?'

'Who is talking here?' a soldier said.

'Do you want a whipping?' said Tony. He began to dismantle his AK-47, undoing springs and screws and in irritation attempted to jam a bullet into a cartridge already full. He told his soldiers that he needed to think, and that he needed to work out how they were going to win this battle or they could all be killed that same night.

'Is there any Islam here?' The general's voice resounded in the marketplace. His arms were raised, his fingers pointing to the sky. 'We need motorbikes and petrol,' the general said, 'so we can defeat the enemy. Will you help?' He knew that the front was in danger of being swallowed by the anti-balaka, that in some hours they could arrive at this place. His boys began to swirl around the marketplace, grabbing motorbikes; petrol was emptied into them from plastic bottles. I was witnessing a scene of procurement in this war, which was so inchoate that a few vehicles poached from poor villagers might make the difference between victory and defeat in a battle. The market smelled of fumes. The general climbed onto one of the bikes, crushing its suspension under his weight, and headed into the jungle with his twenty boys and their heavy weapons. I could hear the roars of the engines after they were out of sight. The people in the market had fallen silent.

I found a government fighter in a white singlet on the dirt road into the jungle. I told him that I wanted to follow the general. He shook his head because he did not understand.

'Aarabiya?' he said.

'Sorry, no Arabic. No French?'

'Sorry, no French.'

'Sango?'

'No Sango.'

'English?' I offered as a last resort.

He slapped my back. 'My friend,' he said, 'my name is Colonel Aktahir and I come from Sudan.' So in this city hardly accessible to the world outside we were speaking the language of the colonizer.

But the colonel refused to let me into the jungle. 'Who will guarantee your safety?' he said.

I told him that I wanted to witness the general's victory. He promised a report of the towns the general would protect. But I knew that if the anti-balaka were winning – why else would the general have arrived at the front? – the government would be brutal, as it had been since the war's beginning, and that with thirty-five men, even well armed, the general could not take on three hundred. What would he do inside that jungle? I had to find a way inside. Perhaps it was possible to take another route.

The boy who had taken me to the new civilization in the jungle, to the houses of leaves, was sitting on the edge of a cemetery dug for victims in Gaga from that past month. Speaking softly so the Seleka would not hear him, he told me that four major towns lay on the road the general had taken – Camp Bangui, Zoé, Dombourou and Carrefour – and that their many thousands of residents were at risk, for the Seleka would assume that they were aiding the anti-balaka. There was another way to reach those towns, on a poor road. You could only walk, or possibly go on a motorbike, and it would take you hours but it was the only other axis, and maybe it was free of the Seleka. A friend of the boy told me that the journey would take a day. Another villager I asked said that it would take fifty hours.

Four days after I saw the government general – he was also Sudanese, Colonel Aktahir told me, and his name was Abdallah Hamat – ride into the jungle from Gaga, I arrived in the early morning at the town of Bekadili. I was accompanied by Lewis Mudge, a Human Rights Watch researcher I knew from Rwanda, here to research recent massacres, and Thierry Messongo, a Central African journalist. I was apprehensive about going to Dombourou and Camp Bangui, the towns in the jungle that General Hamat had likely attacked. I wanted Lewis and Thierry as companions. But they feared the journey would be too dangerous. I was not being helped by the motorcycle drivers in Bekadili, who were themselves afraid to go to a place of recent battle. No information had emerged from Camp Bangui in four days – only rumours of an attack. No survivors had arrived from the town, and no one had gone to see, not even from Bekadili, which was on the main road and had access to motorcycles.

I tried to convince a group of drivers to make the journey. It was their community, their people who had been struck. Should someone not go and see what had happened, and possibly report it?

'We suffer too,' the drivers said to me.

'More than those people in those villages?'

'Yes.'

'All right,' I said, 'that's fine then, we won't go.'

But I waited and watched as they began to chatter among themselves. A man would tell me he was ready; minutes later he would tell me he was too afraid. I said aloud, to no one in particular, that if it grew too dangerous we would turn back before reaching the towns. Two hours later I had three committed drivers. Pack your bags, I told Lewis, we're going in.

Reassured by the drivers' willingness, he and Thierry agreed to come.

The forest was dense and the road almost formless. The drivers kept speaking of a 'highway'; we arrived at the highway, a strip of dirt. Such were the axes that the people used to traverse this country. There were few roads: a strip was so precious that it was referred to as a highway. We rode through tall grass that ripped across and burned our faces. Looking over the driver's shoulder, I could not see the road.

'Is the road still there?' I yelled out.

'Yes, it's here again,' he said.

'Are we all together?'

The drivers exchanged honks. The other motorcycles were at some distance from us. 'Yes we are.'

'How many hours to Camp Bangui?'

'Two.'

'But you said it would be one hour?'

'The road is long, no.'

Near Camp Bangui we passed bundles of clothes on the road, towels and skirts that had been dropped by someone. I saw the small shirts of babies, and my mind conjured images of a mother fleeing with her children, but under the stress of the attack unable to hold on to their things. I thought of the infants hiding in the bush, naked, with nothing to clean them but leaves.

The road forked; to one side was Dombourou, closer to Gaga, where the government might still be present. The other road led to Camp Bangui; we took it, hoping that the soldiers had retreated. A cadaver appeared on the roadside, his eye eaten out and covered in larvae, the body still whole to its toes and fingers. You could see where the head had been shot. Our drivers clicked their tongues. 'The body will curse us,' one of them said.

Camp Bangui was burnt. Casseroles lay on the ground, still filled with food. There were flashlights, towels and bicycles flung from their places; I could still feel the life around me, feel the people who had been sitting and standing in these places, making their tea and fried dough, listening to the radio, talking to their neighbours. The town's homes were roofless, almost all burnt. No one had come to pick up the fallen things that could be useful; no one had come to bury that corpse. From somewhere in the village, from inside one of the homes, we smelled the stench of another decaying body.

Thierry called out, his voice tense; our voices were all strained and seemed somehow solitary. Lewis walked around like a chicken, his arms now flailing, now on his head. Thierry shouted out that it was all right, that the government was gone and that we were friends. He shouted and shouted and in the distance we saw the first person. It was a woman in a red shirt and a black skirt; and she came running down the town's central avenue, looking at each of our faces, as though she was stunned, and stopping for just a moment to shake my hand and say, Thank you, thank you.

It was that first moment of trust; she had been in her place of hiding, she had heard us, believed us and decided to expose herself; and she had survived. At that moment I felt our presence had overcome some portion of the fear, that the people had gained some trust in the community of strangers. More people emerged from the bush, some running towards our motorbikes. 'Do people know what has happened to us?' a man asked me. They said the village had been torched. They said it was General Abdallah's forces that had destroyed the town, and they showed me burnt things that I did not know could burn in this way, whole, like some animal on a skewer: a school, a motorcycle, a human. The citizens had defended themselves against the government and had been winning, when the general, in an act of desperation, employed the method of the Janjaweed in Sudan. He rendered the town uninhabitable, sending the people the message that they should submit, that if they dared to resist, more of their country would be destroyed and more dead would be counted. The Seleka had few fighters – such brutality was its way of occupying the country while they plundered its timber, gold and ivory.

The Republic was burning, here one village and there in the bush another. We could not count how many, and with the people so afraid most of the destruction would never become known. But the villagers told me they would no longer be intimidated. 'We are tired of seeing our women raped and our homes destroyed.' Like the colonizers of old, this government had divided the people – it had entered villages and separated the Muslims from the Christians. The Muslims had to point out the Christian houses, the ones to burn. One community was thus set upon the other. The Muslims were now complicit, and knew that they would be decimated if the government were one day defeated. There was talk in the country of an impending genocide.

The journey to Camp Bangui had taken four hours and it was already three in the afternoon; if we stayed any longer we would not return before dark. 'We should leave,' my driver said. I knew that it was not good for us to be in the jungle, during this war, at night.

The tension of the journey had got to me, and I could not sit properly on the motorcycle. We fell, the motorcycle spun and I had a bloody knee. The driver was mad at me for not sitting properly, he said we were losing balance with the way I was sitting, that I should press closer to him so we were one mass when the motorbike swayed and jumped. But I was not able to hold steady. Two hours in, as we rode through the rivers, and walked through them as well and covered ourselves in mud, after my feet had hit a hundred times little stumps of trees that people had cut to ankle height, so that my shoes were broken and each new impact with a stump made me wince and the soles of my feet could now feel the mud, it all got to me and I told Lewis I needed to stop, I needed to go. He called out to our convoy, 'We have a *caca d'urgence!*' An urgent shit. I got off my bike and trudged, sweating, into the bush and did the job. When I returned I found my driver solemn, for such things can happen to anyone, and he had seen that I had been affected, that my guts had given way; and though I was not able to sit any better for the rest of the journey he would not scold me.

On the road back to Bekadili we passed through a village where men were preparing for revolution; they tilled their fields, tended to their livestock and turned the cranks of their peanut grinders, their rifles slung over their backs. The guns were artisanal, made for hunting small animals; to kill a government soldier they would have to shoot him twice or three times. But the villagers told us that they were the sons of this country and ready to die to reclaim their land from the colonizer, that the test tubes of medicine stuck against their heads and the vials of powder and the leather satchels of herbs that they carried would protect them like the elements of the gods and would make them invulnerable to the government's bullets. Their long-barrelled guns now in their hands, the men said that they would move upon Bangui, that they were not afraid. The battles were only beginning, they told me, and the war would need to get worse before they could be free.

We were driving now by the light of the moon, the engines revving, and I was almost asleep on the back of my driver, unable to take the journey any more, unable to think about that city inverted, its people removed, of that woman holding up her bed and the feeling of shock in the town that had been burned. The leaves in the forest were silver in the light and large like machetes. We saw a hut that was empty. The people, with nowhere to go, were retreating into the bush, and it was from the bush that they would emerge, this burning bush.

# Postscript

Could it possibly be genocide? The question was already being asked when I was in the Central African Republic in November 2013. It remains unanswered. The world has been unable to stop the killings in that country, despite repeated warnings and cries for help. It is as though, through the genocides and massacres of the twentieth century, we have learned little. We are conscious but inert.

Statistics, perhaps, give some measure of what has happened. Twenty per cent of the country's four and a half million people have fled their homes, many to the bush. Tens of thousands of people have been killed, though no one has counted the number of dead.

One and a half million people are at risk of hunger. In May 2014, 100,000 displaced people still squatted in view of the diplomats, journalists and aid workers who flew into the capital's international airport. Some 100,000 anti-balaka were at large, voicing rhetoric that Muslims should be killed. More than 300,000 people, mostly Muslim, have fled to Chad and Cameroon. Entire villages have been emptied. The price of cooking oil has risen from $1.50 per kilogram to thirty dollars. Eight thousand peacekeepers, some working valiantly, have proven ineffective against the violence. A 12,000-strong United Nations force is due to arrive nearly two years after the war began, in mid-September. Ban Ki-moon has said foreign experts are needed to rebuild the nation.

It is now clear that what I was witnessing was the implosion of the country. The anti-balaka I saw in the bush eventually moved on to the capital, Bangui, bringing chaos. Some gained revenge for loved ones they had lost to the Seleka; others instigated their own violence. The Seleka's President Djotodia was forced out of office – largely due to the irritation of Chad's President Idriss Déby, the region's kingmaker – and replaced by Catherine Samba-Panza, a conciliatory figure who would not pressure powerful figures like Déby and former President François Bozizé, whom the Seleka toppled. But the Central African Republic, at this moment, needed the opposite: someone with power, who could stop the state from collapsing, and who could stop the people from killing each other.

Back at home, I have watched footage and seen photographs of lynch mobs operating in broad daylight. Muslims are chased on the streets by men brandishing machetes, as children might chase each other in a game. The victims run in circles, arching their tense bodies away from their pursuers. Spectators stand, hands behind their backs, observing passively as though this was ordinary life. Muslims have been taken apart like toys and burned in the capital's streets. Children have been beheaded. People have confessed to cannibalism.

Many of the people I met on my trip have been killed. Tony Montana, the Seleka boy soldier I met in Gaga, was apparently tortured and murdered by the anti-balaka, as was the Seleka commander Yusuf. The chief of Bekadili was shot dead by the Seleka as they were driven out of the area. The Bekadili *majlis*, a thatched-roof open structure I was given shelter in for one night to sleep under a mosquito net, has been destroyed. The French photographer Camille Lepage, whom I had met briefly, was found dead in May, in a pickup driven by anti-balaka fighters. The brave motorcycle driver who took me to Camp Bangui is, I'm told, still alive.

Muslim leaders who have appealed for restraint have themselves been killed, and as the rhetoric is thus made more violent so are the acts. Bangui was once home to 140,000 Muslims. By the summer of 2014, fewer than one thousand remain. International peacekeepers are informed about spontaneous killings but often arrive too late. A ceasefire agreement signed by the anti-balaka and the Seleka in late July has fallen apart, as both sides have fragmented into groups that have continued attacks.

New peacekeepers may stop some of the carnage. But they also bring risks. This year the peacekeepers – ill-informed, under-resourced and poorly advised – even contributed to the conflict. Suddenly concerned about abuses by Seleka soldiers, international forces began to disarm the government troops. The anti-balaka seized upon the relative calm to mobilize in the bush. Well intentioned and with only a little effort, the peacekeepers thus swung the country to a new disequilibrium. The anti-balaka rose, and the Muslims, who had relied on the Seleka to protect them, found themselves exposed.

Central Africans need a sense of justice. The former President Bozizé and his family are said to command factions of the anti-balaka, while officials in Chad and Sudan are allied with Seleka. Many of these leaders direct their forces from abroad. Sheltered from the rising violence in the Central African Republic, they continue to fuel it, hoping to gain control of the country – but what sort of country do they hope to rule? – or profit from diamonds, ivory and gold during the chaos. There are reports of a slaughter of elephants by the Seleka in southern Central African forests. Gold and diamond mines worked by villagers are controlled by the Seleka and anti-balaka. Forests are being razed to export timber. Sanctions have been imposed by the UN on Bozizé, a Seleka leader called Nourredine Adam and the anti-balaka politician Levy Yakete, but the Central African Republic now operates as a separate world, supplied by traffickers. The sanctions cannot replace local magistrates.

Justice has meanwhile become personal and imaginary. Central Africans kill those they imagine are guilty of crimes, and those whom they imagine will be guilty of crimes.

Facts would help to correct such imaginings. But who knows what happens twenty kilometres outside the capital? There is little information, whether for the formulation of international policy or for immediate life-or-death decisions. Local NGOs like Le Réseau des Journalistes pour les Droits de l'Homme are trying to help civilians who do not know where it will be safe for the night or where to find food or a working hospital.

There are no genocidal pamphlets in the Central African Republic, no radio broadcasts calling for extermination, no gas chambers or industrial killing machines. What we have in this country are identities that have been cleaved apart, and turned upon each other. Bodies are scattered. The twenty people killed in one village are not just twenty, but part of many hundreds and thousands who are being killed across the country. What are we seeing? ∎

August 2014

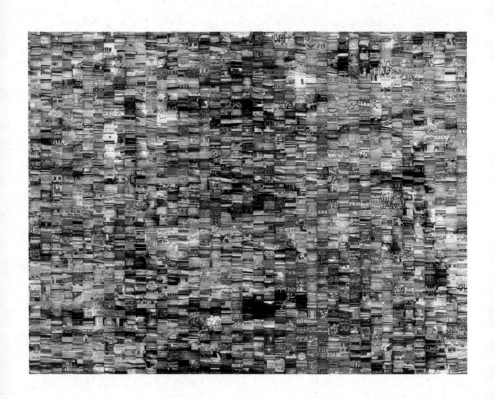

© RASHID RANA
*Language Series 2*, 2010–11
Courtesy of the artist and Lisson Gallery

# BLASPHEMY

## Fatima Bhutto

The Maulana bends down at the washbasin and draws water to his face.

Three times he wets his eyes, small and minutely lashed, three times he turns his head left and right making sure his ears are fingered clean. Ejecting the water from his nostrils, first left then right, he says a prayer over the gargle of his morning ablutions.

*Where there is discord, may we bring harmony. Where there is error, may we bring truth. Where there is doubt, may we bring faith.*

He splashes the water over his arms, covered with the downy white hair of age. He drags out a steel cooking pot so that he does not have to contort himself at the sink, takes off his brown plastic sandals and washes his calloused feet clean.

The Maulana lives like a ghost. He sleeps on the floor of what was once a marital bedroom, comforted by a thin woollen blanket and a mattress shaped by his form over many years. He keeps his windows shut against the valley and his shutters drawn against the neighbours – a degenerate couple who keeps cats that piss and moan until all hours of the night in place of children.

The Maulana's departed wife, his first cousin Bilquis, bore him no children. She was a dutiful wife, she tried. Miscarriage after miscarriage; she tried but failed. He has long since removed the solitary photograph of her that hung on their bedroom wall.

The house is almost empty. He gave away his things many years ago. Gifts from his followers were sent to the mosque, money to the local hospital and food to the poor. The Maulana has no electronics – except for his once-cherished transistor radio, which smells of mothballs and has not been turned on since 1990. The sitting room where the Maulana meets his growing flock of barefooted followers is the only room in the small house that is carpeted, covered by a fraying Persian-style rug.

He takes a glass of goat's milk as his breakfast and wipes his beard dry before leaving the house.

'A*ssalam u alaikum wa rahmatullah wa barakatuh.*' The Maulana softly clears his throat. The radio station is a compact room, rented out to the old man for a small fee by the Department of Tourism. After paying his rent, the Maulana takes no money from his radio show. He paid instead to have the technicians trained and educated and donated the rest to the chai-wallah's *mahr* fund. The little fellow would have had no chance of marriage otherwise.

The Maulana began his professional life listening to the rusted creek of elevated cable cars as they swung and looped over the valley. It never occurred to the Maulana that there was money to be made here. Men like him had long been left out of the drawing rooms where such lucrative deals were made. He was not an important man then.

Four-star hotel chains bought heritage homes from indigent old families and battalions of police were sent from the capital to protect the valley's visitors from its people. Restaurants placed wicker chairs and plastic tables atop the rocky brooks and served cold drinks in glass bottles that had been chilled in the water below. In the daytime the less lazy tourists hiked through the forests, wearing thick boots laced over their ballooning shalwar kameez. At night they gathered around bonfires and sang old Hindi film tunes as they smoked cigarettes lit off the embers. They would never know how much they had disturbed the valley as they trundled through on their vacations.

The Maulana failed out of the madrasa his parents had spent

their savings on. He sat at home, writing and reading, or with the unemployed at various tea houses listening to the languorous voice of Madam Margaret Thatcher on the radio. The Maulana had not seen her face, but he knew from the slow elegance of her words that she must have been a beautiful woman.

BBC Urdu service, dipping and dropping in the valley, often broadcast her statements – free from the hum of a toneless translator – in favour of the holy war Pakistan was fighting.

*I want to say that the hearts of the free world are with you.*

And then, one day, she came to Pakistan. She laughed at the general's jokes and ate a meal of curried goat. She must have been only a few hours away by foot. The Maulana listened, not moving his ear from the warm radio, as Margaret Thatcher wished Pakistan a Happy Eid and her husband, Mr Denis, weighed a Kalashnikov by pumping it up and down in the air. Though he had heard her speaking from London many times, the sound of Margaret Thatcher in Pakistan brought the young Maulana to tears.

*I want to say that we shall never rest till Afghanistan is free.*

After the Maulana's marriage to his cousin, Margaret Thatcher had been overthrown. Deprived of Madam's voice on his radio, he scoured the used-book bazaar for her writing. The Maulana's English improved as he read her, imagining her delicate voice in his head as he mouthed the words wholly devoted to causes such as his.

*I fight on. I fight to win.*

And he would do just that. The Maulana had not wasted any time on the frivolity of youth. There was too much corruption, too much wealth squandered on the cosmetics of the valley. Who spoke for the tribe? Who understood the dangers of a Westoxified elite – running around defending the political benefits of faithlessness and arguing for the most pitiful of freedoms that only codified how long a shirt, how short a hem? The rich and their petty agendas would ultimately fail. Pakistan would be a true Islamic state yet.

*Pakistan ka matlab kya? La illa ha il Allah.*

So the Maulana went to work, patiently waiting, watching the decay of the valley until the moment for revolutionary action was ripe.

The tourists wore woolly sweaters to deal with the mountain chill, they snapped photographs with cheap plastic Konica cameras and asked the Maulana, demoted from cable-car operator to peanut seller, to take pictures of them smiling in the valley they violated.

His fingers were blistered from the charcoal fire, his nails blackened and burnt. The Maulana refused to take their pictures. He would not engage in chit-chat. He did not want to look at the womenfolk, magnified in the cameras' eyes. But their husbands smiled stupidly, unaware of the ruptures they caused in the peanut seller's heart when they trampled through the valley in the dead of summer.

Foreigners came too, though thankfully they tended to leave their women behind. Who were these young men, scrawny boys with dirty blond hair and acne following the Karakoram highway? How could these gangly fools be the inheritors of Margaret Thatcher, a brave and magnificent woman? They had no memory of the glorious jihad their leader had inspired. God will forgive you, the Maulana always told them when they asked for directions or pointed their ugly cameras in his face, but there will be a price.

Today there are no tourists. There is no more hunchbacked seller of peanuts, no uncles in joggers and shalwar kameez carrying children on their shoulders so that they might feel as tall as the pine trees. There are no visitors welcome here.

Ladies no longer wear pink bangles and no longer dance at weddings. A hundred schoolrooms have been burnt. Only the blackboards would not turn to ash.

This is now a valley of the righteous. It has been cleansed of the obscene. The landlords packed their bags with everything but the dirt from their land and fled to Islamabad, the hoteliers abandoned their heritage homes, the wicked have been isolated, the rich defeated.

Madam had been right, you have to fight a battle more than once to win it.

'*Bismillah ah Rahman ar Raheem,*' the Maulana whispers into his microphone, held together with strips of silver duct tape. On his desk lies a pirated copy of *The Downing Street Years*, its spine creased and its shoddily bound pages marked with care. He wears no earphones, but keeps his hands by his ears as if he were praying. After the blessing from the good book, the Maulana begins.

The Maulana sits on the carpet in his living room, pondering his callouses. He counts the rings of dead skin that have collected on his feet and picks at an ingrown toenail.

All around him the men shout.

The young ones are the loudest. *Bismillah, inshallah, mashallah.* They end every sentence like this, even when it doesn't fit. *I am very thirsty, thanks God. I will have a cup of tea, God willing.*

'I heard it, I heard it with my own ears.' Hafiz's skinny legs stick out of the bottoms of his rolled shalwar. He is unbearably excited. 'Maulana Sahib, I heard it myself.'

The Maulana had been so focused on his pedicure that he had missed the boy's pronouncement. All the men are waiting for him to issue a verdict. The Maulana turns to the skinny boy. He has shaved his little moustache off only recently – there is hardly any stubble on his upper lip – and has grown the most basic of beards. This, he thinks, makes him a Muslim.

'Qadir David, Maulana Sahib, he is sending text messages. He sends them to Christians, those in the valley and outside also, but yesterday he sent one to my neighbour Iqbal. Iqbal's one of us, he listens to your show every day, he gives zakat every year to the mosque.' The boy stands up for effect and waves his arms about wildly. 'I am so angry I cannot even begin to tell you what he said.' Hafiz's forehead wrinkles and his eyebrows, one long uninterrupted thread, lift up into his hairline. He pants gently.

The Maulana understands now. He is to be outraged. But Hafiz doesn't inspire him. Qadir David is a decent man; he's stitched the Maulana's clothes for years.

The Maulana sends the tailor his fabric once a year – four cotton shalwar kameez, two for the summer and two for the winter that he recycles until the fabric thins at the elbows and tears. In gratitude, the tailor gifts him a *boski* kurta every Ramadan, delivering the package himself on Chand Raat. Qadir David chooses the colours carefully, nothing too bright, nothing too ostentatious. The fabric alone, spun from the finest Chinese silk, is luxury enough.

The Maulana and the tailor never speak of the cost, of the enormity of the gift. Having so few indulgences, the Maulana allows himself the *boski* kurtas and keeps mothballs in his closet, tolerating the noxious smell for the sake of the beautiful fabric.

The Maulana peels a small bit of dead skin off his heel. 'Don't repeat the sin by spreading the false message, Hafiz. God is listening.'

'I can't, Maulana Sahib, I didn't see it,' Hafiz admits quietly as he sits back down on the floor.

The Maulana scans the room to see if Hafiz has come alone and seeing that he has, wonders who the boy's father is and why he hasn't given him the thrashing he so obviously deserves, shouting up and down in front of his elders like this.

'You brought us all here this afternoon to say nothing?' one man shouts. 'What are we doing here if you didn't even see the message!' The others shake their heads sideways in agreement.

'I didn't see it,' Hafiz says, shifting his legs, 'but Iqbal, my cousin, saw it and he told me. He told me Qadir David is trying to convert Muslims.' Hafiz looks across the room, hoping no one will catch his eye.

'Qadir David? The tailor?'

'Yes, yes the tailor – the one with the daughter.'

'*Pagal ho?* He's an old man, what is he doing sending tax messages?'

'*Arre*, aren't you listening?' someone corrected. 'He's sending text messages. SMS.'

The room rumbles. One of the men laughs out loud. Hafiz feels his hands start to shake. 'Yes, him. Qadir David. He is sending messages across the valley. It's blasphemy.'

The room falls silent. They are all listening to Hafiz now. Except the Maulana, who can hardly stand to look at him. He reminds the Maulana of the reprobate youth he encountered during his days as a peanut seller. Frauds, all looking for something to mark themselves out. The only thing to do with degenerates, Madam said, was to starve them of oxygen.

Qadir David has two khaddar suits of his that he has not yet finished. The Maulana looks back at his feet and picks at the ingrown toenail.

'He speaks about God and Prophets.' Hafiz can sense, as he looks at the men around him, that they are waiting to be provoked. He feels his forehead turn clammy. He has to be careful about what he says next. Hafiz bends forward and on his hands and knees approaches the Maulana. The old man smells of cardamom.

The Maulana feels a fleck of spittle land on his cheek as Hafiz sputters out the secret. The Maulana is repelled by this contact but then he hears the words.

'What?'

Hafiz's mouth is dry. The Maulana touches the boy on his shoulder. 'You are certain?'

Hafiz's jaw tightens. 'I am.' He struggles to remember what he said.

Still holding on to Hafiz, the Maulana looks past him and for the man in the dark blue uniform who always sits at the back of the room. The constable's posture is – at all times – perfectly straight, his pistol respectfully tucked into his shoes by the door.

'Imran,' the Maulana calls. But Imran had not waited to hear his name. He has already dusted off his shoes and clipped his pistol back into its holster.

'Will you file the FIR?'

Hafiz walks towards the police thana, rubbing his hands together for warmth. As soon as the Maulana issued the fatwa, Constable Imran got into his police pickup truck and sped off. He hadn't offered Hafiz a lift. There was only one armed guard in the back of the truck, holding his machine gun like an upturned umbrella. Hafiz could have easily fitted.

The FIR was being filed in his name, he was a big man now. He had the power of the law behind him. Everybody saw how the Maulana hung on to his every word.

In his pocket, his mobile phone vibrates against his thigh. It's Iqbal. *Wat hapned?*

Hafiz stops. He can't walk and type at the same time. He stands in the middle of the street, shuddering and smiling to himself in the cold. *V got him.*

Qadir David stands at the counter. He adjusts the sleeves of the kurta, smoothing out the creases as he lowers the black metal iron. He squints over his glasses, smudged with fingerprints. The cuffs are too big. They will have to be cut.

'Abu?'

'Hmm?' The cuffs are too big and the shoulders too narrow. Qadir David glances at the scrunched-up piece of paper with the chaplain's measurements that he has knotted into the tail of the shirt. It is close to seven. Qadir David struggles to read his own handwriting and wonders if he can alter the shirt by dinner time.

'Abu, the leftover fabric?'

Qadir David looks up from the chaplain's shirt to see Jia standing in the doorway, her black hair thin and greasy. 'What's happened to your hair?'

Jia touches it and makes a face. 'Oil. Ami said.'

Qadir David laughs. He has a full head of freckles, moles, bumpy nicks and cuts from shaving the fluff that collects around the nape of his neck, but no hair.

'So, the fabric?'

Jia is a tall girl. Though she is slender, she worries about her weight and eats only yoghurt for dinner two nights a week. She is pretty, people say, never pausing long enough on a feature that would explain exactly how or why. When her hair is not swimming in mustard oil, it falls in soft waves that she painstakingly irons out every evening after her bath. She is sixteen now and attracting a fair amount of attention. Qadir David's nephew, his brother's boy who lives in Islamabad and works at a travel agency in Jinnah Super, recently expressed an interest.

Qadir David has been very lucky. His business hadn't been struck by the violence in the valley. Oddly, the more that women were confined to their homes, the more outfits they seemed to require. Business was steady, bountiful even.

His wife, Rimsha, was also gainfully employed at the local Sunday school – which met on Saturdays since the security situation had worsened. Soon they would have enough to get Jia married.

'*Beti*, she didn't leave any scraps. You know what these ladies are like –' and he makes a pinched face, arching his eyebrows and pursing his lips. But Jia doesn't laugh.

She looks outside the window now, stained and blotted with dirt just like her father's eyeglasses, to make sure he hasn't followed her here too. There's no sign of him, not a word since she answered his text after school. 'You like clothes?' he said as she begged him to leave her alone and give back her notebook. 'I'll buy you fabric if you talk to me.' He had followed her before, she was sure of it now. She even thought he snapped a picture of her with his camera phone.

Three weeks ago he found out her number and sent her a message.
*U lked nice today. I like yr hairs.*

Jia ignored it, thinking it was one of her girlfriends teasing her. She had gone to school with her mother's mustard-and-sesame concoction in her hair and had smelled like a salad for most of the day. Like the other girls in her class, Jia simply pulled her uniform dupatta over her head, slumped down at the splintering desk she shared with three other students and hoped no one would notice her unwashed hair.

But the messages continued.
*Wat is yr ideal personality type?*
*Can v meet after your tuitions?*
*Wat is yr age? I am 24*
*I luv u*

Jia hadn't answered any of the messages – her mother would be furious if she knew a boy had been sending her SMSs. Her mother might even take away her phone and stop her from going to school. So Jia deleted the messages as they came and took her SIM card out every night.

But then she noticed him outside her school during morning assembly.

As she recited the name of Pakistan's most favourite nuclear scientist, the patron and namesake of the school, she saw his head, his white prayer cap, bobbing up and down outside the school walls. By the time school ended, his friend had joined him and they stood by the rusted gate, waiting for her.

Jia borrowed a chador from one of her classmates and snuck out, peeping through a small slit to make sure the boy hadn't spotted her. He wore the bottoms of his shalwar rolled. His skinny ankles looked unreasonably hairy for his age.

She started leaving school like this most days, the polyester fabric of her chador stretching across her mouth, suffocating her as she tried to breathe.

*Y u don't answer me?*

*U think ur 2 gud?*

*U bitch*

*I am working in pharmacy, gud money*

*I can buy u all fabric u like. Lawn also*

Jia began to get stomach cramps at night. Drawing her knees into her chest while her mother plaited her hair before bedtime, she considered throwing away her phone, asking to move to her uncle's house in Islamabad – for her studies, she would say – and taking to a burqa full-time. She heard stories of acid being thrown in young girls' faces after they had rejected suitors, usually the sons of powerful landlords and politicians. It melted their noses and burned the thin skin of their eyelids, blinding them forever. She lost hours of sleep wondering what she could do to rid herself of the boy with the rolled-up shalwar.

On the walk home this afternoon two things had happened. First, he touched her. When he saw her slip out from under the loose chador, thinking she had lost him as she huddled among her girlfriends, he came running behind her.

'You are hiding from me?'

Jia stopped dead in her tracks. She should have run, but she had never been held like that before. First he touched her, grabbing her arm. And second he spoke to her. She hadn't heard his voice before. He looked like he was about to cry.

Jia freed herself of his grip. 'Sorry,' she whispered and kept walking, quickening her pace. Her friends had all run off – none of them wanted to be caught talking to a strange boy in the middle of the valley. 'Sorry sorry sorry,' Jia repeated it under her breath.

She hoped no one had seen her. Jia thought she had lost him but then she heard him jog up beside her. He was panting slightly. He smiled, a contortion that made him seem younger than his years. Just as Jia allowed herself to look at him, searching for anger in his face, he pinched the notebook.

'You like clothes?' he said fingering the swath of Mrs Amirzai's fabric that Jia had stapled to the page. 'I'll buy you fabric if you talk to me.'

Jia pulled her notebook out of his hands and ran.

By the time she reached home and had run to her room, throwing her satchel on the floor, he had texted.

*Lawn also. Very gud quality. Three piece suits.*

*I know Gul Ahmed, Sana Safinaz, pink suit, red suit, how many styles u want?*

Jia looked at his number, she didn't know his name. She punched the reply button. Her long nails clicked against the keys:

*I am alrdy engaged*

She bit the skin at the corner of her lips and pressed send.

She hasn't heard from him since then.

Hafiz sits uncomfortably before the constable. The police station is empty and cold, the wooden window frames are broken. There is a strange smell in the air, like stale cigarette smoke and mould. His chair has no cushion, no wheels like Imran's chair. Constable Imran hasn't even offered Hafiz a cup of tea.

'Did you see the message in question?'

The constable's uniform is starched and pressed. His hair is partitioned and pomaded so that it sticks to his head and shines like silver when the light catches it.

Hafiz shakes his head. 'My uncle Iqbal saw it.'

Constable Imran lifts his eyes off the paper he is filling out in triplicate, black sheets of carbon paper placed neatly underneath the original.

'You said your cousin told you about the blasphemous message.'

'Yes, that's what I mean.' Hafiz nods, trying to remember what he said. 'Same thing only – we're the same age so I call him my cousin. But he's also my uncle.'

The constable looks at him squarely. 'And your neighbour?'

Hafiz looks back at the irritated police officer and says innocently, 'Which neighbour?'

Constable Imran puts the pen down and speaks very slowly. 'At the Maulana's house you said it was your neighbour who showed you the message.' He lifts an eyebrow. 'Remember?'

'*Haan*, we live near each other also.'

'What did your uncle cousin neighbour say was in the message?'

Hafiz laughs, stretching his legs out under the constable's desk. 'I can't possibly repeat, Constable Sahib. I have conveyed the message to Maulana Sahib and he will tell your goodself Sahib if you please.'

Imran leans across his desk. '*Sala*,' he swears in a low, menacing voice. 'What did the message say?'

Hafiz straightens his shalwar kameez, smoothing it over his lap and adjusts his white prayer cap. He moves his body to meet the constable's over the desk and murmurs the blasphemous matter as relayed by his cousin uncle neighbour friend into the police officer's ear.

'Cycil.'
   The Maulana called the youth to his living room once all the men had left. Cycil Nazir Ali was surprised to hear from the Maulana and he kneels before him now, shifting his weight over his buttocks. He is not used to sitting on the floor like this.

'I have asked you here for a very important task.'

Cycil doesn't know what a task is and how he's supposed to procure one for the Maulana. The air smells of camphor, sweet and sickly. He blinks nervously.

'You are a good boy.'

The Maulana has known Cycil since he was a schoolboy. Bilquis used to give the neighbourhood children reading lessons. Cycil used to bring Bible stories for her to read to him. The boy would sit in her lap and she would trace the words with her fingers so he could follow along. For a moment, a second only, the Maulana remembers his khaddar fabric, probably still folded in the tailor's cupboard. How will he retrieve it now? An unsettling shame comes over him.

'And I need to tell you something that will greatly upset you. I am sorry about this.'

The Maulana pauses for emphasis. He has learned this from Madam too. Cycil looks anxious. He would do anything for him now.

'The Christians have taken advantage of our kindness here in the valley. Twenty-two cases have been filed this year alone. Two Hindus and one Muslim have been accused but the rest have all been Christians.'

The Maulana pats Cycil's knee.

'I know, I know you are a good boy. And that is why I am afraid this news will upset you. But one of your own has committed the most grievous of sins, the most terrible.'

The Maulana sips from a glass of goat's milk with honey. It soothes his voice in the evenings.

'Qadir David, the tailor. He has been spreading lies about Islam.'

He pushes a copy of the FIR towards Cycil, who blinks as he reads Constable Imran's perfect penmanship. The Maulana examines the carpet underneath him as the boy reads. It is an unnecessary extravagance. He thinks of several homes that would benefit from the comfort of its warmth.

'I'm sorry, Maulana Sahib. So sorry . . .' Cycil stutters. They will be rounded up, forced out of their homes. 'We don't agree with this. We don't agree with what he has done.' He will have to move his elderly parents quickly. He wonders where the deed to their house is. Cycil is too polite to ask how much time they have till the news spreads and the Christian mohalla is lit up in flames.

The Maulana edges closer towards the boy. 'Yes, I know. I know you will find a way to show this to the men of the valley.' He wonders if Cycil remembers Bilquis, if he thinks of those hours spent reading at her feet.

*Where there is discord, may we bring harmony. Where there is error, may we bring truth. Where there is doubt, may we bring faith.*

The Maulana strokes his beard. It was one of Madam's best speeches. No matter how one said it – in English, Pashto, Kohistani or Urdu – there was no discounting the power of the great leader's words. 'Law and order is a social service, *beta*. You must perform your part.'

'Yes Maulana Sahib. Please, we will take care of it. Please leave it to us.' Cycil searches the Maulana's face for assurance. 'We will bring faith. Ours is no different.' The Maulana smiles and with the smallest tip of his head, consents.

'But may I ask,' Cycil continues uneasily, 'what did he say?'

Resting his palm on the young man's knee for balance, the Maulana leans forward and speaks the profane secret so that only Cycil can hear.

Before he can bolt the door shut, his wife runs into the shop. Rimsha's face is covered in sweat.

'It's you,' she says, fumbling with the bolt, turning her back to her husband until she's sure she has secured the rusted lock. 'They are coming for you.'

Qadir David holds the chaplain's freshly pressed shirt against his belly. He doesn't understand.

'Section 295-C.'

Outside, a fire has been lit. He can smell the smoke – the burning rubber of the tyres, the petrol like aniseed and charcoal. Someone is firing a pistol; he can smell the sulphur. Somewhere in the distance glass is breaking.

'What are you saying, Rimsha?'

His wife covers her mouth to muffle her sobs.

There is shouting outside. He hears it getting closer.

'Blasphemy,' Rimsha whispers.

Qadir David will not remember this, but his fingernails tear through the alterations he has just made to the chaplain's shirt, cutting into the now perfectly measured sleeves.

'Me?'

It makes sense now, the luck. The fortune he has enjoyed for so very long. Some said that it was colour that faded first in the valley, but it was not true. The valley pears were still a spotted green and the apricots that grew in the orchards still the palest orange. There was colour still in the valley. No men, not even those who spoke with the voice of God, could deprive the valley of the lightness of snow. But they took something else. Not colour but certainty.

Qadir David no longer had the certainty of a lucky man. He never knew where he stood; he had no way of knowing when he was an outsider – an interloper – and when he belonged.

This was not his fate alone.

Muslims, it was worse for them. They had new enemies now. The only way to be sure of loyalty, to know who belonged and who did not then, was to fight everywhere, on every front.

'It's a mistake.' Qadir David places the shirt on the counter, smoothing it down with his palm.

He picks up his mobile phone. He has thirteen messages, eight missed calls.

'How should I have committed blasphemy?'

He drops his voice as he says the word.

Qadir David looks at the mobile phone in his hands. He does not want to read the messages.

There is a loud banging on the door. Rimsha wraps her dupatta over her head, covering her ears. Her eyes are pinched shut. 'We are done,' she mumbles, shaking her head. 'Thy kingdom come, thy will be done,' she hurries, remembering the prayer. 'Our father who art in heaven . . .' but saying it backwards and skipping words.

Qadir David thinks of the Maulana whose clothes he has sewn with his own hands. He thinks of the raw silk he has woven into yards of thick cotton, only to make one shalwar kameez for the Maulana, the wool he has processed and dyed into shawls for the winter months, the burns from the iron.

The banging is harder now. Somebody shouts the tailor's name. It sounds like Cycil, the bricklayer's son.

'What do they say I've done?' Qadir David wonders where Jia is. What will she think of her father when she hears the news? Qadir David feels his throat constrict and his stomach clench with fear. How will he protect her from this? They will shame him in front of his daughter.

They will kill him.

How will Rimsha raise Jia alone? Just last week she slapped her for some minor infraction. The girl had hidden her telephone under the bed and her mother assumed she was trying to keep some boy's late-night calls a secret. She hit her first and looked at the telephone second.

They will kill him and destroy his family.

Qadir David's mind races back to every conversation he's had in the past week. The chaplain. The rickshaw-wallah, the dyer, the customers. It must have been a customer. He must have said something, done something. He must have looked where he shouldn't have. Made a comment, held a measuring tape too tight.

He has lived here all his life. Qadir David has never left the valley. He will beg the Maulana's intercession. They are simple men, they understand each other. It is the only way.

'What did I do?' he repeats the question. The mobile phone rings. Rimsha can't hear her husband over her forgotten prayer.

'Rimsha.' Qadir David shakes his wife, edging her closer to him and away from the door. 'What are they saying I did?'

Rimsha opens her eyes slowly and brings her face closer to her husband's. Resting her chin slightly on his shoulder she cups a palm around his ear and whispers the words.

The constable stands before the Maulana. He adjusts his belt, making sure his phone, keys and holster are secure.

'The accused blasphemer, Mr Qadir David, Christian, s/o Junaid David, inhabitant of union council seven, Swat, Khyber Pakhtunkhwa, age fifty-two, employed by goodself, and possessor of ID number 00-004-538-9178, born on –'

Constable Imran coughs. 'The charges are on the next page, Maulana Sahib.'

The Maulana nods and licks his thumb. A thread of spit follows his finger to the paper.

'The accused blasphemer, Mr Qadir David, has wilfully failed to protect religious feelings. According to Hafiz, s/o Abdur Rahman, inhabitant of union council –'

Cough.

'– nine, Swat, Khyber Pakht–'

'Bottom of the page.'

The Maulana arches an eyebrow and pauses his slow, deliberate reading to look at the constable. 'You should have that cough fixed, Imran.'

The constable hangs his head in apology and sneaks a peek at his watch. He saw two burning buses on the way to the Maulana's. If he doesn't get the warrant issued, the tailor will be dead by the time he arrives to arrest him.

'Under Section 295-A of British Indian Penal Code, Mr Qadir David, s/o –' the Maulana pauses and reads silently to himself for a moment – 'is accused of committing the malicious act of deliberately outraging and insulting religious beliefs. Under Section 295-B of

Pakistan Penal Code, Qadir David is charged with wilfully defying the Holy Quran or an extract of it, verbally or through written means, in this case cellular.'

The constable smiles. He had added that last bit.

'Under further amended Section 295-C of PPC, complainant is charging Mr David with making derogatory remarks against Prophet Mohammad (PBUH) in spoken, written, and/or cellular form.'

Ten years. Life. Death. A, B, C. The case is airtight.

Hafiz considers the bolts of fabric lying before him and the yards of soft material draped across his shoulder. Real lawn. Not the fake stuff the fellow down the gully sells. On the radio, hidden behind bottles of 7-Up, Hafiz hears the Maulana's voice.

'. . . this is a necessary law, a wholesome law. A law that protects the people from those who . . .'

Twelve hundred for a suit, the Afghan trader insists. Around them merchants pull down their shutters. There are crowds coming through the cramped gullies.

'Hurry up yaar.' The Afghan is anxious to roll away his priciest fabrics. He can smell fire. 'They thrashed the jeweller for not closing his shop in time,' he says softly. 'Gave him a real beating, broke a few fingers.'

'It could have been worse,' Hafiz says, leaning back into his plastic chair.

They are screaming now, grown men are rushing through the gullies, screaming.

The Afghan taps the counter. He doesn't have all day to deal with this spoiled brat. He keeps an ear on the radio. He has a family to get home to.

Hafiz smiles as he strokes the orange-and-yellow cloth. He is in no hurry. ∎

# THE ATLANTIC WALL

## *Ianthe Ruthven*

'When the combat ceases, that which is does not
disappear, but the world turns away.' – Martin Heidegger

The Atlantic Wall – the chain of World War II fortifications
stretching from the Norwegian Arctic to France's western
frontier with Spain – is one of Europe's least acknowledged
monuments. Built for the most part between 1942 and 1945, it is
the largest construction project in history to have been executed
in so short a time. An enduring physical legacy of the world's most
notorious regime – committed to murder on an industrial scale – the
concrete monoliths that still litter the coasts of Norway, Denmark, the
Low Countries and France are stark reminders of the darkest period
in modern history.

From a strategic viewpoint, the vast network of batteries and
bunkers is a material testament to the folly of Adolf Hitler's military
enterprise: given Allied air supremacy, fixed defences were useless.
On D-Day, 6 June 1944, the bunkers and casemates commanding
the landing beaches offered only limited resistance.

Hitler took an obsessive interest in the Atlantic Wall, sketching
designs and planning installations down to the smallest details. Yet
far from reflecting his preference for neoclassical grandeur – evoking
the power and glory of Rome – the fortifications are infused with a
modernist aesthetic. The command post at Batz-sur-Mer in Brittany
– a structure of receding horizontal planes with a cantilevered roof

– is reminiscent of Le Corbusier's concept of a house as '*une machine-à-habiter*' (a machine for living in) while the massive Oldenberg battery at Calais resembles the ground-hugging contours of Henry van de Velde's masterpiece, the 1914 Werkbund Theater in Cologne.

A few batteries have been converted into museums that attract tourists along with students doing courses in twentieth-century history. But the majority lies neglected in fields and woods, perched on cliffs or sinking beneath the sands, incongruous monoliths, the detritus of history. ■

# WHERE THE
# WORLD WAR BEGAN

*Joseph Roth*

TRANSLATED FROM THE GERMAN
BY MICHAEL HOFMANN

The World War began in Sarajevo, on a balmy summer afternoon in 1914. It was a Sunday; I was a student at the time. In the afternoon a girl came round; girls wore plaits in those days. She was carrying a large yellow straw hat in her hand, it was like summer coming to call, with hay, grasshoppers and poppies. In her straw hat was a telegram, the first special edition I had then seen, crumpled and terrible, a thunderbolt on paper. 'Guess what,' said the girl. 'They've killed the heir to the throne. My father came home from the cafe. We won't stay here either, will we?'

I didn't manage to be quite as deadly serious as her father who had left the cafe. We rode on the back platform of a tram. Out in the suburbs there was a place where the tram brushed past some jasmine bushes that grew close to the track. We drove along, jingle-jangle, it was like a sleigh ride in summer. The girl was light blue, soft, close, with cool breath, a morning on an afternoon. She had brought me the news from Sarajevo, the name was visible over her, picked out in dark red smoke, like an inferno over a clueless child.

A year and a half later – strange how durable love could be in peacetime! – there she was again, surrounded by smoke, on the goods station, platform 2, music was blaring out, wagons screeched, locomotives whistled, little shivering women hung like withered wreaths on green men, the brand-new uniforms smelled of finish, we were an infantry company, destination secret, but thought to be Serbia. Probably we were both thinking of that Sunday, the telegram, Sarajevo. Her father hadn't been to a cafe since, he was in a mass grave.

Today, thirteen years after that first shot, I am seeing Sarajevo. Innocent, accursed city, still standing! Sorry sheath of the grimmest catastrophes. Unmoved! No rain of fire has descended on it, the houses are intact, girls are just going home from school, though plaits are no longer in fashion. It's one o'clock. The sky is blue satin. The station where the Archduke arrived, Death waiting for him, is some way outside the city. A wide, dusty, part-asphalted, part-gravel road leads left into the city. Trees, thickly crowned, dark and dusty, leftovers from a time when the road was still an avenue, are now irregularly sprinkled along its edge. We are sitting in a spacious courtesy bus from the hotel. We drive through streets, along the riverbank – there, that corner is where the World War began. Nothing has changed. I am looking for bloodstains. They have been removed. Thirteen years, innumerable rains, millions of people have washed away the blood. The young people are coming home from school; did they learn about the World War? I wonder.

The main street is very quiet. At the top end of it is a small Turkish cemetery, stone flowers in a small garden for the dead. At its lower edge an oriental bazaar begins. Just about the middle of it, facing one another, are two big hotels, with cafe terraces. The wind browses indifferently through old newspapers and fallen leaves. Waiters stand by at the doors, more to verify than to assist the tourist trade. Old policemen lean against the walls, recalling peace, the pre-War. One has whiskers, a ghost of the old double monarchy. Very old men, probably retired notaries, speak the Army German of Austrian days. A bookseller deals in paper and books and literary journals – mostly for symbolic purposes. I pick up a Maupassant from him (although he has Dekobra in stock as well) for a night ahead on a train without a wagon-lit. We get to talking. I learn that literary interest has ebbed in Sarajevo. There is a teacher who subscribes to a couple of literary weeklies. (It's good to know that such teachers still exist!)

In the evening, there's the *passeggiata* of the lovely, chaste women. It's the *passeggiata* of a small town. The beautiful women walk in twos and threes, like convent girls. The gentlemen are continually doffing their hats, people here know one another so well that I feel a threefold stranger. I might almost be watching a film, a historical costume drama, where the people don't know one another, the scenes of their greetings have been left in the cutting room, one is a stranger among strangers, the auditorium is dark; only the bright, garish intervals frighten me. It might be good to read a newspaper, to discover something about the world that I have left behind in order to see something of the world.

By ten o'clock everything is quiet, there's the distant glimmer of a single late bar down a side street; it's a family gathering. Across the river, on the Turkish side, the houses climb up in flat terraced trays, their lights dissolve in the fog, they remind me of the wide staircase to a lofty wide altar.

There is a theatre, opera is performed, there is a museum, hospitals, a law court, police, everything a city could want. A city! As if Sarajevo were a city like any other! As though the war to end all wars hadn't begun here in Sarajevo! All the heroes' graves, all the mass graves, all the battlefields, all the poison gas, all the cripples, the war widows, the unknown soldiers: they all came from here. I don't wish destruction upon this city, how could I? It has dear, good people, beautiful women, charming innocent children, animals that enjoy their lives, butterflies on the stones in the Turkish cemetery. And yet the War began here, the world was destroyed, and Sarajevo has survived. It shouldn't be a city, it should be a monument to the terrible memory. ■

© RONAN CANTWELL

# THE ALPHABET OF BIRDS

## S.J. Naudé

Sandrien is the only white woman in Bella Gardens. She is in fact the only white person in town. *An establishment for the accommodation of women travellers*, reads the website of Bella Gardens. *The most luxurious home for females*, reads the brochure in the dim entrance hall. One could mistake it for a refuge for unwed mothers.

Her hostess is Mrs Edith Nyathi, who introduces herself as a widow and retired matron of Frere Hospital. She never stops talking about her 'second life'. She raises her eyebrows and drops her head forward when pronouncing the phrase. The guest house is her pension, she says, 'my little egg'. The number of maids in her employ permits her to relax with a cigarette on the veranda during the day; sometimes, late in the evening, with a cigar. Mrs Nyathi does not raise her voice to any of the maids – a phalanx of demure village girls, ready to fry up sizzling English breakfasts or to polish baths and wooden floors to a high gloss. When she calls to one of her girls, it is in the same cooing voice she uses to address her guests.

The colonial veranda of the sandstone house offers a view over the village. Except for the college buildings at the top of the slope, the guest house is the grandest building in Vloedspruit. Corrugated-iron shacks hug the slope. Dotted between them are Basotho-style rondavels with thatched roofs. Lower down, where it is colder and where the watery waste collects, there are rows of government houses built of cement bricks, some with rickety lean-tos. Others have clay-plastered rondavels in the backyards. A village of *pondokkie*, *kaias* and *strooise*, Sandrien thinks. The hovels of natives. But these are words from a different time, words her mother would have used. They sit strangely on her own tongue.

In the mornings Sandrien walks up the hill to the training college of the provincial health department. She is attending a refresher course, lasting six weeks, to prepare rural nurses for 'the major challenges in primary health care today'. *Our Health Revolution* is the title of their newly printed textbook; it has laughing faces of different races on the cover. The classes begin at nine. At eleven, tea and sandwiches are served; at one there is a two-hour lunch break. In between, they fit in sessions about everything from vaccinations to smears to the physiological effects of different classes of antiretrovirals.

Her jaw drops the first time she sees the lunch provided by the college to the students and personnel. Samp, pap, rice, three varieties of vegetables, three kinds of meat. Deep, steaming pots.

'Is it all for us?' Sandrien asks the younger woman next to her.

'We have to eat, *meisie*,' she answers, and prods Sandrien with her elbow. The woman's earrings sway. 'Lerato,' she introduces herself, tucking an extra can of Coke under her arm. 'I'm a nurse from the Free State.'

The first few days Sandrien sits by herself on the steps. At first, she eats her food with a spoon. Then she starts using her hands, like the others. Why not?

On the third day Lerato joins her. 'You white girls don't get very hungry, do you?'

Outside the fence a few half-starved children with snot on their upper lips stand gaping.

When Sandrien hands some of her food to the children through the fence, Lerato clicks her tongue: 'Stop that!'

'But look at them! They're famished.'

'Just you wait. Tomorrow the whole town's children will be here.' Lerato points to the fence. 'Just behind that fence, all of them, tomorrow.'

'But then we must feed them. We have enough. More than enough.'

'Eish, you people.' Lerato clicks, more loudly this time. 'I know your type. You're like the crowd in my hospital. Charity doctors from Scandinavia. They don't know this place.'

Lerato gets up, her plate still half full.

'I'm not from Scandinavia,' Sandrien says to Lerato's enormous back. 'I'm from the Eastern Cape, from the banks of the Gariep.'

'I admire the fact that you are dedicating yourself here; you must have had many other opportunities,' Sandrien says to Dr Shirley Kgope, the course leader, during morning tea, gesturing with her eyes towards the rows of shacks below the college buildings. Shirley Kgope, although originally from the Eastern Cape too, studied medicine in a drab city in the American Midwest, and is also a microbiologist.

'Why not?' says Dr Kgope, sounding weary of this kind of conversation. 'It is where I am most needed.' She takes a sip of tea. 'It would be more interesting to know what brings *you* here.'

Dr Kgope's cup tinkles in the saucer. Thick-rimmed porcelain cups, like in a teachers' common room.

'Why not?' Sandrien smiles. 'By the way, how did it happen that the training college here has such extensive facilities?'

'It was originally designed as a teachers' college,' says Dr Kgope. 'Everyone knew that all the teachers' colleges would be closed shortly, but the place was built nevertheless. It stood empty for a few years.'

'But why?'

Dr Kgope rubs her thumb over her forefinger like a cashier counting money.

'Bribes?'

'Draw your own conclusions.'

Dr Shirley Kgope bends down to straighten the lines down the back of her silk stockings. Teatime is over. They pick their way through goats on the veranda to get to the seminar room.

'We should tell Mr Mabunda to fix the fence,' says Dr Kgope, kicking goat droppings from the tiles.

'Why are you here?' Mrs Nyathi asks with sly, amused eyes when the two of them are drinking brandy alone late that evening. Tonight she is smoking a cigar. Like two gents in a members' club they sit in deep armchairs.

'You're not the first to ask,' answers Sandrien. 'For the training, of course!'

Mrs Nyathi shakes her head. 'No, no, I mean why are *you* here?'

She gestures with both hands towards Sandrien's body. Towards her skin colour, in fact.

Sandrien sits back in the armchair. Two months ago, she had returned home to the farm called Dorrebult, her palate shredded by chemotherapy. She had spent three months in Bloemfontein. She stayed on her own in a guest house, within walking distance of the hospital.

When she returned to Dorrebult, nothing was left of the weaving mill. The tables and looms stood there gathering dust. The yarn – the wool and the mohair – everything, gone. Just a few loose filaments on the cement floor.

'Where have they all gone?' She looked at her husband accusingly. 'Grace, Brenda, Xoliswe, the rest?'

Kobus shrugged. 'There's nothing left of the weaving business. What did you expect? You were the heart of it. Surely you know that.'

'But it was for them, as much as for me. How could they just let go of it?'

Kobus touched her elbow in passing. He put on his hat and drove off to his cattle. In the shafts of sunlight pouring through the windows, his footsteps had stirred up fragments of fibre that kept floating and shimmering.

Sandrien is surrounded by Mrs Nyathi's fragrant smoke. She is picking at loose threads on her chair cushion.

Over two years she had built up the weaving mill. Poured a new concrete floor for the old barn, punched new windows into the walls for light. She went to work at a community weaving project in Grahamstown for a few months, acquainting herself with market size, potential sales points, marketing channels. Back home she met with each of their neighbours to assess attitudes. Most of the farmers were relieved at the opportunity for their labourers to earn an extra income, their burden of responsibility perhaps somewhat lightened. She spoke to the women on each of the farms, made sure the men were not present. The coloured women seemed more enthusiastic than the Xhosa women, but ultimately so many turned up that she could not take all of them.

She taught them what she had learned, weaving shoulder-to-shoulder with them until her hands were raw. Some of the women learned quickly; about half kept at it and became highly adept. Together with the five who remained, she developed the project. Colours and designs were adapted as she received orders from shops in Franschhoek and Dullstroom and Clarens. Blankets in natural, earthy colours; monochrome rugs with subtly varying textures. *Handwoven by women from the Eastern Cape* on the back of the label, underneath her brand name: *Glo-fibre*. A paragraph about Glo-fibre's environmentally friendly practices.

The business started growing; she was getting enquiries from Europe and the Middle East. When she got her diagnosis, she called Grace in and told her. Grace was the only one of her personnel who had a high school education; she was bright and dedicated.

'I have to go away for treatment. While I'm gone, you must be the driving force behind the project, Grace, the linchpin.'

Grace promised solemnly, her tall frame tilting slightly forward.

There was little time. For two weeks, she trained Grace in aspects of administration and management. 'Showing you the ropes, no pun intended.' Grace did not laugh. Carefully she took Grace through the order books and her list of suppliers, showing her how to make entries, explaining everything.

Mrs Nyathi's eyes are shining. She is observing Sandrien, as if sharing the memory.

Sandrien considered asking Kobus to take over, but she knew he would not be able to manage it with the cattle. And he would not understand what the mill demanded.

'Anyhow,' she said to Grace, 'it would run counter to the spirit of this if I involved my husband, or one of the other farmers' wives.'

She looked Grace in the eyes, pressed Grace's hands against her chest. 'I have trust in you. In your heart you know the value of this, what it means.'

Grace and the other women sang for her when she left. She was embarrassed; it was not as if she was facing death. Prior to the mastectomy and treatment she in fact radiated health. When she got back and found the mill abandoned, it didn't take long to find out why. She was shocked at how ill Grace was.

She changes the subject, and expands on her answer to Mrs Nyathi's original question. 'I am here for retraining, of course; I'm rusty. Before, I spent years as a nurse in intensive care in a private hospital in Grahamstown. I want to work again. I have to earn money.'

Mrs Nyathi's eyes are sharp.

Sandrien clears her throat. 'Perhaps,' she says and touches her throat, 'I am here to become acquainted with the textures of loss.'

Mrs Nyathi laughs and her neat feet stir, her cheeks as lovely as a baby's.

A thunderstorm wakes her. She pulls away the curtain. Lightning flashes across currents of brown water running down the mountain. The currents branch out into a delta, flowing around some of the little houses and straight through others. She opens the window; the curtains billow into the room. In her nightgown she stands before the storm.

After the incident with the children, Lerato no longer sits with her at mealtimes. Sandrien now piles the food extra high on her plate every lunch and gives it to the children. She hands them rolled balls of pap through the fence. Later she holds out the plate for them to take the food themselves. Their hands are smaller, and move more easily through the tightly woven fence. As Lerato predicted, the numbers have swollen. There is a small crowd. Two of the littler ones have even wriggled through the hole made by the goats. Sandrien looks around. On the veranda a group of her fellow students are watching, hands on their hips. Lerato walks towards them, arms swinging, earrings swaying. She hits the fence with an open hand so that it rattles from one corner post to the other. The children scatter in all directions. The two small ones on the inside start crying. 'Bloody goats and children!' she shouts, but her anger is really aimed at Sandrien.

Sandrien walks away without a word, round the back of the classrooms. She will not shed a tear; she won't. In front of her a furrow has been dug into the hillside, directing water around the building. In the furrow there are two heaps of rubbish. One consists of hundreds of Coke cans, the other of smouldering plastic.

'I am Walter Mabunda.'

She quickly rubs tears off her cheeks. The man approaches and stands next to her, too close. He takes her hands between his. She stiffens.

'Why doesn't someone start a recycling project here?' she says, her voice more vehement than she intended. 'It could mean money, jobs.'

'Perhaps you should do it.'

'But I'm just here for a few weeks.'

He shrugs his shoulders. 'Managing this facility is a demanding task. I have only these two hands.'

She loosens hers from his.

'I presume you're staying in Bella Gardens?'

She looks at him. A charming voice. In his mid-fifties, she estimates, a good ten years older than she.

'Yes, at Mrs Nyathi's.'

'Hmm, such a good hostess. But,' he laughs lazily, 'she governs that establishment with an iron fist, I tell you. The girls who work there, they toe the line. Ooh, very scary,' he says in an unexpected alto voice, eyes wide. 'She can be withering – blistering.' He suddenly strikes her as somewhat camp. Below his beer belly, neat folds have been ironed into his slacks. His shoes are shiny.

'Mrs Nyathi has been a model of courtesy.'

'By the way, we must ask you not to lure the children.' His voice is sympathetic, soothing. 'They are a nuisance. We cannot take on responsibility for the entire community.'

The storms over Vloedspruit are fiercer than anything Sandrien has known. At night, lightning draws nerve patterns across the skies. Fountains burst from the slopes as if through a dam wall. Lower down, small buildings regularly wash away. The government houses remain standing, but mud is building against their walls. She is getting used to the rhythms here, even the storms. Her daily routine is not devoid of minor joys. Mrs Nyathi's substantial breakfasts, the morning classes at the college, the teas and lunches, the unpredictable – and often perplexing – conversations with Mrs Nyathi at night on the veranda. She is getting used to the maids with their quiet eyes, furiously polishing or scurrying down the corridor, possibly instructed to remain invisible to guests. Her fellow students' social codes remain a mystery, though. As soon as she thinks she has started forming bonds of friendship, she is excluded again.

Sunday afternoons, when the other girls are out and she is not in the mood for Mrs Nyathi's company, or when the maids' unseen presence unnerves her, she goes for long walks. She breathes mountain air deep into her lungs after the rain. Children run naked through puddles and mill around her. They tug at her hands or clothes, search her pockets. She hands out money or sweets. She feels embarrassed, like the Western heroine in a Hollywood African fantasy: hand on the little khaki hat, children's profiles etched against

THE ALPHABET OF BIRDS

her linen dress. Cows with bony rumps struggle up the slippery slope. One afternoon she realizes most of the village market next to the government houses has been washed away.

Wherever she walks, little dogs run after the children and dart around her feet. They yap and yelp, dodging her footsteps.

'Why are there only small dogs here?' she asks Mrs Nyathi one afternoon.

Mrs Nyathi holds up her palms, as if saying: Isn't it obvious? She makes a gesture as if bringing food to her mouth. 'They get eaten, don't they? The big ones.'

She is reluctant to call home. On a Sunday afternoon she calls Brenda, Grace's daughter, who is looking after Sandrien's elderly mother. Brenda is sulky.

'Missus Karlien is walking around with garden shears, trying to cut flies. She refuses to let me change her bedding. Sometimes she eats off the floor.'

The shadow of one of Mrs Nyathi's maids flits down the corridor. Sandrien regrets making the call. Once a week Kobus calls from Dorrebult. He talks about his cattle, about their daughters in Bloemfontein. She invokes platitudes, talks about her accommodation, the nursing course, the storms. She keeps it vague. She wants to keep this place – this respite – separate. They do not talk about the illness, or the time she spent in Bloemfontein. That belongs to the past.

When Sandrien encounters Mrs Nyathi in the dim rooms of Bella Gardens, the same ritual always repeats itself.

'You still enjoying your wonderful stay, Mrs Gouws?'

Without fail, she answers: 'I am having the most wonderful time in this establishment of yours, Mrs Nyathi.'

Then Mrs Nyathi laughs, nodding her head as if they share a secret.

But this afternoon she catches Mrs Nyathi unawares. When Sandrien enters, she hears a loud voice in the bathroom. A new voice. It is Mrs Nyathi shouting at one of her maids in Xhosa. When

Sandrien quietly passes by in the corridor, Mrs Nyathi turns around and smiles. The girl is in shadow behind her. Sandrien can see the whites of her eyes. Mrs Nyathi pushes the door shut. Silence. From the bathroom, after a while, the unmistakable sound of a slap.

The other nurses in Bella Gardens are polite, but keep their distance from Sandrien. In the mornings, when they stroll to the college, they cluster together, chattering. Around the table in the evenings the girls and Mrs Nyathi speak a mix of English, Sotho and Xhosa, so that Sandrien only catches the occasional snippet. On week nights, they mostly retire to their rooms.

On Saturdays, Mrs Nyathi brings someone in to do their hair extensions in the sunshine on the veranda. At dusk there is chit-chat and giggling in the rooms of Bella Gardens. Vapours of perfume drift down the corridor. The maids sneak by on their toes, trying to get a glimpse of all things shiny and fragrant. With jingling bangles the girls trip through the lounge on silver heels. They make snake-like movements to the beat of inaudible music, initially ignoring Mrs Nyathi, who is looking on and keeping the rhythm. She keeps nodding her approval, over and over again, animated by an infectious exuberance. Then something strange happens: the air starts moving differently around the bodies. As if against their will, the girls start dancing to Mrs Nyathi's beat. They arrange themselves in relation to her, creating a formation with her at the forefront.

The taxi's hooter breaks the rhythm. To prevent mud getting on stockings, the driver picks up the girls at the end of the paved garden path. Music flows out when the white taxi door opens. Arms hang out the windows once they're inside.

'Yes,' says Mrs Nyathi to Sandrien when they are left sitting alone on the veranda, the village lights and fires below them. Her eyes are moist, searching for the taxi, its music fading among the houses. 'When I was a young nurse, there were also good, good times.'

Tonight she is wearing a headcloth, bright textile from West Africa.

'Where do they go at night?' Sandrien wants to know.

'There are places across the border in Lesotho,' Mrs Nyathi says, 'where you can have a lot of fun.' Her eyes widen and her head nods forward. 'A *lot* of fun.'

Mrs Nyathi looks askance at Sandrien, sips her brandy.

'How about you? You're still young enough. Don't you sing and dance, don't you sometimes seek out a little fun, fun, fun?' Mrs Nyathi shakes her head, pouting her lips as if talking to a baby.

Sandrien turns her head away, as if interrogating the thickening darkness. She uncrosses her legs, crosses them again. 'No,' she says slowly, 'my body refuses music. I only came close to singing when agony was at its worst. Then I made small noises under my breath. Yes, when I was ill, I sang like that, if you can call it singing.'

Mrs Nyathi stares at her. 'I sang for my patients sometimes, at night when they were dying.'

A tiny trail of sound, Sandrien thinks, illuminating the route.

Mrs Nyathi gets up and goes inside. She leaves her glass half full on the table, perhaps annoyed that Sandrien has permeated the air with such sudden gloom. Sandrien stays until the fires of Vloedspruit burn out one by one. She is a revelation to herself in Mrs Nyathi's company.

Through the veils of sleep she is waiting for the precipitation. She can hear thunder in the distance. She wakes up; it has arrived. Roaring against the corrugated-iron roof and windowpanes. She jumps up and opens the curtain. The ground is white. Hailstones are bouncing off the roofs. She is standing there, her body like a lamp, waiting for the glass to break. Moments after Mrs Nyathi pulls her away by the arm from behind, it happens: glass flying where she was just standing.

The moment the hailstorm has passed, Mrs Nyathi summons some of her maids. They appear out of the rain to nail wooden boards to the broken windows. They clean up and dry the floors, change wet linen.

Sandrien falls asleep again.

When she walks through Vloedspruit one last time the next morning, she notices the extent of the damage. Glass and blades of corrugated iron slice into the ground. A woman stops her at the market premises. The parts of the market that were still standing before have now gone too. The woman waves her arms. She is arguing animatedly, as if Sandrien is the cause of the floods, and responsible for repairing the market. Sandrien gives her money. The woman will not let her go. She sinks down on her knees in the mud, holding Sandrien back by her sleeve.

A downy feather descends on the kneeling woman's forehead. Sandrien looks up. Feathers are floating on the breeze. She shakes loose. She follows the feather trail. Like seeds at harvest time, down is hovering above the marshy area next to the river. Men are wringing the necks of herons and hacking off heads with pangas. Sometimes more than one blow is required. Dozens of waterbirds are dotted around, flapping with broken wings or trying to escape on snapped legs. The men do not even have to run to catch up with them. ∎

# Salad Days

How easy then, the fun house at Lincoln Park
before it grew into a field of weeds, you could buy
five tickets for a buck from a blank face in a booth
and enter the dark with your brother to be scared
by tilting floors, phoney doors, corpses
bursting out of coffins, and once out into blue sky
dash breathless to your mother and father, dazed,
you could have called them salad days,
but why would you – no one in your family
had read Shakespeare – so you bought
French fries, doused them with malt vinegar,
the four of you, competing for your share
of potatoes improved by salt and grease,
and nothing in those early evenings free
of care could have prepared you
to be the last one left, the one
with grief to spare.

© MIE MORIMOTO
from *pH*, 2013
Courtesy of Misako & Rosen, Tokyo

# IN THE SHADOW
# OF THE HOSPITAL

## Tim Winton

In 1995 veteran folk singer Loudon Wainwright III released a typically mordant song in which he catalogued the births, breakdowns, deaths and near misses of friends and family. Somehow all the health campuses of memory coalesce as a single monolithic entity, a site of inescapable mortality. *That hospital,* Wainwright senses, will never be done with him; it will always be there, waiting.

Hospital. The word itself carries historical notions of shelter, respite and hospitality. The modern institution remains a refuge, a place of deliverance. It's a bulwark against chaos. Anyone who's ever needed a hospital in a hurry knows the other-worldly sanctuary it promises. In the Greek islands thirty years ago I once sat in a small boat holding my infant son's scalp together with my thumbs as we beat into a gale towards the prospect of harbour and hospital. Although the clinic we were trying so desperately to reach was a seedy little affair I'd previously avoided, during that rocky passage it became in my mind a citadel of hygiene and expertise. *In extremis,* we yearn for that hospital, and yet at any other time, if you're anything like me, the very word brims with dread. Like the ageing Canadian strummer, I have a lifelong preoccupation with *that hospital,* an aversion I refuse to call a phobia.

As a child of safe, prosperous Australia, my earliest notion of hospital was that it was a mysterious reservoir of bounty. This was where mums and dads got their babies. And though I'd apparently come from there myself, I'd never been back to see. Grown-ups spoke of it as a place where broken arms were fixed, where sick people went to get better; it was amazing what they could do these days. On rare visits to the city when a parent pointed out some bland tower as a hospital I struggled to match it with the miracle factory I'd imagined. But by the time I was five I knew better. Hospital was trouble. You didn't want to go there because if you returned at all you came home in ruins.

I was still a small boy when my father suddenly disappeared. He just didn't come home from his shift. It took a long time for me to understand that there had been an accident. My mother tried to reassure me. So did the policemen who came to the door every day. They all said my dad would be okay – he was doing fine, the folks in the big city hospital were looking after him, it was incredible what they could do these days. He'd be back in no time. We just had to sit tight. Well, he wasn't back in no time, not even a long time, and all those other words of comfort began to sound like lies. Our little brick-veneer bungalow in the outer suburbs of Perth had never felt so empty and isolated. As the weeks went by I started to think hospital was a place from which people could not return. If Dad was doing so well there, why was Mum crying all the time? And if this was the best place for him right now, why couldn't I visit? He was sleeping, they said. But wasn't that what they told kids when people were dead and they were just too scared to say? Even after someone came by with the startling news that Dad was finally awake, I was told there would be no visits. And the weeks rolled on.

Then one day a big white armchair appeared in the lounge. It seemed to take up half the room. Mum said we were having a special visitor. And that afternoon a pale and wizened creature was carried into our house and carefully lowered into that new chair as if made of glass. His eyes were the colour of broken red bricks and he breathed through a hole in his neck. If I squinted a little he looked a bit like my dad, but he was so much older and too feeble-looking. My father was a big, strong, vigorous man. And yet everyone in the room – the off-duty coppers, the blokes from the hospital and even my mother – kept saying his name over and over: Johnny, John, John! They shook their heads in wonder and joshed with him, laughing as if this was a great day indeed. But I didn't really recognize him. I took everyone's cue and played along. If anything I was a little afraid of this husk in our midst. If this really was my dad, something awful had happened to him. He'd been carted off to hospital and sent home as a wreck.

Dad's recovery was long and slow. There were always crutches by the bedroom door, pills on the bedside table, bandages on the bedspread. Under his bed lay a slippery carpet of X-rays and some days he looked as ghostly and indecipherable as them. There were always doctors' appointments, visits to this specialist or that therapist. Finally the crutches gave way to the awful walking stick. And then the stick disappeared and he was suddenly plausible again. We had him back.

But now and then during my primary-school years, Dad would have to go in for more surgery, and any time he was taken back to hospital I felt a chill of panic. That lingering doubt was always there. What if he didn't come back? And what if he came home a stranger again?

As if picking up on my anxiety Mum eventually took me to visit him during one of these sojourns. At the time he was recovering from a bone graft, and that visit is my first memory of the inside of a hospital. I remember being nervous. But the reality was worse than what I'd imagined. It was like a descent into the netherworld: the grand entrance, the high desks and hard lights, all those flat, stern faces peering down. I shrank against my mother as she led us through a maze of corridors. Nurses' shoes squawked on the lino. The opaque windows had threads of steel in them as if the patients were captives. In the long open ward with its ranks of steel-framed beds, there was a gauntlet of horrors to be traversed before I could see my father. It was as if there was a price to be paid for visiting.

In the sixties an orthopaedic ward in a big public hospital was

a confronting environment for an adult, let alone a child. Visits by
children were discouraged. For patients there was no privacy, and
even with those ghastly curtains the nurses ricked around beds at
crucial moments, there was precious little discretion. On that long
walk, with coughs and moans and pulleys and pins and plasters at
every turn, I felt the first onset of the weird tunnel vision I am still
subject to as a visitor in hospital wards. It was as if I were walking
down my own tiny hallway from which the lurid tableau of men in
traction and wing-headed matrons were excluded. But what I could
not see loomed larger in the mind. Behind the death rattle of curtains,
I imagined limbs plastered into Gothic contortions, hypodermic
needles the size of bike pumps, bandaged heads in which black
mouths gaped and pulsed like anemones. With all those horrors, real
and imagined, it seemed quite a distance to travel. I pressed so hard
to my mother's hip she could barely walk.

After this ordeal the eventual sight of my dad with tubes snaking
from his hip wasn't quite so bad. Beneath his bed bottles collected
tawny liquid like the juices of a lamb roast. Dad hoisted me up and
showed me the plaster and the gruesome antiseptic stains on his
skin. He pointed out where the pipes went in. It was gross but it was
nothing like the charnel house I'd just been through. When our time
was up I didn't want to go. I bawled and said I missed him. But the
truth was I didn't want to walk back down that ward.

Years later I saw a movie by Dalton Trumbo that brought all that
childhood horror back to the surface. *Johnny Got His Gun* is about a
quadruple amputee, a soldier reduced to a helpless trunk. Mute and
alone with his fevered thoughts, he lies on a bed encased in plaster, just
a pair of eyes and a silent screaming mouth. From the first glimpse
this character was like something bursting in from the banished
periphery. For Trumbo, of course, he was meant to be exactly that;
a reminder that boys pay the price for the wars of old men. But to
me he was personal: a memory and a nightmare, the image that once
danced out of bounds beyond the walls of my panicky tunnel vision.
Man or boy, whenever I had to visit someone in hospital a version of

that Gothic effigy lurked at the edge of consciousness.

As a family we had our share of waiting-room nights and long days in car parks – puncture wounds, fractures, births and miscarriages, episodes of pleurisy, osteomyelitis, asthma and meningitis – yet somehow I managed to avoid admission all the years of childhood. Sometimes it seemed I was paying for this apparent immunity with traumatic visits. My infant brother emerging from a coma, his mouth a nest of ulcers. My grandmother writhing and raging after her catastrophic stroke. The day I stumbled into the burns unit by accident. Hospital seemed like a constant presence. But I was only visiting.

And then one morning at eighteen I woke up on the inside. I had no idea where I was or how I got there. There was a bloke gurgling and moaning beside me. I tried to get up but there was no power in my body; it was like a nasty dream. I tried to speak – to the man in the next bed, to anyone, really – but all I could produce was a croak. For a few moments I lay there, taking the room in, trying not to panic. Every surface had a ghost. I couldn't focus. My room-mate sounded as if he were dying. My hair was full of biting insects, my head hurt, my face hurt, my back and legs hurt, my belly felt as if it had been perforated with something blunt. I really needed to piss but I couldn't get up. I knew I wasn't paralysed; everything was working in a way but I was stuck. I felt ruined. Confused, frightened, angry, I began to cry.

Eventually someone arrived to see what the fuss was about. A glass of orange juice appeared. The drink was cool but it stung my chapped lips and I spilled some down my chest, unable to lift my head sufficiently. Soon afterwards I puked it all back up.

I didn't remember the accident. By all accounts I was lucky to be alive. The convulsions were gone but I was still badly concussed and there were ongoing tests on my innards. Those weren't whiskers on my chin; they were sutures. And the bees in my hair were thousands of fragments of windscreen glass.

The guy next to me died or was moved elsewhere; it wasn't clear.

Nothing looked right, nothing felt right. If I dropped off I couldn't tell, when I woke again, whether I was still in the same day. I felt like a very old man, feeble, addled, at the mercy of others. I couldn't think straight and all I could fix upon was the idea of fleeing. Yes, hospital was awful to visit, but it was far worse on the inside.

If you're an inpatient, acute illness does you the oddest favour; it takes up all mental space and serves as a buffer between you and the institution. Once the worst of the pain and fear have receded, however, your ordeal is not over; it merely changes shape. Of course nothing is more hellish than extreme pain and ungovernable terror, but nobody can prepare you for the challenge of recovery. That's the long game.

For one thing, unless you're out of your head on drugs there's no rest to be had in hospital. When the trolleys aren't crashing and scraping in the hectic daylight hours – all those drug carts, food wagons, theatre gurneys – the noise at night is both sinister and cruelly promising. As you lie awake in the wee hours the squeak of castors in the distance telegraphs the news that something is coming, coming, coming. Something better, something awful, some food, some unspeakable procedure. You're hooked up to machines that whine and burp and chirp and the same nurses who sternly tell you to get your rest will bellow and gossip outside your door all night. So you're exhausted. And on top of that you feel like a captive, so you're agitated. Whatever you want is perpetually unavailable: better pain relief, a pillow that hasn't previously done service as a sandbag, an open window, a view, some news, some better news. The only thing worse than visitors is other patients' visitors – or no visitors at all.

In hospital you become needy, greedy, callous. While you'll concede the necessity of tapering off the painkillers, you'll always find the decline too steep, too sudden. Even knowing how awful it is to be a hospital visitor you glory in showing friends the sutures and staples and you laugh boorishly when they lurch away in horror. Suffering is supposed to be ennobling, but being in hospital could make even a saint cruel and peevish. Perhaps it's the enclosed world, the peculiar internal logic, the infantilizing effect of being confined to your room, ordered into bed, wearing pyjamas, for goodness' sake, having baby food delivered and sometimes spooned into your mouth. No wonder so many great novels have been set in hospitals. From the paralysis and recrimination of Solzhenitsyn's cancer victims to the pettiness and moral vacancy of Endō's lung patients and their doctors, or the murky circus world of Kesey's mental ward, the healing institution harbours the bully, the whiner, the snitch and the cowardly accomplice. Wars and hospitals; it's a surprise we write about anything else. Hospitals make rich fictional settings because from the inside they are such chillingly plausible worlds unto themselves. They have their own surreal logic, their own absurd governance, their own uncanny weather, and the impotence and boredom they induce is hard to match anywhere else but prison or the military.

No wonder so many terminally ill patients prefer to die at home. Perhaps it's not the prospect of expiring in the company of loved ones and familiar surroundings so much as the thought of being a civilian again with notional command over the immediate environment. As an experience of powerlessness there is little to rival a stint in hospital.

As fate would have it, I married a nurse. I don't know what it says about me, but there it is. After every shift at the big suburban campus where she trained, she brought the ward home with her – in stories, in bruised silences and in the smells and stains of people suffering and dying day in and day out. That was all the hospital I needed in my life, though now and then I relented and met her for lunch in the cafeteria. But I was rotten company; I was forever distracted, fidgeting, flinching at the clash of trolleys and the sight of patients wheeling their IV stands between tables. My wife worked until a few weeks before our first child was born. It must have been strange for her cancer patients, being ministered to by such a young and hugely pregnant woman. Soon she was back at work, while still breastfeeding. Once or twice a shift, I drove our son to the campus so she could feed him on her breaks. He and I spent many hours lurking in the car park, spooking the security guards as we waited for her to emerge from Oncology. When she came rushing out into the fresh air she was as hungry for our baby as he was for her, and as she lay back in the passenger seat with the child at her breast, she kept me up to date with the trajectories of patients I felt I knew but would never meet. She smelled of antiseptic and sweat and things I didn't care to guess at, and it was odd to be with her in those minutes, feeding our baby with those strangers struggling and mostly dying a few floors above us.

For five years we lived in the very literal shadow of a big teaching hospital in the port city of Fremantle. Like all institutions it managed to be bigger than the sum of its parts. It wasn't just a health campus. At times it was more like a mill or a power plant. It filled the summer air with screams and sirens and the drone of cooling towers. It was an implacable presence. The beige mass of its buildings blocked the winter sun. Having previously lived in a rural community too small for a pharmacy, let alone a doctor, the proximity of a hospital was supposed to be reassuring, even for the likes of me. After all, I had three small kids now and I'd done more than my share of driving through the night to get medical help. I told myself: this is great – really; we can walk across the street to Accident and Emergency.

As it turned out the hospital didn't just offer safety; it provided a startling amount of free entertainment. It was a twenty-four-hour soap opera. Whether their problems were large, inconsequential or totally imaginary, the people who visited the building operated in an unrelievedly histrionic register and this operatic mode wasn't always dictated by crisis, although there was never any shortage of that. It seemed as if the aura of the institutional precinct brought out something different in people, something that altered them from their workaday selves, as if hospital didn't simply license them to behave differently but required it. And the variety of people a public hospital draws into its orbit hour by hour is hard to credit. In the time it took to get the groceries from the car to the house, you could meet a football star, a weeping woman with a painted moustache and too many fingers and a man with a steel bolt protruding from his forearm.

Our hospital was not the modern, discrete, Australian campus set in awesome suburban isolation like a hyper-mall, surrounded by a vast moat of car parking. This was the inner city, a neighbourhood of narrow streets and workers' cottages, and the hospital had long outgrown its original footprint. The old Victorian building was buried amid hulking brutalist slabs. They didn't just tower over the surrounding streets; they seemed to project outward. With the A&E opposite the local primary school and the new mental health unit directly opposite our house, the institution dominated the environs. In a medical precinct some of this institutional colonization is unavoidable – the nasty signage, the ever-present uniforms and flashing ambulances – but there were occasions when overzealous security guards or high-handed management gave locals like us the feeling that we were suspects and intruders in our own neighbourhood.

The place had its own microclimate. In summer the buildings steamed and shimmered and in winter they trapped squalls and spat out vicious, roof-rattling downdraughts. But this was only one form of weather. Approaching the place, within a block or two, you could feel the atmosphere become feverish and the closer you got to the foot of those towers and their yawning electric doors the more you noticed the vortex of suffering and need that sucked and boiled around you. There was electricity in the air. Latent havoc. Within a few moments our street could change from circus to battlefield. With its aura of hope and dread, it was peculiarly volatile, especially at night and on weekends. Negotiating it required vigilance.

On any street in any city, there's a human story walking past you every moment but it's usually withheld. However, in the lee of a hospital the social camouflage slips away. What's usually disguised is on display. Where else do people bear their own narratives so openly? Body language is heightened, almost balletic. Patients who step out for a fag by the taxi rank will pace and smoke and weep like actors from a film noir. Out on the forecourt, visitors, frightened relatives and self-admitters exist in a zone well outside their usual reserve. All discretion deserts them. Sometimes their basic competencies forsake them, too: they drive as if in a trance, park like rubes who've never been at the wheel before. And sometimes they don't even park; they simply abandon the car across or even in your driveway, keys, luggage, shopping and all. People literally carry their troubles on the pavement before you: the sick and shrieking child, the disoriented parent, the demon that hisses in their ear. From all those sliding doors – the locked ward, the A&E, the palliative unit – the anguished spill onto the street in haunted shifts, dazed by news good, bad or incomprehensible. They stagger into traffic, they stumble, they faint. At the kerbside shocked and grieving families unravel in public, erupting in vituperative brawls. I've seen people flog each other with cardigans, shoes, bunches of flowers.

The A&E entrance was like the door to a bright-lit hell. On the way home some nights, I crossed the road to avoid it. The sick and wounded came in ambulances, taxis, shopping trolleys. In the small hours of the weekend patients and supporters beat the glass doors, threatened and bashed the staff or crawled bleeding and intoxicated through the hedges around the ramp until eventually the hedges themselves were removed. I woke one night to the sound of an outpatient ramming the doors of the mental health unit with his car in a desperate bid for admission. I once stood at an intersection, waiting for the light to change, watching a woman in a car a metre away scream without pause. She was right beside me at eye level in the passenger seat, flailing and writhing. She gripped the seat belt with both hands as if it were the only thing preventing her from flying from the vehicle and bursting into flames. Her face bore the clenched solitude of untouchable suffering. It was as palpable as radiant heat. At the wheel the woman's friend wept. They were fifty metres from help, at the mercy of a single red light that seemed as if it would never relent. Just standing there, healthy and pain-free, I felt ashamed. I wanted to turn away, walk in another direction, but before I could move the light changed and they were gone.

Sometimes you see the worst in people. And it's a surprise to sense how quickly your tolerance and fellow feeling are eroded. You can still find some pity in your heart for the woman who regularly defecates in public because you know she's at the mercy of impulses beyond her control. But for those whose derangement is entirely recreational you end up feeling only disgust. As you step around the puddles of blood and the shitty nappies and the needles and broken glass and the pools of piss of a standard Saturday night, it's hard to spare the emerging wounded much sympathy; you just want them to bugger off and take their squalid fun elsewhere.

Despite all this bad weather, kindness still prevailed, even if it sometimes took a little concentration to notice it. It was both tonic and lesson to see how strangers comforted one another as they waited to be collected on the forecourt, how they dandled the babies of weary mothers and offered each other unexpired time on their parking tickets. The forbearance of nurses and paramedics was remarkable. Beneath their brusque drollery there was great care and courage. Every morning on the way to work I saw nurses and doctors emerging into the light wearing the long night on their faces and in their scrubs and I felt frivolous heading off to my safe, dull day's work.

All the years I lived next door to Fremantle Hospital I barely crossed the threshold. But in time its influence grew too oppressive for me. Like the grey noise of the cooling towers, its grim presence was unceasing. Even my wife admitted that the precinct was wearing at her nerves. We didn't move far. And yet, the distance of just a few streets was telling.

But the shadow falls wherever you are.

I got a message one day from an old friend. We'd been estranged for some years. He shocked me by announcing he was in hospital and that he could see my roof from his room. The silver flash of corrugated iron was like something burning in his mind, he said, and he needed to see me. Would I come?

It was only as I walked down the ward, feeling that ancient flutter of dread, that it dawned on me just how ill my friend might be. When I was allowed into his room I thought I'd made a mistake like the time I had bumbled into the burns wing. Sitting on the bed, staring out the window like a captive and dressed only in a nappy, was a tiny man, emaciated and entirely bald. Wrong room. Again! What a dunce I was. I was half turned to leave when he called my name.

I didn't need to be told how close to death he was. He said what a provocation to conscience it was to be trapped here in this room staring at my roof and how glad he was now that he'd been assigned this room. Before he grew too weak to continue, we made our peace and said our goodbyes. Afterwards I often looked up at that dreary tower as the sun lit up its windows and thought of others staring out in hope and regret as the rest of us went about our day, oblivious. All that yearning spilling down amid the treetops and roof ridges, a shadow I'd never properly considered before.

That kind of yearning came to mind the day I paced the halls of another hospital awaiting the birth of my first grandchild. We were in Melbourne, half a continent away, but the building felt only too familiar. Even before the talk of complications took hold I hated the place. It gave me the creeps. The air was all wrong. Well, there was no air. I was agitated. For hours there was no news at all but I couldn't sit down, couldn't eat, couldn't relax. Every few seconds the lifts in the corridor kept chiming demonically. After a while that cruel, festive sound drove me down to the end of the hall where I pressed my hands and face against the glass, staring out at the strange, flat city below as if there might be relief down there. What a sight I must have been. Wearing the gormless imploring look I was used to seeing on the faces of others. Eventually my long-suffering wife took me out to an astro turfed courtyard where at least the air was real and the open sky merciful. And that's where he found us, our eldest son, the colicky boy we nursed in the hospital car park all those nights a lifetime ago, holding his tiny squinting daughter in the sunshine.

I still have to steel myself for a hospital visit. Sadly I need to do it now more often than ever. People have breakdowns, heart surgery; they get cancer or simply wear out. And they're still having babies. The wind bloweth where it listeth, as the old book says, and the shadow falls likewise.

'Here,' my father said one afternoon, pressing my palm against the egregious new lump in his scarred old chest. It was his new pacemaker. He was in the recovery ward of a private clinic. 'They can do amazing things these days,' he said.

They can. And they do. In an earlier era he'd have been long dead. Mum brought him home the next day. From that hospital. ∎

© PIERRE-OLIVIER DESCHAMPS / AGENCE VU
Casa Milà, Barcelona, Spain

# BOOKS AND ROSES

## *Helen Oyeyemi*

Once upon a time in Catalonia a baby was found in a chapel. This was over at Santa Maria de Montserrat. It was an April morning. And the baby was so wriggly and minuscule that the basket she was found in looked empty at first glance. The child had got lost in a corner of it, but courageously wriggled her way back up to the top fold of the blanket in order to peep out. The monk who found this basket searched for an explanation. His eyes met the wooden eyes of the Virgin of Montserrat, a mother who has held her child on her lap for centuries, a gilded child that doesn't breathe or grow. In looking upon that great lady the monk received a measure of her unquestioning love and fell to his knees to pray for further guidance, only to find that he'd knelt on a slip of paper that the baby had dislodged with her wriggling. The note read:

1. You have a Black Madonna here, so you will
   know how to love this child almost as much as
   I do. Please call her Montserrat.
2. Wait for me.

A golden chain was fastened around her neck, and on that chain was a key. As she grew up, the lock of every door and cupboard in the monastery was tested, to no avail. She had to wait. It was both a comfort and a great frustration to Montse, this . . . what could she call it, a notion, a suggestion, a promise? This promise that somebody was coming back for her. If she'd been a white child the monks of Santa Maria de Montserrat might have given her into the care of a local family, but she was as black as the face and hands of the Virgin they adored. She was given the surname Fosc, not just because she was black, but also because her origin was obscure. And the monks set themselves the task of learning all they could about the needs of a child. More often than not they erred on the side of indulgence, and held debates on the matter of whether this extreme degree of fondness was a mortal sin or a venial one. At any rate it was the Benedictine friars who fed and clothed and carried Montse, and went through the horrors of the teething process with her, and rang the chapel bells for hours the day she spoke her first words. Neither as a girl nor as a woman did Montse ever doubt the devotion of her many fathers, and in part it was the certainty of this devotion that saw her through times at school and times down in the city when people looked at her strangely or said insulting things; the words and looks sometimes made her lower her head for a few steps along the street, but never for long. She was a daughter of the Virgin of Montserrat, and she felt instinctively and of course heretically that the Virgin herself was only a symbol of a yet greater sister-mother who was carefree and sorrowful all at once, a goddess who didn't guide you or shield you but who went with you from place to place and added her tangible presence to your own when required.

When Montse was old enough she took a job at a haberdashery in Les Corts de Sarrià, and worked there until Señora Cabella found her relatives unwilling to take over the family business and the shop closed down. 'You're a hard-working girl, Montse,' Señora Cabella told her, 'and I know you'll make something of yourself if given a chance. You've seen that eyesore at the Passeig de Gràcia. The Casa Milà. People call it La Pedrera because it looks like a quarry, just a lot of stones all thrown on top of one another. An honest, reliable girl

can find work as a laundress there. Is that work you can do? Very well
– go to Señora Molina, the *conserje*'s wife. Tell her Emma Cabella sent
you. Give her this.' And the woman wrote out a recommendation that
made Montse blush to read it.

She reported to Señora Molina at La Pedrera the next morning,
and the *conserje*'s wife sent her upstairs to Señora Gaeta, who
pronounced Montse satisfactory and tied an apron on her. After that
it was work, work, work, and weeks turned into months. Montse had
to work extra fast to keep Señora Gaeta from noticing that she was
washing the Cabella family's clothes along with those of the residents
she'd been assigned. The staff turnover at La Pedrera was rapid; every
week there were new girls who joined the ranks without warning, and
girls who vanished without giving notice. Señora Gaeta knew every
name and face, even when the identical uniforms made it difficult for
the girls themselves to remember each other. It was Señora Gaeta
who employed the girls and also relieved them of their duties if their
efforts weren't up to scratch. She darted around the attic, flicking
the air with her red lacquered fan as she inspected various activities.
The residents of Casa Milà called Señora Gaeta a treasure, and the
laundry maids liked her because she sometimes joined in when they
sang work songs; it seemed that once she had been just like them,
for all the damask and cameo rings she wore now. Señora Gaeta
was also well liked because it was interesting to hear her talk: she
swore the most powerful and unusual oaths they'd ever heard, really
unrepeatable stuff, and all in a sweetly quivering voice, like the song of
a harp. Señora Gaeta's policy was to employ healthy-looking women
who didn't look likely to develop bad backs too quickly. But you can't
guess right all the time. There were girls who aged overnight. Others
were unexpectedly lazy. Women who worried about their reputations
didn't last long in the attic laundry either – they sought and found
work in more ordinary buildings.

It was generally agreed that this mansion the Milà family had
had built in their name was a complete failure. This was mostly
the fault of the architect. He had the right materials but clearly he

hadn't known how to make the best use of them. A house of stone and glass and iron should be stark and sober, a watchtower from which a benevolent guard is kept on society. But the white stone of this particular house rippled as if reacting to a hand that had found its most pleasurable point of contact. A notable newspaper critic had described this effect as being that of 'a pernicious sensuality'. And as if that wasn't enough, the entire structure blushed a truly disgraceful peachy-pink at sunset and dawn. Respectable citizens couldn't help but feel that the house expressed the dispositions of its inhabitants, who must surely be either mad or ceaselessly engaged in indecent activities. But Montse thought the house was beautiful. She stood on a corner of the pavement and looked up, and what she saw clouded her senses. To Montse's mind La Pedrera was a magnificent place. But then her taste lacked refinement. Her greatest material treasure was an egregiously shiny bit of tin she'd won at a fairground coconut shy; this fact can't be overlooked. But there was also Señora Lucy, who lived on the second floor and frequently argued with people about whether or not her home was an aesthetic offence. Journalists came to interview the Señora from time to time, and would make some comment about the house as a parting shot on their way out, but Señora Lucy refused to let them have the last word and stood there arguing at the top of her voice. The question of right angles was always being raised: How could Señora Lucy bear to live in a house without a single right angle . . . not even in the furniture?

'But really who needs right angles? Who?' Señora Lucy would demand, and she'd slam the courtyard door and run up the stairs laughing.

Señora Lucy was a painter with eyes like daybreak. She told people that she was fifty years old and gave them looks that dared them to say she was in good condition for her age. (Señora Lucy was actually thirty-five, only five years older than Montse. One of the housemaids had overheard a gallery curator begging her to stop telling people she was fifty. The Señora had replied that she'd recently attended the exhibitions of some of her colleagues and now wished to discover whether fifty-year-old men in her field were treated with reverence because they were fifty or for some other reason.) Aside from this, the housemaids were a bit disappointed with Señora Lucy. They expected their resident artist to lounge about in scarlet pyjamas, drink cocktails for breakfast and entertain dashing rascals and fragrant sirens. But Señora Lucy kept office hours. Merce, her maid of all work, tried to defend her by alleging that the Señora drank her morning coffee out of a vase, but nobody found this credible.

Montse found ways to be the one to return Señora Lucy's laundry to her; this sometimes meant undertaking several other deliveries so that her boss Señora Gaeta didn't become suspicious. There was a workroom in Señora Lucy's apartment; she often began work there, and then had the canvases transported to her real studio. Thirty seconds in Señora Lucy's apartment was long enough for Montse to get a good stare at all those beginnings of paintings. The Señora soon saw that Montse was curious about her work, and she took to leaving her studio door open while she etched on canvas. She'd call Montse to come and judge how well the picture was progressing. 'Look here,' she'd say, indicating a faint shape in the corner of the canvas. 'Look here.' Her fingertips glided over a darkening of colour in the distance. She sketched with an effort that strained every limb. Montse saw that the Señora sometimes grew short of breath though she'd hardly stirred: a consequence of snatching images out of the air – the air took something back.

Montse asked the Señora about the key around her neck. It wasn't a real question, Montse was just talking so that she could stay a moment longer. But the Señora said she wore it because she was waiting for someone; at this Montse forgot herself and blurted: 'You too?'

The Señora was amused. 'Yes, me too. I suppose we're all waiting for someone.' And she told Montse all about it as she poured coffee into vases for them both. (It was true! It was true!)

'Two mostly penniless women met at a self-congratulation ritual in Seville,' Señora Lucy began. The event was the five-year reunion

of a graduating class of the University of Seville – neither woman
had attended this university, but they blended in, and every other
person they met claimed to remember them, and there was much
exclamation on the theme of it being wonderful to see former
classmates looking so well. The imposters had done their research,
and knew what to say, and what questions to ask. Their names were
Safiye and Lucy, and you wouldn't have guessed that either one was a
pauper, since they'd spent most of the preceding afternoon liberating
various items of priceless finery from their keepers.

These two penniless girls knew every trick in the book. Both
women moved from town to town under an assortment of aliases,
and both believed that collaboration was for weaklings. Lucy and
Safiye hadn't come to that gathering looking for friendship or love;
they were there to make contacts. Back when they had toiled at honest
work – Lucy at a bakery and Safiye at an abattoir – they'd wondered
if it could be true that there were people who were given money
simply because they looked as if they had lots of it. Being blessed with
forgettable faces and the gift of brazen fabrication, they'd gone forth
to test their theory and had found it functional. Safiye loved to look
at paintings, and needed money to build her collection. Lucy was an
artist in constant need of paint, brushes, turpentine, peaceful light
and enough canvas to make compelling errors on. For a time Lucy
had been married to a rare sort of clown, the sort that children aren't
afraid of: *After all, he is one of us, you can see it in his eyes*, they reasoned.
*How funny that he's so strangely tall.* Lucy and her husband had not
much liked being married to each other, the bond proving much
heavier than their light-hearted courtship had led them to expect,
but they agreed that it had been worth a try, and while waiting for
their divorce to come through Lucy's husband had taught her the
sleight of hand she eventually used to pick her neighbour's pocket
down to the very last thread. The night she met Safiye she stole her
earrings right out of her earlobes and, having retired to a quiet corner
of the mansion to inspect them, found that the gems were paste.
Then she discovered that her base metal bangle was missing and

quickly realized that she could only have lost it to the person she was stealing from; she'd been distracted by the baubles and the appeal of those delicate earlobes. Cornered by a banker whose false memory of having been in love with her since matriculation day might prove profitable, Lucy wavered between a sensible decision and a foolhardy one. Ever did foolhardiness hold the upper hand with Lucy; she found Safiye leaning against an oil lantern out in the garden and saw for herself that she wasn't the only foolish woman in the world, or even at that party, for Safiye had Lucy's highly polished bangle in her hand and was turning it this way and that in order to catch fireflies in the billowing, transparent left sleeve of her gown. All this at the risk of being set alight, but then from where Lucy stood Safiye looked as if she was formed of fire herself, particles of flame dancing the flesh of her arm into existence. That or she was returning to fire.

They left the reunion early and in a hurry. Having fallen into Lucy's bed, they didn't get out again for days. How could they, when Lucy held all Safiye's satisfactions in her very fingertips, and each teasing stroke of Safiye's tongue summoned Lucy to the brink of delirium? They fell asleep, each making secret plans to slip away in the middle of the night. After all, their passion placed them entirely at each other's command, and they were bound to find that fearsome. So they planned escape but instead woke up intertwined. It was at Lucy's bidding that Safiye would stay or go. And who knew what Safiye might suddenly and successfully demand of Lucy? *Stop breathing. Give up tea.* The situation improved once it occurred to them that they should also talk; as they came to understand each other they learned that what they'd been afraid of was running out of self. On the contrary the more they loved the more there was to love. The lovers spent Christmas together, then parted – Lucy for Grenoble, and Safiye for Barcelona. They wrote to each other care of their cities' central post offices, and at the beginning of April Safiye wrote of the romance of St Jordi's Day. *Lucy, it is the custom here to exchange books and roses each year on April 23rd. Shall we?*

Lucy happily settled down to work. First she sent for papyrus and handmade a book leaf by leaf, binding the leaves together between board covers. Then she filled each page from memory, drew English roses budding and Chinese roses in full bloom, peppercorn-pink Bourbon roses climbing walls and silvery musk roses drowsing in flower beds. She took every rose she'd ever seen, made them as lifelike as she could (where she shaded each petal the rough paper turned silken) and in these lasting forms she offered them to Safiye.

The making of this rose book coincided with a period in Lucy's life when she was making money without having to lie to anyone. She'd fallen in with an inveterate gambler who'd noticed that she steadied his nerves to a miraculous degree. He always won at blackjack whenever she was sitting beside him, so they agreed he'd give her 10 per cent of each evening's winnings. This man only played when the stakes were high, so he won big and they were both happy. Lucy had no idea what was going to happen when their luck ran out; she could only hope her gambler wouldn't get violent with her, because then she'd have to get violent herself. That would be a shame, since she liked the man. He never pawed at her, he always asked her how Safiye was getting on and he was very much in love with his wife, who loved him too and thought he was a nightwatchman. The gambler's wife would've gone mad with terror if she'd known how close she came to losing her life savings each night, but she didn't suspect a thing, so she packed her husband light suppers to eat at work, suppers the man couldn't even bear to look at (his stomach always played up when he was challenging Lady Luck), so Lucy ate the suppers and enjoyed them very much, the flavour of herbed olives lingering in her mouth so that when she drank her wine she tasted all the greenness of the grapes.

From time to time Lucy paused her work on the rose book to write and send brief notes: *Safiye – I've been so busy I haven't had time to think; I'm afraid I'll only be able to send you a small token for this St Jordi's Day you wrote about. I'll beg my forgiveness when I see you.*

Safiye replied: *Whatever the size of your token, I'm certain mine is smaller. You'll laugh when you see it, Lucy.*

*Competitive as ever! Whatever it is you're doing, don't get caught.
I love you, I love you.*

On April 23rd, an envelope addressed in Safiye's hand arrived at
the post office for Lucy. It contained a key on a necklace chain and a
map of Barcelona with a black rose drawn over a small section of it.
Lucy turned the envelope inside out but there was no accompanying
note. Safiye's map led Lucy to a crudely hewn door in a wall. This
didn't look like a door that could open, but a covering for a mistake in
the brickwork. The key fitted the lock and Lucy walked into a walled
garden overrun with roses.

'And what about your own key, Montserrat?'

Lucy's key gleamed and Montse's looked a little sad and dusty;
perhaps it was only gold-plated. She rubbed at it with her apron.

'Just junk, I think.'

'**M**ontserrat, have you seen the newspaper?' Assunta called out
across the washtubs.

'I never see the newspaper,' Montserrat answered through a
mouthful of thread.

'Montserrat, Montserrrat of the key,' Marta crooned beside her.

The other maids took up the chant until Montse held her needle
still and said, 'All right, what's the joke, girls?'

'They're talking about the advertisement that's in *La Vanguardia*
this morning,' said Señora Gaeta, placing the newspaper on the lid of
Montse's work basket. Montse laid lengths of thread beneath the lines
of newsprint as she read: *Enzo Gomez of Gomez, Cruz and Molina
awaits contact with a woman who bears the name Montserrat and is in
possession of a gold key one and one half inches in length.*

Without saying another word, the eagle-eyed Señora Gaeta picked
up a scarlet thread an inch and a half long and held it up against Montse's
key. The lengths matched. Señora Gaeta rested a hand on Montse's
shoulder, then walked back up to the front of the room to inspect a
heap of newly done laundry before it returned to its owner. Montse
kept her eyes on her work. It was the only way to keep her mind quiet.

The solicitor Enzo Gomez looked at her hands and uniform before he looked into her eyes. Her hands had been roughened by harsh soap and hard water; she fought the impulse to hide them behind her back. Instead she undid the clasp of her necklace and held the key out to him. She told him her name and he jingled a bunch of keys in his own pocket and said, 'The only way we can find out is by trying the lock. So let's go.'

The route they took was familiar. Gomez stopped walking and rifled through his briefcase, pulled out a folder and read aloud from a piece of paper in it:

> Against my better judgement but in accordance with the promise I made to my brother Isidoro Salazar, I, Zacarias Salazar, leave the library of my house at 17 Carrer Alhambra to one Montserrat who will come with the key to the library as proof of her claim. If the claimant has not come forth within fifty years of my death, let the lock of the library door be changed in order to put an end to this nonsense. For if the mother cannot be found then how can the daughter?

Enzo put the folder back into his briefcase. 'I hope you're the one,' he said. 'I've met a lot of Montserrats in this capacity today, most of them chancers. But you – I hope it's you.'

A gallery attendant opened the main gate for them and showed them around a few gilt passages until they came to the library, which was on its own at the end of a corridor. Montse was dimly aware of Enzo Gomez mopping his forehead with a handkerchief as she placed the key in the lock and turned it. The door opened onto a room with high shelves and higher windows that followed the curve of a cupola ceiling. The laundry maid and the solicitor stood in front of the shelf closest to the door. Sunset lit the chandeliers above them and they found themselves holding hands until Gomez remembered his professionalism and strode over to the nearest desk to remove the papers from his briefcase.

'I'm glad it's you, Montserrat,' he said, placing the papers on the desk and patting them. 'You must let me know if I can be of service to you in future.' He bowed, shook hands and left her in her library without looking back, the quivering of his trouser cuffs the only visible sign of his emotions.

Montse wandered among the shelves until it was too dark to see. She thought that if the place was really hers she should open it up to the public; there were more books here than could possibly be read in one lifetime. Books on sword-swallowing and life forms found in the ocean, clidomancy and the aurora borealis and other topics that reminded Montse how very much there was to wonder about in this world: there were things she'd seen in dreams that she wanted to see again and one of these books, any of them, might lead her back to those visions, and lead her further on. For now there was the smell of leather-bound books and another faint but definite scent: roses. She cried into her hands because she was lost: she'd carried the key to this place for so long and now that she was there she didn't know where she was. The scent of roses grew stronger and she wiped her hands on her apron, switched on a light and opened the folder Enzo Gomez had handed her.

This is what she read:

> Montserrat, I'm very fond of your mother. I was fond of everyone who shared my home. I am a fool, but not the kind who surrounds himself with people he doesn't trust. I didn't know what was really happening below stairs; upstairs we are always the last to know. Things could have been very different. You would have had a home here, and I would have spoiled you, and doubtless you would have grown up with the most maddening airs and graces. That would have been wonderful.

As I say, I was fond of everyone who lived with me, but I was particularly fond of Aurelie. I am an old man now – an old libertine even – and my memory commits all manner of treacheries; only a few things stay with me. Some words that made me happy because they were said by exactly the right person at exactly the right time, and some pictures because they formed their own moment. One such picture is your mother's brilliant smile, always slightly anxious, as if even in the moment of delighting you she wonders how she dares to be so very delightful. I hope that smile is before you right now. I hope she came back to you. I first met her soon after she'd been abandoned by her travelling companion, a musician she'd accompanied from her home town of Paris. I believe this musician to be your father. And that, I'm afraid, is all I know about that.

Please allow me to say another useless thing: Nobody could have made me believe that Aurelie ever stole from me. The only person who could possibly have held your mother in higher esteem than I did was my brother, Isidoro. He wrote to me about your mother, you know. He told me I should give my library to her. Then he told me she'd be happier if I gave it to her daughter. *Do it or I'll haunt you to death,* he wrote. The rest of this house is dedicated to art now; it's been a long time since I lived here, or visited. But the library is yours. So enjoy it, my dear.

Zacarias Salazar ∎

AN
INTERNATIONAL
CONSPIRACY
OF GOOD
WRITING

From Brazil to Sweden,
Japan to Turkey, *Granta*
has international editions
in twelve languages across
three continents. Read the
best new writing from
around the world.

# GRANTA
THE MAGAZINE OF NEW WRITING

granta.com/about/international-editions

© ZHOU HONGBIN
*Aquarium 02*, 2008
Courtesy of Magda Danysz Gallery, Shanghai/Paris

# HARE IN LOVE

## Sam Coll

From the beach, the Mad Monk passed as a shadow over many miles of dunes, the pampas blades bowing backwards to admit him through. And in the sky dark clouds began to rally – and in the wings of his nose came the scent of storm. So he abandoned the plains of dunes in favour of a seashore cave, a humble shelter for his noble head. And in this cave he resided for some short duration of days, as the rain came down to drench the land, and the wet of the weather to welcome him. And in that cave he built from some logs and branches a fire for himself, one that he lit from a spark of some stones he scraped, and the warmth it lent, and the light at night it gave, were pleasing to his senses. And for food he fed on some crabs that ambled naively into that cave, lured by the firelight. He cooked their flesh in the flame, and ate heartily, relishing the crunch of their crabby shells under his iron canines. And for dessert he dined on an earthworm, seasoned with sea salt, made juicier through liberal sprinkling of the silvery slime of snail (it was his custom to collect such slime). And when he was not eating or sleeping or surveying the storm's progress, he would doodle on the walls of the cave, anointing his fingertips with pigments of his own produce, and making bold strokes on the flatter sections of stone. He drew dragons and demons, visions of the otherworld and of paradise, sometimes even attempting

the beloved face of Watt once known. And sometimes he took stabs
at sketching his own self, though through lack of a mirror, the results
were mediocre. Still and all, he found it a pleasant pastime, and he
reckoned he would improve, through dint of sheer persistence.

And one day there came into the cave a darting Hare, whom the
Mad Monk caught easily, and would have killed and cooked and
eaten, had not the Hare, who possessed great powers of persuasion,
made a moving appeal for his life to be spared. He was young, and
his whole life lay before him. What is more, he knew the Mad Monk
of old, so he claimed, for when a baby he remembered having been
introduced to that same worthy gentleman by his father, one of the
pillars of the haring community, who had dealt with fairies and druids
and shamans and suchlike singular folk, of whom the Mad Monk was
one of the more colourful. His father had hailed the Mad Monk a
hero such as might redeem the world from the ruin with which it
flirted, and he made it plain to his impressionable son that such was
the sort of chap he would have him try in his own little life to live up
to, and strive to emulate, for all he never could nor would. And as long
as he lived the young Hare would never forget the words of his father
apropos that paragon of all earthly creatures, that glory of the world
and God in man.

So thus did the loquacious Hare plead his case and charm the Mad
Monk through flattery and flowery words and cloying compliments,
and though outwardly the Mad Monk affected to disdain the praise,
within he was secretly delighted. And when the pageant of praise was
winding down, the Mad Monk bade the Hare be quiet, and run along
like a good fellow and leave him alone – 'for my appetite that once
yearned for your flesh is dissipated and quenched, so well wrought
your roguish ruse of waffle'.

But the Hare, getting cocky, would not leave. He had come to the
cave with a specific purpose, to seek advice from a man known far
and wide to be wise.

'Hang on now, my hopping hare of bandy bow legs! Leaving aside
whether or not I do be wise, how is it that you came to know that

advice such as you seek would be readily found from one such as me in this particular godforsaken cave of all caves on the coast?'

The Hare smiled, knowing something the Mad Monk didn't, and elaborated. The Mad Monk's coming was no secret among the learned. For months prior to his landing, the advent of his return had been much spoken of. It all began when a ghost was seen wandering the hills, caressing the goats, murmuring sweet nothings in their ears and babbling unto them prophetic gobbledygook to make their hairs stand on end. This ghost took the shape of a bald old man with a very long beard and glowing eyes, who spoke in lofty language, foretelling his brother's impending arrival to redeem the wretched.

The Mad Monk started at the employment of the word 'brother' with reference to this prophet, and felt a chill to his heart. For he recognized in the description the person of his own dead brother Elijah, who knew all, and of what he knew told only a little, and that little whenever and to whomsoever few he chose. And he felt a quiet horror then.

The Hare continued. The appearance of this spectral soothsayer was surely a portent, and the goats had not been slow to spread what he said. They told other goats, goats overheard by donkeys, who told other donkeys, who told the asses, who told the horses, who told the cattle, who told the pigs, who told the sheep, who told the dogs, who told the cats, who told the rats, who told the mice, who told the geese, who told the chickens, who told the ducks, who told the swans, who told the herons, who told the cormorants, who told the otters, who told the jackdaws, who told the –

'Enough,' said the Mad Monk with some firmness. And then he felt a great weariness that gave way to doubt, and to the threshold of terror. For the weight of expectancy was doomed to dog him now, in a way it would not have done had his coming to the country been made in secret. But contrary to his wishes, the multitude both high and low had long known, and thanks to the gossiping of his brother's ghost, the numbers of those in the know had day by day the greater grown. And they expected much of him, more than any mere mortal man, more than even his own immortal self, the very God in man, could ever live up to. And now his strong shoulders began sadly to sag, under strain from all the daunting weight of promise they sweating bore.

Sitting there brooding darkly, scratching his beard, digesting all he heard with a liberal dose of doubt, the Mad Monk forgot about the cocky Hare seated there before him on the floor of the cave, by light of the flickering fire, eagerly eyeing him, awaiting the moment when the old man would ask of him at last the precise advice his youthful ignorance had sought.

And then the Mad Monk shook himself, remembering of a sudden something the youth had said, with regard to the reason for his coming to the cave.

'Sorry about that, lad,' he said more amiably. 'Me mind's a muddle, I'm afraid. Thanks for the telling. But I seem to recall that you had need of advice to ask me? I beg you, pray, spit it out, and we'll see what needs or can be done, if anything at all.'

The Hare grew shyer, a faint blush stealing to his furry cheeks.

'Dear sir,' he said, hopping gingerly in his shyness from one hare's foot to the other. 'It is long past the last March's mating season. My fellows and brethren males, as is common and can only be expected, went mad with mating, impregnating females all over the shop with proper impunity. And being as I was at the time newly come of age, it was my expected duty to do ditto. And I tried. But somehow, for whatever why, I could not bring myself so to do as they did. My heart was not in it. I failed in my function.'

'You are impotent, I take it?' said the Mad Monk drily, stifling a yawn, with a sneer to his voice, already feeling a bit bored.

The Hare blushed redder and blanched. 'Oh no, no, not at all – or at least, not always – only sometimes – intermittently impotent it is I am, you might well say. But I –'

'I see.' The Mad Monk cut across him, doing his best to be indulgent. 'Well now, Lordy knows this is a vexing matter, but not so new that I have not met it scores of times before. Your affliction is as old as the hills, as old as tyrant time, that traitor time in many men the primary cause. Cannot say I have ever known it personally, this sapping of the vital spirits, no, not I, who was always from birth a virile bounder enviably laden with a lucky loot of the bindu, but I've always done my best to help the poor bastards who are less lucky. A quiver of aphrodisiac arrows it was once my pleasure to keep, which arrows I administered with glee to the wretches, that they may know again the joy of fecundity. Is that why you have come? Because I must have you know, those arrows are stowed away in my desert hideaway in care of the Puck, who will be coming later, who may or may not bring them. I make no promises. I give thee no false hopes. In the meantime, I can cook up a potion of potency that may alleviate thy malady, if only temporarily, until the cure more lasting may come. Or not. Nothing is certain. Will that do? Is that all?'

Throughout this disinterested expostulation, the Hare wrung his paws and ground teeth in dismay for having got the emphasis and the wording wrong.

'No, sir, that is not all,' he said finally, raising his nervous head to face down the godly yellow eyes of eagle, set in the fine face crackled by light of fire's flame. 'My concerns go beyond the mechanical squirt of seed. For I, uncommonly among my kind, have higher aims in mind, not so easily brought off, when you are an animal as I am.'

'Higher aims,' the Mad Monk drawled, tasting the sounds. 'That sounds funny. Can't say I've met many hares as yourself who ever bother to aim higher, who care to do more than their allotment of life permits, and their cast of mind allows, they who do no more than feed, and fuck, and try not to get killed. You begin to intrigue me, boy. In what way, then, is it that you aim higher and do so differ from your flat-headed peers?'

'It will sound ridiculous for me to say it,' the humble Hare said shyly, 'but say it I must. Unlike my contemporaries, I did not care to bound from bed to bed and from woman to woman, leaving in my leaky trail a wake of children. For, you see, there's ever only been one for me. Bare but one. Only one especial lady for whom

I ever had any attention or deep affection, any real care at all, ever since birth. It is more than physical – it is spiritual, if you'll allow me to say so. Only for her would I squander my goods, do deeds of service and run errant errands. Only for her would I lend my life in sacrifice if the barrel of the hunter's cruel gun at her were pointed, if it meant I would die so long as she would remain and live and last. For her alone do I feel the noblest of sentiments, the greatest gift and the most galling curse, making of all my life a melancholic agony, and making me mad, mad, mad, madness that knows not the calendar's dictation nor the schedule of the seasons, madness beyond mere March, a lasting passion that never leaves me.'

His little voice broke, and he hesitated. And the Mad Monk felt a quickening excitement to hear the Hare so speak, whose eager eyes bulged as his fervour grew, tall the shadow he threw on the cave's craggy walls, dark shadow forged by the firelight that flickered (night by now had fallen thickly), as he spoke with feeling of his nameless passion, erect ears aquiver as they tautened and pricked.

And in the quiet of hesitation, the patter of rain and sound of storm filled the gap and howled, as the Mad Monk knelt forward closer to the Hare, to whom he now whispered hoarsely, his curiosity to satisfy: 'And what is the name of that feeling of which you speak?'

The Hare shivered; swallowed; then said: 'Love, sir.'

And the Mad Monk sighed; and shut his eyes; and spoke slowly: 'Ah . . . yes. Love. Sweetest of dreams, our life's bitterest mystery, our foremost misery. I know the feeling well, old as I am, and have felt so oft in my time its prick and sting, its brief and intermittent bliss that will so swiftly turn to rancour, that yet will come again to be a craving for sating, wringing our anguished hearts until we can take no more – though forever always we eternally do come back for more. Only ask the ages, and you shall see it is so. It is the oldest of ailments, the most delicious, the most destructive, affecting all manner of men from all walks of life high and low from top to toe. Still and all, for such as yourself, I mean a Hare, to speak of it so finely, is decidedly rare. Please elaborate, my boy – impart unto me the circumstances – the state – the condition of this love – the nature and character of this lady on whom you would shower it – and tell me how real – how true – how lasting this love – do but tell me all this, and ask my advice, and we shall see for sure how I might help, if help I can, as I hope I can.'

With quiet tears, the Hare expanded, and the Mad Monk with shut eyes nodded and sighed in sympathy, swaying from side to side as he listened to the Hare speak impassioned of his lady love, the one and only, a darling damsel with luscious legs and floppy ears, so sweet, so kind, so gently tender her nature, possessed of a pair of eyes, and a speaking voice, that were the most beautiful and divine he had ever been blessed to behold, or ever had the happiness to hear. She was as young as he was, lived not far nearby, and he had known her from their infancy, they were childhood friends who bonded as babies, who grew up together amid the tall grass of hill and dale and vale, among whose blades and thickets they tumbled and played their childish games, knowing not a care in the world – until, slowly but surely, over the years there was begot in his aching heart a bubble of love for none but this fairest lady, love that grew and grew, giving him now, in the throes of his young manhood, nothing but the vilest spleen. And the core and crux of his angst was his deep uncertainty as to the pitch and degree of her feelings for him, his awful doubts as to whether what he felt was fully reciprocated.

And the Mad Monk sadly smiled to hear this, recognizing the seed of the oldest story – the potential unrequited that ever beguiled, ever destroyed.

The Hare, by his own admission, had not the requisite cockiness to make his move to stake his claim, to pluck his pick and take his choice and bewitching woman woo – so greatly in cowardice did he fear her rebuttal. And she had recently begun to disgust him by her seeming fickleness, having, during the month of last March when high on her first heat, gone about gadding with the other braver boys, hopping around and pulling hairs, earning a reputation as a ready ride. Already pregnant, she was expecting now a batch of babes –

SAM COLL

begat in delirious frenzy, their fathers gone away elsewhere, to fresher pastures for ploughing, such as knew no love. And relations nowadays between himself and herself were strained – he wondered had she done it all just to make him jealous, to spurn him on to claim her as she knew (she must know) he dearly wanted to, or whether indeed he were wasting his time and ought to swallow pride and strive to quash his doomed and futile impotent love. And wondering whether indeed she were only just another fickle hare-brained female fool, happily ignorant of any higher feeling such as that selfsame love he felt, that made him so miserable.

The Hare fell quiet and waited for the advice to be dispensed. But it did not come. Still the Mad Monk sat on silent with eyes closed, seeming to be sleeping. The Hare wondered had he bored him overmuch. But he was mistaken to wonder thus. For the Mad Monk had heard all intently and interestedly, and now was in the midst of formulating a scheme, cogs and wheels grinding and clacking as he thought things through. For he was of the opinion that it was not mere advice the young Hare needed, verbal advice that could get lost, or be misunderstood, or ignored, or forgotten. Rather, practical and active assistance, such as at which he excelled, was needed. For he was since time immemorial one of the most devoted servants of true love in all its forms, and the very best friend and encourager of young love in particular. He liked this young Hare who had given him valuable information, and the picture painted of his passion's plight had touched the old man keenly, and he was determined to do well by him. In his strong heart warm sentiment stirred, and he decided that, once more again, as so oft before he'd been, it was meet that he, the Mad Monk, should be matchmaker one more time.

'Come, boy,' he said, opening his eyes, 'no more dallying. Let us make tracks. Take me to the place where this lady lives. By the mass, I must glimpse this girl with mine own eyes afore I do more. And then – then – I shall well make it worth thy while.'

And these words puzzled the Hare – yet also excited him – and kindled in his starving soul a smidgen of hope. And so they got up to

240

their feet, and stretched and sighed, and the Mad Monk fashioned a crude umbrella to shield them from the waning storm, its spokes of stick and its tattered canvas dried seaweed, and blew out in a breath the fire no longer needed, and bade fond farewell to his doodles and daubs on the craggy walls, and picked up the little lithe Hare not half so cocky, who fitted snugly in his large palm where he would not get so wet, and in such manner arrayed did the Mad Monk and the Hare quit the cave and go out into the world, in search of the lady that the latter loved, the woman who, through the machinations of the former, he might somehow still win. ■

© MACARENA YAÑEZ

# TOURIST

## *Andrea Stuart*

The first time I was spooned by another woman I could not sleep. I was used to the contours of men: their length and strength, their flatness and hardness. Instead curled around me was a body even smaller than my own; soft breasts pressed against my narrow back. Even the room smelled different, the intense pheromones of masculinity replaced by a cloud of oestrogen with a top note of Chanel No. 5. I felt the way travellers do as they try to sleep on their first night in a new place: disorientated and disturbed; the sounds and smells unfamiliar; the sensations unnervingly foreign.

As I lay there, eyes wide open, I went over and over the preceding seduction, in which I was entirely complicit. Meeting the woman I shall call Carla, a petite redhead with a fashionable pixie cut; getting to know her, both of us subtly fanning the burgeoning spark of interest that we shared; everything finally coming together on this evening, the setting a fashionable new restaurant in Chelsea, the dramatis personae two women in their early thirties, one black the other white, heads leaning in towards the other, a certain self-consciousness initially but the conversation flowing, the unmistakable body language of a connection being forged.

We continued to talk for hours in a state of increasing captivation until only the waiters were left, and made our way into the cool summer night, the joint cab ride to her place now a foregone conclusion. When we got back to her flat she made me wait at the door for a moment, until I was ushered into a bedroom, where I was confronted by the classic *mise en scène* of amour: a bed, wide and low; a long mirror on a big wooden dresser and candles, candles everywhere. When we kissed our mouths tasted of wine. Though I had dabbled with a few other girls, as so many heterosexual women did in order to appear cool and alternative, she was the first 'real' lesbian I had ever slept with and I was almost frightened.

When I left her bed the following morning and walked out onto the south London streets, I bristled with a curious paranoia. I felt that everyone who passed me could see last night shimmering on my skin. In particular I examined men's gazes, as most young heterosexual women habitually do, watching myself being watched, wondering whether I was still wanted, although I had betrayed them, and broken the contract of desire I shared with them. And in my traitor's heart I felt both shame and triumph at my conduct. Shame because I was a deviant, and triumph because I had got away with it.

How did I end up in this sapphic tryst? Me, perhaps the most avid heterosexual in the world, a girl whose mother dubbed her 'boy crazy' as a teen; a girl who had her first boyfriend at eleven and never looked back? From my earliest adolescence, males were my hobby, and my female friends and I did little else but talk and speculate about them. Every interaction with the opposite sex was dissected; every nuance of their behaviour weighed and measured. I was so immersed in this pursuit, so utterly intoxicated with it, that I was only a little shocked – and secretly rather pleased – when my university lecturer suggested my most suitable future career would be that of a courtesan.

I can't really explain my apparent volte-face. Or rather, there are many explanations: some competing, some complementary, all ultimately unsatisfactory. There was, for example, the predictable backstory of heterosexual heartbreak. The long-term boyfriend that

I had met at university and loved madly if not well, who had left me after nearly ten years, breaking my heart into a million weeping pieces, and replacing me with a woman who was my doppelgänger. The depression that followed flattened me like a tsunami. When I finally admitted to my therapist that I was involved in a lesbian relationship, she diagnosed me as being 'in manic flight from heterosexuality', proving how simultaneously accurate and irrelevant therapy can be.

My friends concurred with my therapist. Surely my interest in women could only be explained by the break-up. Clearly I was hurt, in retreat from the dangers of the heterosexual romantic battlefield. To most of them, women were a safe, almost chaste, choice. People frequently make this assumption: that being with a woman is 'easier', less intense, like having a best friend that you sleep with. They equate romance with emotional turbulence, and emotional turbulence with the difference and threat represented by men. They cannot imagine that a woman can tear another woman's heart and soul into shreds.

I was scarred by love. But who among us is not? And the truth was that by then I had had a couple of years to recover, with a few enjoyable affairs with men under my belt. The bruises had healed, as much as psychic ones do, and I was back out there. But my return to the heterosexual arena was disappointing. I couldn't get over the feeling that I had been there and done that. It all felt a bit lacklustre. After hearing the same old lines, and playing the same old games, I was, I realized, bored.

The idea that our sexual predilections might turn on such a shallow thing as boredom is almost a heresy. Especially as 'born that way' has been a central tenet of the gay rights movement in the West. Surely, the campaign strategy asserts, we are born with certain things fixed in place, our sexuality as immutable as our race and therefore equally undeserving of hostility. And indeed, the evidence seems to be stacking up that this may be broadly true for men. But not for women. And for this woman, at least, I seemed both turnable and ready to be turned. I craved something different, something new. I felt like a jaded traveller searching for a new destination; I wanted to explore customs and cultures different from my own.

Looking back, I realize I had always been bi-curious. I had vague crushes on girls as well as boys in my early teens but none that were so intense that a whiff of disapproval could not dispel them; I transferred my interest exclusively to boys with no discernible sense of grief and with great alacrity. I was always fascinated by alternative lives, however. As a voracious teen reader I was beguiled by books like Radclyffe Hall's *The Well of Loneliness* and Edmund White's *A Boy's Own Story*, which explored the drama of being a sexual outcast: those forced to lead a hidden life. I was also drawn to the burgeoning struggle for lesbian and gay rights. Despite the pervasive homophobic climate of my youth, in both London and the Caribbean, I didn't understand why an alternative sexual preference should be a source of shame. Later I read Freud and was convinced by his theory that bisexuality was the norm, and monosexuality the product of social conditioning; to put it another way, that all infants are born into a state of sexual fluidity, requiring shaping by sociocultural forces in order to assume conventional gender roles.

It wasn't just sexual autonomy I craved, but intellectual freedom. I was an ardent feminist, it was the nineties and third-wave feminism was blowing across the cultural landscape like a fresh wind. And I was utterly transfixed by the pleasure-loving, sex-positive model of feminism that the third-wavers espoused. I dreamed of being a writer, and was looking for a way to lead a free life: that, for me, meant a creative life that allowed me to pursue my intellectual ambitions. I was in flight from domesticity too, trying to work out how not to take on the conventional role of someone's mother and someone's wife. Even more than this I did not want to lead a life 'predicated on the threat and promise of men' as Toni Morrison wrote in her novel, *A Mercy*. I wanted to possess what the novelist Colette called a 'virile femininity', to combine my dresses and heels with independence and autonomy: a woman in control of her own body, who pursued her own ambitions, and was the captain of her own life.

I particularly resented the sexual restrictions put upon women.

Whereas men were expected to define themselves through their interactions with the outside world as well as the active exploration of their sexuality, women always had to weigh up their daring desires against the mores of social decorum. A roguish man who displays a restless drive to overcome individual limitations, confront danger and explore the world, as well as enjoy a certain amount of sexual meandering, is tolerated, even admired in our society: a similar woman is still branded a slut. So my curiosity about lesbianism was an accomplice of my feminism: a path that allowed me to be sexual and free.

I was a passionate rebel against women's lot, full of aspirations and fantasies, fearful of being trapped in roles that I felt were not of my own making – the 'good' woman, the domestic goddess, the dutiful wife – and eager to express my aspirations for female freedom. I was inspired by intellectuals and artists, performers and outlaws: those women who escaped the destiny to which their gender had consigned them. I had a restless craving for change, love and motion. My dreams were born of women's repressed wildness, their craving for adventure and a profound longing to transcend the complex limitations that govern our lives.

Whatever the commingling of reasons which meant I finally opened this new door, I came to believe that if you do not allow your longings to emerge into the light, you potentially sacrifice the person that you could become. Or as that mad sage Blake once wrote: 'It is better to murder an infant in its cradle than to nurse desires unacted upon.'

We met a few times a week, mostly at her place. Those passionate, curious, experimental nights! Clothes on the floor; bodies covered in a sheen of sweat, white sheets tangled beneath us. The sex was a revelation, not least because there was no script. Back in the nineties, heterosexuality was already overdetermined to the point of becoming banal, but lesbian love was an exhilarating vista of possibility – a *tabula rasa* waiting to be written on, a terra incognita begging to be explored. Hard as it may be to believe now, magazines like *off our backs* and sexperts like Susie Bright were mapping out truly unknown territory – hence the question that all lesbians inevitably faced: 'Just what it is that you do in bed?' A query that never failed to make my blood boil, not least because it signalled such an extraordinary lack of imagination but also because it implied that love between women was merely aimless fumbling, and 'real' sex could only happen with a penis.

This not knowing was delicious and frightening. The fear of getting it wrong, of being exposed as a neophyte, gradually overcome by experimentation and practice and growing confidence into a Ready Brek smugness when you had finally sussed the code. In those days before anything and everything was available on the Internet, there was a real sense of being a member of a highly restricted club – that you could walk around, carrying snugly against your glowing heart the secret knowledge, and nobody would ever guess. No Bletchley code-breaker was more proud of their work than I.

And how wonderful it was to learn something new. The pleasure of being a novice again was unutterably thrilling. Learning to love her woman's body, I felt like an explorer, a composer, feeling my way one caress at a time. The sex was like a jazz riff, one note suggesting another, until we created a complete melody. Of course, today with the proliferation of representations of 'girl-on-girl action', designed entirely as a masturbatory aid for men, lesbian sex is in danger of being co-opted as a heterosexual practice, one that vacates the radical challenge lesbianism has traditionally represented. For 'lesbian existence', the poet and academic Adrienne Rich once wrote, 'is both the breaking of a taboo and the rejection of a compulsory way of life. It is also a direct or indirect attack on the male right of access to women.'

Where before I had eroticized the difference of men, I discovered that I was also stimulated by familiarity and symmetry. Sex with a woman was more intuitive. Indeed the narcissism of lesbianism, the mirroring of identical bodies and body parts, is a profoundly underrated pleasure. As I watched the sensations skip across her face, I could see that her responses were mine. I not only had the power but the skill to evoke this pleasure, and I felt almost as if I was experiencing them myself.

M y relationship with Carla was a passport into a new world and I realized almost immediately that Lesbos was indeed another country, and that I would have to learn a whole new set of traditions and codes of behaviour if I was to survive there.

The populace was inscrutable. Lesbians generally do not recruit, or rush to garland newcomers with floral wreaths. Introduce yourself to the community and watch it fold its arms and raise one eyebrow. I scoured the available guidebooks, trying to find the connection between the radical queers of *Square Peg* magazine and the flannel-shirted heroines of Naiad Press novels. Once I thought I'd got the essence of the look, the talk, the swagger, I ventured forth – only to discover a bewildering array of people and styles: young and old, white, black, Asian, Mediterranean, Latina. Some were politically conservative, others left of centre. There were models and mothers, married women and bisexuals, a lesbian for every day of the year, all of them apparently more 'in the know' than I.

There was also a new dress code to master, with new cultural meanings, particularly since self-presentation is an exceptionally vexed issue in the lesbian world, not least because it is clothing that in many points in history, and in many circumstances, has signalled not just a woman's lesbian identity, but what kind of sex she enjoys.

So I had to rethink myself sartorially. It was not a simple task. I have always been ultra-feminine in my self-presentation, fascinated by fashion, working at various times on its fringes, and the thought of having to cut my hair and buy Doc Martens made my heart sink. It was such a sore point that I joked with friends that if it were a choice between lesbianism and my very feminine (and expensive) wardrobe, I would choose the latter. It was not entirely in jest. And the waste of good tailoring was a side issue. What I meant was that I would not give up conventional femininity and the social confidence it gave me. My frocks and make-up had helped me negotiate the hostile society into which my Caribbean family had migrated, and helped to disguise my rather masculine professional ambitions in a misogynist world – my desire to be autonomous, bold and free. Mercifully my timing was good. This was the era that saw the emergence of the lipstick lesbian, when a corseted Cindy Crawford pretended to shave a besuited k.d. lang on the cover of *Vanity Fair*. The mainstream was spotlighting lesbianism at last; suddenly the feminine lesbian was the star of the stage.

There was also a new language to be learned. Even though I was a 'het', I thought I was au fait with the lesbian lingua franca; after all I knew that a 'femme' was a lesbian who presented in a feminine way while a 'butch' presented in a masculine way. But of course it was more complex than that. A femme could also be a 'top', who prefers to take the more active role in sex, while her opposite, the 'butch bottom', preferred to be passive in bed. Then there was a 'stone butch', who did not allow her bedmate to stimulate her and gained pleasure solely in pleasing her partner, and the 'pillow princess', who liked only to receive. There was the 'tomboy femme', who enjoyed sports as well as shopping, the 'soft butch' who mixed female and male presentation; the 'diesel dyke', the most masculine of lesbians, as well as the more recent tags such as 'boi', who played with the masquerade of masculinity, and her African American/Afro-Caribbean counterpart, the 'stud'. All of which were different from the transsexual, for whom the script that one is a woman in a man's body, or vice versa, is 'solved' primarily by the medical transformation of the body, rather than the innumerable masquerades of sexual difference that those who were ambivalent about their gender exploited over previous centuries.

Exposed over time to these various types, I developed more epicurean sexual tastes. For the outside world the butch, a woman who is seen to be pretending to be a man, is a derided creature, the victim of scorn and hostility. But it is different in the lesbian world. I found that I was curiously touched by women who tried to look like boys, with their upturned collars and cropped hair. How feminine and vulnerable they seemed beneath their masculine disguise. Indeed, as Colette once noted, there is something seductive about a person of ambiguous or dissimulated sex. Especially when they shared the courtliness of a well-bred man, and the sensitivity of a woman.

Like other subcultures, the lesbian world of the late 1990s had its own venues and pastimes. But it was a scene that was in transition, one that was struggling to emerge from the shadow of its more powerful gay male counterpart, and thus was assertively claiming the right to 'women only' space. And I discovered to my fascination that all over London, and indeed the entire country, was a network of discreet nightclubs publicized by lesbian word of mouth or listings in particular magazines. Some were scuzzy dives replete with women who had tattoos on their forearms (this was before being inked was compulsory) and settled their romantic dramas with fisticuffs; others were exclusive and stylish and very, very cool.

One of my favourites was called the Ace of Clubs, which was a night held bimonthly in a basement beneath London's historic and ritzy Burlington Arcade. With its underground setting, its low ceilings and worn wine-coloured carpets, it felt rather like a dingy womb designed to protect its clientele from intrusion, sightseers, prying eyes. Here the noise of the outside world and its hostility and judgements were entirely blocked out. But when I frequented it, it was already regarded as old-fashioned and passé, a throwback to a community that felt stigmatized, ashamed and fearful: a monument to lesbian life past.

More popular then was a bar – I forget now its name – which you accessed by a narrow alleyway on a street in the fashionable area of Covent Garden. Once through the dark passageway, it was bright and well lit, open and airy: no apologies, and no secrecy. The clientele here was more cosmopolitan, often professionals working in the media. The dress code was tomboy chic. The most voracious of the punters here were the married women, who approached you with the hunger of wanderers stranded in a desert, desperate and aggressive and sad.

It was succeeded in popularity a few years later by the Box, which perched on the busy junction of London's Seven Dials only a few yards away. As its name suggests it was glass on three of its four sides, entirely visible to the numerous passers-by, its mirrors multiplying the women inside, making them seem even more numerous, more busy, more self-assured. The evolutions of these venues were a marked indication of how the lesbian community's confidence had grown and developed in just a few short years.

Unwittingly, I had joined an international network. When I went abroad, friends would give me a heads-up about other places where lady lovers gathered. So in Los Angeles a friend of a friend dropped me off at a Venice Beach bar where the waitress informed me that I had just missed Jodie Foster, who had roared away on her Harley minutes before. I sat there among the smug handful of patrons who had made a successful sighting, nursing a pineapple juice alone, feeling like a disappointed birdwatcher who had just missed seeing the rarest of species: the celebrity dyke. While on a night out in Paris a friend and I ferreted out a club in a disused town hall, utterly devoid of any glamour, where the bar was tended by solid girls in Hawaiian shirts; we went on to an exclusive establishment in one of the best arrondissements, where you could not enter without a referral. Here the clientele looked like Catherine Deneuve, with a few butches as handsome and slick as Alain Delon. And I was desperately grateful that I had squandered my food allowance on the sleek designer dress I was wearing, even if I was too shy for the first hour to approach anyone. When an immaculate blonde eventually spoke to me I was so tongue-tied that I could barely respond. She wouldn't give me her number; she didn't want her husband to know what she was up to, but she took mine, though I never returned her call (I was worried about her husband too).

And when in New York, I tracked down a club in the Meatpacking District before it was gentrified, where an eclectic crowd, including black dykes the size of fridges and their only slightly smaller girlfriends, danced alongside cyberpunks, models and strippers.

Screens of lesbian porn, made by women for women, flickered their libidinous images in each corner. There I danced all night with a girl with long, black ringlets and the most beautiful breasts I had ever seen.

And the parties! The frisson of the forbidden, the unleashing of repressed longings, made them often unbearably exciting. I remember one such night, in a flat in north London, where the hostess had hand-picked a group of gay and bisexual women that she thought were particularly attractive, butch as well as femme, which turned into a spontaneous orgy. A handsome cropped-haired woman slipped off the stiletto shoe of a gorgeous blonde and gently kissed her feet; another girl performed an impromptu strip. Soon girls were slipping in and out of toilets together, and it ended finally with trios and quartets taking over the available bedrooms, enjoying each other in the semi-light. While the living room, denuded of most of its furniture, was colonized by a foursome on the floor, and two couples intertwined on the matching couches.

At the most select of these gatherings it was understood that famous lesbians could be open with their lovers without fear of being outed. This code of discretion was rarely betrayed, since, during those years, many women were closeted to some degree, whether at work or in their personal lives, and therefore were similarly vulnerable to treachery. So you would meet a legendary soul singer, or a Shakespearean actress, or a best-selling author, many of whom were on the arm of their female significant others.

The intensity of these occasions was only heightened by the incestuousness of the lesbian milieu. If the mainstream world worked on the theory of six degrees of separation, the lesbian world worked on two degrees. Everyone you met, or lusted after, or rejected, would inevitably recur in your life. Everyone had slept with someone you had slept with; or was currently sleeping with the woman you were once with; or wanted to sleep with the woman you were currently with. In this world everyone knew about your past and speculated about your future. I was captivated by the clandestine nature of this milieu: a kind of sexual Cosa Nostra.

Carla and I were together for two years, but the cracks in our relationship were evident relatively early. During one of our pivotal arguments she accused me of being 'a tourist in her lifestyle'. Tears flooded my eyes, and I was suffused by a sense of outrage, and self-pity. How could she accuse me of that? As if I were some vulgar experience junkie just out for a new thrill. But of course she was completely right. I was a tourist, and I had used her as a guide to explore this unknown new territory. But she was not without blame. I discovered later that she had a history of 'turning' straight girls, a pastime similar to that of the older male roué who favours seducing young virgins. In both cases the power one wields is intoxicating. But it has its own perils. Straight women on the turn are poor bets as long-term partners, because at this early point in their journey they are usually so vulnerable and uncertain that they are not yet ready to commit to an openly lesbian life.

I certainly was not, and this was to prove a major stumbling block. Carla had lived a gay life for a long time; I had barely lost my training wheels. And I was a black woman who already offered altogether too much 'otherness' for any social occasion: I wasn't sure that I wanted to be a *Daily Mail* joke. I had suffered judgement enough and I was not ready to step even further away from societal approval. That she grew impatient with my ambivalence was unsurprising. I too feared that I was a dilettante, a dabbler, a coward, who would inevitably retreat into the safety of heterosexuality. We split, as so many lesbians did, pulling the plaster off slowly, rather than ripping it off fast.

It would be a couple of years later, in another relationship, that I officially came out. By then the secrecy of my lesbianism was no longer a thrill but a cross. I felt that hiding something so significant about myself cut me off from those I loved. And I was tired of concealing my real life from my family and fed up with living a double life. It did not go as I had planned. I wandered into my mother's bedroom in the house in which we were holidaying. She was reading a book on her bed. I sat down and said, 'There is something I want to discuss with you.' She put the book down and sat up, propping herself up against the pillows. I perched on the south-east corner of the bed, and said, after a long pause, 'I think I prefer women.' Knowing that I was referring to 'the friend' who accompanied me on the trip, she replied, 'Of course you prefer women; *everyone* prefers women. You just can't marry them.'

I was totally taken aback. Even more so when she added: 'For God's sake, don't tell your father. It would kill him.' Over the following months, my rather urbane father took me out for a series of lavish lunches in fashionable London restaurants, in which he cheerfully declaimed on the fact that there were all different kinds of people, with all different kinds of desires and sexualities and wasn't that what was wonderful about the human race? After the third such lunch I finally realized what he was trying to tell me. That it was all right. He knew about my sexuality, and it was not going to kill him, contrary to my mother's trepidation.

The legacy of this story? I would like to be able to tie it up neatly. Twenty years on, I can see that my break from sexual convention facilitated my shift into the rather nonconformist path of being a writer. Not least because becoming an outsider is the greatest gift an author can be given. My first lesbian relationship was empowering for me in other ways. I realized that it is not just men who bring the impetus for sex (or, as feminist rhetoric would have it, 'carry the phallus'): that women freed from the weight of heterosexual conventions are just as active agents of desire. (These conventions of course have changed in recent years but it seems to me that women were freer in our time than now, before porn had made it de rigueur for women to indulge in certain sexual practices, whether they want to or not; and where slappings and stranglings are signals of 'hot' het sex.) It also freed me from the obligation so many straight women feel, to privilege appearing and seeming sexy over obtaining genuine pleasure, a compulsion that has only increased in recent years with the influence of the sex industry.

Sometimes, I wonder if I have been a tourist my entire life. When I migrated to Britain as a teenager, I mourned the sense of belonging, which was left behind with my island home. But once the grieving was over, I realized that my adult identity, in this new place, was inextricably tied up with being an interloper. And as with lipstick lesbianism my timing was good. In the 1980s, for perhaps the first time, outsider status had become politicized and glamorized under the rubric of identity politics. And thus one would attend conferences where people would explain proudly that they were of African origin or gay rather than be embarrassed about it, or explain that while they were white, they were Welsh, not English. To be mainstream was an insult; being on the margins was ineffably cool. And so to my surprise I found a home there on the edges. Now for me being on the inside feels uncomfortable; I feel that conformity may trap me within social mores I am not in tune with, like an insect trapped in resin.

My lesbian identity is a response to that, but also, paradoxically, it has led me to a place called home, a place buttressed by my partner and my children, my writing and my politics. Ironically of course, I have in many ways replicated a rather conventional familial structure, except with two women as heads of the household. And my days are regulated, largely as my mother's were, by the care and love of children. And though I have found in these ordinary maternal pleasures a balance that levels out the solipsism and neurosis that is often a feature of a creative life, I realize that I remain a restless spirit. Home feels, as it does for so many women and men, at times both a place of safety and a trap.

In truth not belonging has become my belonging. It is the space that I feel most comfortable in; too much predictability makes me chafe and struggle. I remain essentially a tourist, a traveller, someone who longs for new scenarios and new challenges. I yearn for the opportunity to unmake myself and then remake myself again just to see what the pieces look like when they fall, a craving that is mercifully met, at least in part, by the vicissitudes of the writing life.

As to my sexuality, my lesbian desires did not simply replace the old heterosexual ones. Instead they layered one upon the other like turf over soil. The way that I usually explain it is that I like Thai *and* Indian food. In the past we would talk about bisexuality, while today we speculate on women's sexual fluidity, their erotic plasticity. Whether one describes oneself in these more fashionable terms, or more archaic ones like heterosexual and homosexual, they do not fully capture the shifting mosaic of our longings; for what we want changes in different circumstances at different times in our lives. This paucity of language and understanding is important because what lovemaking gives us is more than just pleasure, or the pursuit of the overhyped orgasm. It is about the longing for contact, the need to be seen and validated, to climb beneath the skin, even, and counteract that existential loneliness that plagues us all.

Thomas Wolfe famously wrote, 'You can't go home again.' And this certainly was true for me. The woman I met a few years later, and am still with, left me breathless. As Judith Butler wrote in *Undoing Gender*, 'One does not always stay intact. It may be that one wants to . . . but it may also be that despite one's best efforts, one is undone, in the face of the other, by the touch, by the scent, by the feel, by the prospect of the touch, by the memory of the feel.' This new love, a beautiful, accomplished and committed lesbian, who shared my political proclivities and intellectual interests, meant that I was turned for good. I could not, and did not want to, return to the heterosexual fold, despite its privileges. It was now impossible to find my way back to where I had come from, or the person I had been: and this new self, this new place, had become my home.

Psychoanalyst Adam Phillips has posited that we all have double lives: the life we actually live and the one that we have renounced. I chose to jettison the more conventional heterosexual life that I could have lived, in favour of the lesbian life that I now lead, despite the ambiguity of my desire. And like everyone else who contemplates the road not travelled, I am sometimes haunted by that decision, and mournful. But it was the right one; I took the path that I could least bear to relinquish.

As to the pleasures of the life that I have chosen: I come back again and again to the writer Colette, a woman whose writing career was hijacked by her first, and much older, husband who published her work under his name, until she escaped into a lesbian relationship with an aristocratic older woman. She never returned to her bourgeois existence, and became the champion of adventurous women. Her slim volume, *The Pure and the Impure*, remains the most lyrical and sophisticated book on sexuality I know. She had this to say about lesbian relationships:

> Perhaps this love, which according to some people is outrageous, escapes the changing seasons and the wanings of love by being controlled with an invisible severity, nourished on very little, permitted to live gropingly and without a goal, its unique flower being a mutual trust such as that other love can never plumb or comprehend, but only envy; and so great is such a love that by its grace a half century can pass by like a day of 'exquisite and delicious retirement'. ■

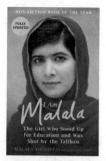

## I Am Malala
### by Malala Yousafzai

The best-selling memoir of Nobel Prize nominee Malala Yousafzai, the schoolgirl who stood up to the Taliban and became a worldwide symbol of courage and hope. Her shooting sparked a wave of solidarity across the globe for the right to education, freedom from terror and female emancipation. This is Malala's inspirational story.

**Weidenfeld & Nicolson** | £7.99 | **PB**

## An Amorous Discourse in the Suburbs of Hell
### by Deborah Levy

She is an angel, flown from Paradise. He an accountant, dreaming of a white Christmas. She attempts to fly him away, while he holds on tight to all he knows. Deborah Levy whips up a storm of romance and slapstick, of heavenly and earthly delights, in this poem about freedom and the search for the good life. A beautiful gift.

**And Other Stories** | £7.99 / $12.95 | **HB**

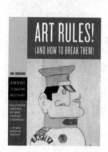

## Art Rules! (And How to Break Them)
### by Mel Gooding

A spectacular new box book from Redstone Press, *Art Rules!* offers a completely new key to enjoying and understanding contemporary art by showing how it is made. The box contains forty-two illustrated, interactive cards and an original book, *Modern Art: Inside Out.*
www.theredstoneshop.com

**Redstone Press** | £19.95 | **Box book**

## The Vegetarian
### by Han Kang

'A startling new novel . . . *The Vegetarian* is a story about metamorphosis, rage and the desire for another sort of life. It is written in cool, still, poetic but matter-of-fact short sentences, translated luminously by Deborah Smith.' Deborah Levy, author of *Swimming Home*
'*The Vegetarian* is hypnotically strange, sad, beautiful and compelling. I liked it immensely.' Nathan Filer, author of *The Shock of the Fall*

**Portobello Books** | £12.99 | **PB**

Every surviving ex-Kumari, sitting in order of age, being honoured
at the old royal palace. Rashmila Shakya second from right.
Kathmandu, Nepal, 2007
Courtesy of the author

# LIVING GODDESS

## Isabella Tree

'The Word has been made man, but the world will be saved when
the Word shall have been made woman.' – Guillaume Postel

Kathmandu, 1983. I was eighteen. In the Office of Controlled
Immigration where my three school friends and I extended our
visas, billboards shed notices like autumn leaves – photos of missing
persons, stolen passports, wanted men: drug traffickers, art thieves,
fraudsters, lost souls. One night Charlie and Somerset stumbled
across a corpse. At first they thought the guy was sick, slumped as
he was in a doorway down a side street, head lolling to one side,
dreadlocks looped across his face as though he had just passed out.
Only venturing closer did they see the needle hanging from his arm
and the unmistakable greyness of his skin. You just knew, Somerset
said, visibly shaken. He was no longer there.

From behind his desk at Peace Air Cargo, our friend Simi – font
of local knowledge and liaison with our landlord – congratulated the
boys on doing nothing. You go to the police, he said, and you end up
in jail yourself. How long would it be before the authorities found
the body, and would the gigantic rats that scurried up and down
our street like fat little terriers get there first? The body could be the
face on a poster, his parents – like ours – hoping for news.

My parents had been among the first tourists to visit Nepal in
the 1950s, shortly after the borders opened to the outside world.
My father's pen-and-ink drawings of the pagodas in Kathmandu's

Durbar Square, the Golden Temple of Pashupati and the great domed stupa of Swayambhu covered the walls of their bedroom. My mother told me of leopards among the rhododendrons, a sloth bear stealing into her bed in the Royal Hotel, a gigantic blancmange called Rana's Bouche shaking with their laughter at the dinner table. When she left her stockings hanging over a chair the Nepali chambermaid had passed out – she'd thought the strange, pale *bideshi* – foreigner – from across the Black Water, with short-cropped hair like a man and legs like a stork, had taken off her skin.

Nepal, now a honeypot for Western hippies, had modernized in thirty years but beneath the surface ancient traditions still ran deep. Our flat on Freak Street, in the nucleus of old Kathmandu, had electricity but no running water, and the lavatory was a noxious hole under the stairs. But there was a roof terrace and spectacular views from both rooms, one on top of the other, looking onto the open expanse of Basantapur Square – once the royal elephant stables – and the towering pagoda-temples of the main Durbar Square. Every morning we opened our shutters onto the old royal palace of Hanuman Dhoka, its stuccoed facade reminiscent of Belgravia. The seven-roofed Basantapur Tower, where once the king had surveyed his kingdom, threw long shadows in the afternoon. And across the way was the house of Kathmandu's Living Goddess. We could see her at night, a little child in red, running past the windows on the second floor. Another world on our doorstep.

One day we stepped into her courtyard. We followed a trickle of devotees passing through the entrance and, mounting the steps between snarling stone lions, ducked our heads beneath a doorway carved with tiny human skulls.

Inside, away from the jangling of rickshaw bells and cries of street vendors, it was blissfully quiet. A jasmine shedding its flowers over a tiny Buddhist stupa in the centre released a wisp of nostalgia over the mustiness of pigeon guano. This was as far as we could go. A sign – ENTRY TO HINDUS ONLY – above a door in the corner admitted the Goddess's devotees but no foreigners. From somewhere inside the building, behind roof struts carved with ferocious multi-armed goddesses, came the ringing of a handbell.

A tour guide joined us in the courtyard with his group. 'Please – put away your cameras.' Then he called up to the third floor. 'Eh, Devi!' Moments passed. We waited, staring up in unison, each cough, footfall and beat of a pigeon's wings echoing like a thunderclap.

Without warning a small child appeared at the window. She could have been six, eight, nine years old. It was impossible to tell. She gazed sternly down at us, pouting slightly, looking mildly inconvenienced. Her eyes were huge, exaggerated with thick lines of kohl reaching all the way to her temples. She was dressed entirely in red, her lips bright red; her hair bound up tightly in a topknot; gold ornaments around her neck and bangles on her wrists. Her tiny fingers, their nails painted red, clasped the wooden rail across the window frame with the command of a captain at the ship's helm. There were awed murmurs and even some applause. The child's expression did not falter. Lowering his voice, the guide explained, 'She does not smile. If she did, it would be an invitation to heaven, and you would die.'

Just as suddenly she was gone, reabsorbed into the shadows, leaving a flutter of red curtains.

Nepalis call her 'Kumari' – the word for a virgin or unmarried girl. Her name is on shops, banks and beauty products. We were told she embodies a powerful goddess protecting Nepal and its people. She has the power to cure illnesses, to remove obstacles in the way of happiness, to bestow blessings on the pure of heart. She can punish the wicked with a single withering stare. On festivals she wears a third eye in the middle of her forehead. All-seeing, all-knowing, she is said to have eyes in the past, the future and the present. A change in her mood can predict earthquakes, floods, political unrest. Every year the King of Nepal was duty-bound to come to the Kumari's house, kneel at her feet and beg her blessing to rule.

She is chosen at the age of three or four, taken away from her parents and installed in her palace where she is looked after by a family of caretakers. She leaves the building only to attend festivals a dozen or so times a year. Her feet must not touch the ground, so she is carried in a palanquin or pulled by teams of farm labourers around the streets of the city in a massive temple chariot made of gold. She mustn't bleed. Special care is taken to see that she does not bruise or accidentally cut herself. If she does, the spirit of the Goddess residing inside her leaves and she becomes mortal again. Eventually, with the first blood loss of puberty, she is dismissed and another little girl is found to take her place. Her connection with blood empowers her. People with blood disorders, and women suffering from miscarriages or haemorrhaging, come to her to be healed.

There was little more anyone on Freak Street could tell us. The world of the Living Goddess, a tradition centuries old, is bound up in Tantra, the esoteric practice running through the backbone of Hinduism and Buddhism in Nepal.

As a teenager, still struggling to know myself, I couldn't help seeing her through the prism of the culture in which I had grown up. She was a child, so to me, in my journal, she was 'Christ-like', 'innocent', 'untainted by the overwhelming desires of the adult'. She was young and feminine, therefore 'shy', 'vulnerable' and 'submissive'. I assumed she represented some kind of 'sacrifice', an 'atonement for the sins of the world'; that she must be, in some way, a 'victim'; her connection with blood that of the sacrificial lamb.

I looked at her and saw myself at her age, not so long ago, at my first school, a Catholic convent – a very different place but a religious institution nonetheless where, until the age of thirteen, I had felt trapped and frustrated, and permanently guilty; where the Virgin Mary, passive, compliant, puritanical, uncomplaining, asexual, had been an object of both awe and alienation. 'I'm not sure what I feel about secluding anyone from normal life,' I pondered in my diary on the Kumari's behalf. 'She becomes mortal with the capacity to have children and once more her foot is allowed to touch the defiled soil as she walks out to lead as normal a life as she can after such deprivation.'

A s we fell in with a routine of cafe life and wanderings I took
to visiting the Kumari's house almost every morning, often on
my own. Sometimes she would appear at her window. Other times
I would lose myself, instead, in the carvings around the doorways
and windows – multi-armed goddesses in warrior poses, poised to
strike down a demon. I would listen out for the ringing of the puja
bell, imagining the little Goddess alone on her lion throne, mistress
of her universe, the priest kneeling on the floor before her, arrows of
sunlight from the lattice windows piercing clouds of incense. I longed
to know what she was thinking, what she did all day when she wasn't
performing rituals. Where did she come from, and where did she go
when, eventually, on the cusp of adulthood, she was dismissed?

The rumours on Freak Street were speculative and caustic. 'You
know they give her drugs and alcohol,' a flower child, well past the
bloom of youth, told me one day. 'How else do you think they get a
toddler to sit still through all those rituals?' The word on the street
was soma – the legendary narcotic, the stuff of fantasy, mentioned
in the Rig Veda. The hippies had been trying to find it for years. 'No
one will marry an ex-Kumari,' Simi insisted. 'Men who have tried
in the past have died on their wedding night with their heads burst
out.' Westerners had more prosaic but equally dark suggestions:
ex-Kumaris were trafficked to brothels in Bombay and Bangkok, or
ended their lives as indentured slaves.

F ourteen years later, I returned to Kathmandu. I had married
Charlie, one of the friends who had shared the flat on Freak
Street. Our first child, a daughter, born in 1995, was now two years
old – approaching the age at which a Kumari would be chosen. I
didn't know what chance I had of finding out more, but something,
I felt, was coming to fruition. Something in my own life had shifted,
or at least changed my way of seeing things.

Rashmila was seventeen. She had been dismissed as Living
Goddess five years earlier. A chance conversation had led me to her
door. An introduction would be easy, Laxminath, my friend, said

– his cousin lived next door. He could translate. The stories we'd heard on Freak Street all those years ago, which still headlined the Nepali newspapers and which had even found their way into Western magazines, were, he explained, unfounded. Ex-Kumaris were not abandoned or trafficked abroad but returned home to their own families. Most of them were married and had children, and even grandchildren, of their own. They belonged to the Shakya clan – an affluent, well-educated Buddhist caste of Newars living in the old courtyards around Durbar Square. There were generations of them living near our old flat.

The Newars, now a minority in Nepal, are the original inhabitants of the Kathmandu Valley. They trace their ancestry to the Kirata, a Himalayan people mentioned in the great Indian epics like the Mahabharata. Over the centuries they have adopted practices of both Buddhism and Hinduism, but what most characterizes them is their belief in an omnipotent Mother Goddess – a tradition a million miles from a compliant Virgin Mary and Almighty God. Belief in a Supreme Goddess and the practice of worshipping her in the form of a living child is one of the fundamental differences between Newars and other Nepalis who – like our old friend Simi – subscribe to a more orthodox form of Hinduism. The reason we'd been unable to find out about the Living Goddess on Freak Street was that we hadn't been talking to Newars. Laxminath himself was a Newar and, though he earned a living teaching Nepali, his first language was Newari.

As she sat between her parents on their living-room sofa Rashmila Shakya's shyness was palpable: gaze averted, fingers twisting in her lap. Unused to meeting foreigners, and to the very concept of having to explain herself, the former Kumari seemed lost for words. She stared into her lap, or simply smiled. Occasionally, with effort, she would utter a few tiny sounds that had Laxminath leaning forward in his seat trying to catch them. Her parents, used to this process, retrieved her utterances, almost telepathically it seemed, speaking for her.

Four little girls had been put forward by Shakya families for selection. The royal astrologer had scrutinized the candidates' horoscopes. Rashmila's had all the positive signs. After a few days she had been sent for a physical examination by the royal priest's wife, to check that she had no blemishes or imperfections that would make it unsafe for the Goddess to inhabit her. After a tantric ritual in the old royal palace during which the Goddess was 'pulled' inside her, she was installed in the Kumari residence.

I asked Rashmila if she had been upset at being separated from her parents, her home, her siblings. Something was stirring inside me, a sense of shared experience, perhaps; the spectre of abandonment, the dichotomy of a double life. She leaned across to her father. She was too small to remember, he said. It had clearly been hard for her mother, however. 'I couldn't cuddle her when she became Goddess,' she said. 'I could kneel at her feet like any other devotee but I couldn't talk to her. The first few times I went to worship her I cried.'

The caretakers at the Kumari House had become Rashmila's family. The main caretaker, Gyan Devi Shakya, had become her surrogate mother, sleeping by her bed, dressing her, bathing her, feeding her, teaching her to read. When she wasn't on her throne Rashmila would play with Gyan Devi's children and grandchildren – they became like her own brothers and sisters. She had been reborn, I suggested. No, her parents insisted, this was not another life. It was karma, the life that was meant for her.

What was it like to be a goddess? I asked, aware that my question was unanswerable. She had felt different, Rashmila finally replied, via the convoluted responses of her parents. She had felt like a goddess. Whenever she put on the *naga mala* – the golden serpent necklace that she wore for special rituals – she had felt stronger, and bigger. She had never felt like smiling then, or talking. She had felt the Goddess's power inside her. It was this conviction, this feeling inside, which governed the Kumari's stillness while she was on her throne. Had she ever been frightened? No, she said. A goddess does not feel afraid.

'What did you think about the foreigners coming to see you in the courtyard?'

Rashmila warmed to this question. She had always been curious about them. They seemed to dress very strangely. Their hair seemed wild and odd, all different colours and often untidy. Sometimes she was tempted to call down to their Nepali guide to ask where these people came from, why they came to see her – didn't they have goddesses in their own land? But she knew she had to stay silent and to be careful not to smile or she might visit misfortune on them.

Had she ever predicted disasters? There was one time, her mother said, when Rashmila had been afflicted by headaches and mood swings. It was 1989 and the People's Movement had begun to push for democracy in Nepal. Violence had erupted in the city. The King had sent special supplications to the Kumari palace and offerings to all the *pithas* – the 'power-places' of the Goddess in the valley – but still Rashmila's headaches didn't lift. Eventually, after months of curfews and rioting that left dozens of people dead, and the Living Goddess in a state of increasing distress, the King submitted. He announced he was ready to accept the role of a constitutional monarch. Nepal had become a democracy, and Rashmila's headaches disappeared.

At twelve years old, as soon as she showed signs of reaching puberty, Rashmila had been dismissed. At first, she hadn't understood what was happening to her. The caretakers had told her she was going home. But home, to her, was the Kumari palace. The priests and the caretaker's son – the young man she considered her brother – had brought her to this strange house down winding backstreets. She had been ritually disrobed of her red dress, her crown and her golden necklaces and bracelets and anklets. In a final act of dissolution, the priest had released her topknot and let down her hair. Rashmila begged to be taken back to the palace. She had wept inconsolably and stayed in her bedroom for days, refusing to eat or talk.

Eventually, with patient coaxing, her sisters had built bridges. The first time they took her outside, into the streets of Kathmandu, Rashmila had been flummoxed by the people and traffic and uneven pavements. Used to the smooth wooden floors of the Kumari palace, and in shoes for the very first time, she had clomped about, avoiding potholes like a prancing horse.

What about marriage? I asked. Rashmila blushed and stared back at her hands. It was too soon to consider such a step, her father said gently. 'She wants to go to college,' he said, 'to study architectural engineering.'

I looked at Rashmila sitting next to her mother on the sofa. Just five years earlier, in the year Rashmila had been dismissed, I had found myself sitting in a similar position, on a sofa, next to the stranger I had learned was my biological mother. I had recognized the shape of my hands, my own fingernails, in the hands – only nineteen years older than mine – that had just made me tea. The same eyebrows, the same eyes. Mannerisms from somewhere deep in my DNA. I realized, now, that it was this resolution that had returned me to Kathmandu. The restlessness I had felt as a child – always looking for a hole in the fence, my adoptive father used to say – had vanished when I stepped across the threshold to my biological mother. There were grainy black-and-white photographs of me, a baby in her arms, taken by her lover, my father, a married man, in the six weeks we had had together. She had wanted a proper portrait taken but had fled the photographer's studio in tears when he asked her to bring me back when I could hold my head up by myself. Her father, a vicar, had extended Christian charity only so far as to baptize me so I wouldn't go to hell. There was no question of her keeping the child. She had asked her lover to trace the number plate of the car that drove me away from the mother and baby home. That way she knew the part of the country where I began my new life. She knew I was in loving hands: the first concern of my adoptive mother when she and my adoptive father came to collect me from the matron had been, how is the baby's mother?

Meeting my biological mother, I realized, had opened me to the possibilities of connection and reconciliation, and to the breadth and depth of maternal instinct – perhaps, even, to the agency of fate. Afterwards, I had returned to my adoptive parents, to my childhood home, to my father's drawings and my mother's stories, to everything I loved and knew as my own. A weight had been lifted. I knew who I had been and who I had become. ∎

Kent and grandson, Henry, 2011
Courtesy of the author

# THE MAKING OF A WRITER

## Kent Haruf

Henry David Thoreau at the opening of *Walden* said: 'I should not talk so much about myself if there were anybody else whom I knew as well.' I take that as my authority and my defence for what I'm going to say.

I was born in the steel mill town of Pueblo, Colorado, in the war year of 1943, and I was born with a cleft lip. It was sewed up, and more than that, my parents didn't know what to do, how I should be taken care of, what should be done with me. There was no money – my father was a Methodist preacher – and after a day or two it was decided to send me to Children's Hospital in Denver where I stayed for about a month. Money was collected from churches in Colorado to help pay for the expenses. During the war, gasoline was rationed, even if my parents could have afforded to buy gas, so my mother came to see me by train, the two times she could come. At the hospital I was fed out of a paper cup since I couldn't drink from a bottle, and that's how I was fed when I was taken home. Sometime later the surgeon was supposed to do more work on my lip and nose, but he died in a plane crash and my parents took that as a sign of God's will, and so nothing more was done.

In the summer of 1943, my family moved out onto the high plains of eastern Colorado and that was where I grew up. For twelve years we lived in three little towns out there. And of course it was those towns and that landscape and the culture of that specific place which has had so much influence on me and my writing. During that period of my life out on the high plains, I was more or less a happy kid, I think, and I survived childhood with only a few hard lessons that I still remember. One was: don't you be a show-off, and I have tried to abide by that injunction ever since, with all its contradictions and complications.

So: I was more or less a happy kid – until about the age of twelve. Then the scar on my lip and my flattened nose became matters of embarrassment and humiliation for me, and matters that set me apart from people around me – I can still remember certain moments that make me want to cringe and squirm even now – and from that time on until I was almost thirty my impulse was to hide my face behind my hand whenever I was out in public. I learned to live completely inwardly in those years. I wouldn't show anyone anything of myself. I never told anyone anything. The last thing I wanted was to draw attention to myself. If you had told me when I was fourteen or when I was twenty-two that some day I would come to regard my cleft lip as a gift, I would have said you were a fool and completely and utterly crazy. But, the truth is, I have come to think so now, to think that perhaps those years of unhappiness and isolation and living inwardly to myself have helped me to be more aware of others and to pay closer attention to what others around me are feeling. Which are good things if you are trying to learn how to write fiction about characters you care about and love. When I was about twenty-nine I had a little surgery done on my face, which really didn't fix much physically, but the surgery turned out to be a kind of mental and spiritual internal corrective, and I've rarely given my face any thought since then. Of course for these last forty years, I've covered up my lip with a moustache.

After I finished high school I went off to college, and I went away from home gladly, but really knowing nothing. I was as ignorant and green as any eighteen-year-old kid can be. But during my college years things began to change for the better. I entered college thinking I wanted to be a biology teacher, but once I took American literature classes, and once I began to read Faulkner and Hemingway, my life and my intentions were changed forever – I knew that I wanted to spend the rest of my life reading great writing and thinking about it. I was just shocked by what Faulkner and Hemingway could do on the page – it was as if the words they wrote were raised up off the page, as if there were a kind of shimmering aura about them, as if the stories were holy, and sacred, the most important matters in the world to know about – and I've never gotten over that feeling, and I don't want to. In college I was lucky to have the kind of English teachers that I needed. They were not really scholars, but men and women who were passionate about literature, and what they insisted on was the passionate appreciation of the story or the poem itself, and not some theory about it. All this was a great discovery for me – just what I needed and it came at a time when I was ready for such a discovery. You have to be available and open to such moments, I think, and I was. And of course the story or poem is what I still need today, every day.

After college I lived in a village in Turkey for two years as a Peace Corps volunteer, and taught English to middle-school kids who didn't need it and would probably never meet another English speaker in their lives. But the Turks were very kind to me and in many ways were like the religious and conservative people I'd grown up with out on the high plains of Colorado. It was in this time while I was living alone in a foreign country that I began to try to write stories myself. The stories were awful little things: imitative and reductive and sentimental. But that was my beginning. Toward the end of my time in Turkey, I applied to the Iowa Writers' Workshop. But I wasn't accepted.

When I came home I enrolled in graduate school in English at the University of Kansas in Lawrence, and I got married. But I found that the way professors and students talked about literature in graduate school was not what I wanted and I quit in the middle

of the second semester. This was in the spring of 1968. The war in
Vietnam was raging, and once I no longer had a student deferment
I got caught up by the draft. I hated what my country was doing in
the war, and I certainly didn't want to kill anyone and didn't want
to be killed myself. I applied to my draft board back in Colorado
as a conscientious objector, but didn't expect my application to be
accepted because I had applied so late, and I told myself that I would
go to prison instead of allowing myself to be inducted into the army.
I never had to find out whether or not I would actually do that. The
draft board in my small home town decided it was legal, what I was
applying for, and decided I meant what I said (my father had been a
preacher in that town, a fact which didn't hurt), and they granted me
the classification.

Then, in lieu of military service, I spent the next two years as an
orderly in hospitals (for a while in Denver at Craig Rehabilitation
Hospital) and as a house parent in an orphanage in Helena, Montana.
My first daughter was born in Helena, and during all that time I
still was trying to write stories – and I sent the stories off to the big
slick magazines and they all came back. But once in a great while,
a rejection slip had a line or two from the editor, and I took each of
these lines as encouragement and kept them in a special folder.

After those two years were over, I applied to the Iowa Writers'
Workshop for a second time and before I ever heard anything from
the workshop I moved myself and my wife and daughter out to Iowa
into an old farmhouse in the middle of winter and got a job as a
janitor in a nursing home, and after a few weeks I went up to the
workshop office and told them I was there. I kept writing and kept
sending them new stories to be added to my application, and in May
I got a letter saying that they had accepted me into the programme.
In retrospect I think I was accepted sort of on probation and out
of astonishment – to think that someone would move to Iowa with
his wife and baby daughter in the middle of winter with no money
and with no job, that person must be desperate. And I was. I was
desperate to learn how to write fiction.

I think it's fair to say that I made some progress that first year because I was given a fellowship for the second year. I took workshops with various writers, including one with John Irving, and the way they all taught writing then was different from what teaching tends to be now: they didn't mess around with your manuscript; what they did was more descriptive than it was prescriptive. They told you what they thought worked in a story and what didn't and left it up to you to figure out how to fix it. There were good students there, too, people like Denis Johnson and Stuart Dybek and Tracy Kidder and Jane Smiley and Ron Hansen and T.C. Boyle and Joe Somoza, and you learned as much from them as you did from the teachers. I came out of the workshop encouraged to think that maybe I could write a little bit – that kind of encouragement was very important to me – and I started a novel while I was there. One chapter of that beginning novel was set in what I for the first time called Holt County, and it was in that chapter that I discovered where I wanted to set all my stories from then on.

Then I spent the next eleven years trying to learn how to write well enough that someone would actually pay me to publish what I'd written. Of course I was also working to make a living for my growing family – my other two daughters were born when we lived in Madison, Wisconsin – and all that time I was trying to write as often as I could. I finished the novel I had begun in the workshop, and Harper & Row looked as if they would publish it – they paid me a little money when it was about half finished – but they decided in the end not to publish it, and I was very disappointed and discouraged about that. But now I am grateful that that book was never published. I would be embarrassed to have it out in public; it was a bitter autobiographical story and I don't feel that way any more, and besides it wasn't very good. So: I kept working to make a living, mostly as a teacher – I taught for seven years in a country school in Colorado, again out on the high plains – and gradually started another novel, and wrote it down in the coal room of our house, over three summers between school years. I had learned how precious time was, so that in those summers I became very disciplined and very religious about writing and wouldn't do anything else in the morning except write. And I still feel that way about the hours when I'm writing. When I'm working on a novel I will work seven days a week and won't let anything interfere with my routine.

When I finished that novel I wrote John Irving to ask if he would connect me with his agent, and he said he would. He said he had sent fifty writers to his agent and he hadn't taken any of them, but maybe he'd take me. And he did: I got a telegram from the agent (there were still telegrams back then) and he said he was impressed by the book and wanted to represent it. That was a great day for me. The book was *The Tie That Binds*, and after a few months I got a call from an editor at Holt, Rinehart and Winston and he said they wanted to publish the book. That was another great day. The book came out in the fall of 1984. Except for one very tiny story, that was the first thing I ever had published. By that time I was forty-one years old and had been writing as hard as I could for almost twenty years. If I had learned anything over those years of work and persistence, it was that you had to believe in yourself even when no one else did. And later I often said something like that to my graduate students. You have to believe in yourself despite the evidence. I felt as though I had a little flame of talent, not a big talent, but a little pilot-light-sized flame of talent, and I had to tend to it regularly, religiously, with care and discipline, like a kind of monk or acolyte, and not to ever let the little flame go out.

After that first book was published I could then find teaching jobs in colleges and universities and it became easier to find time to write while still making a living. Meanwhile, my first marriage ended and Cathy and I found each other, and my three girls were making their own grown-up lives, and moving on, going to various colleges, and travelling all over the world.

In the 1990s I taught in the MFA programme at Southern Illinois University in Carbondale, where John Gardner and Richard Russo had both taught before, and I wrote *Plainsong* over about a six-year period while I was there. But earlier in that decade, before Cathy joined me in Illinois, I was living in a trailer court in a one-room trailer; I was very poor, still trying to support my family even though we weren't living together any more, but I was happy nevertheless. Across the road from me in the trailer court was a family who were all mentally disabled. Darrell and Retta and their little boy, Kevin. I used to help them a little by driving them to the grocery store and to their appointments with Social Services. On one of those trips, Retta said to me: 'Well, Keinnt' – she always called me Keinnt – 'Well, Keinnt, what do you do for a living?'

And I said: 'I try to help students learn how to write better.'

And she said: 'Well, Keinnt, Darrell says I write too small.' She thought of course that I was teaching penmanship. Which, in truth, probably would be more useful than trying to help anyone learn how to write convincing lies and literary fictions.

Now for the last thirteen years Cathy and I have been back in Colorado, in Salida, and I wrote *Eventide* and the prose parts of the photography book Peter Brown and I did together called *West of Last Chance*, and I wrote this new novel *Benediction*, working out in my writer's shed in the mountains, heeding my hours, and I feel as if I've been very lucky in my life.

And I want to think, as Darrell warned Retta: over the years I have tried not to write too small, and I want to believe I have tried not to live too small, either. ∎

AUTHORS' FOUNDATION
GRANTS AND AWARDS
&
K BLUNDELL TRUST
AWARDS
*(open to writers under 40 years of age)*

Next closing dates –
**30 April** and
**30 September 2015**

Full guidelines available from
www.societyofauthors.org
020 7373 6642

THE
SOCIETY OF
AUTHORS
GRANTS

# HARD TIMES?

**For more than 200 years the Fund has provided hardship grants and pensions to thousands of writers at all stages of their careers.**

**If you are a published author – novelist, biographer, poet or playwright – the Royal Literary Fund can offer financial assistance.**

**For more information contact:
Eileen Gunn
020 7353 7159
eileen.gunn@rlf.org.uk
www.rlf.org.uk**

**All enquiries are treated in the strictest confidence**

Registered Charity No. 219952

The Royal Society
*of* Literature

**TUESDAY 9 DECEMBER, 7PM**

## Lionel Shriver

*in conversation with*

## Fiammetta Rocco

Lionel Shriver reflects on the state of American fiction, and her scepticism about creative writing degrees.

**£12 / £8 / FREE FOR RSL MEMBERS.**

RSL Membership is open to all.

BATH
SPA
UNIVERSITY

**www.rslit.org
020 7845 4679**

THE
*Writing*
PLATFORM

## DIGITAL KNOWLEDGE
## FOR WRITERS

Find out about our bursary programme for writers and technologists at

www.thewritingplatform.com

QUT
Queensland University of Technology
Brisbane Australia

BATH
SPA
UNIVERSITY

LOTTERY FUNDED

Supported using public funding by
ARTS COUNCIL
ENGLAND

# CONTRIBUTORS

**Anthea Bell** is a translator from German and French. Her translations include works by E.T.A. Hoffmann, W.G. Sebald, Stefan Zweig and the Franco-Belgian comic book series *Asterix*.

**Fatima Bhutto** was born in Kabul, Afghanistan. She is the author of *Songs of Blood and Sword* and *The Shadow of the Crescent Moon*.

**Sam Coll** earned a BA in English & Art History and a master's in Anglo-Irish literature from Trinity College, Dublin. 'Hare in Love' is an extract from *The Abode of Fancy*, his first novel.

**Mark Doty**'s new collection of poetry, *Deep Lane*, is forthcoming in 2015. He teaches at Rutgers University and lives in New York City.

**Louise Erdrich** grew up in North Dakota and is a tribal member of the Turtle Mountain Chippewa. Her novels include *Love Medicine, The Plague of Doves* and *The Round House*. 'Domain' is part of a forthcoming novel, *Future Home of the Living God*.

**Adam Fitzgerald** is the editor of the poetry journal *Maggy*, and the author of *The Late Parade*. Recent poems can be found in the *New Yorker, Poetry, Boston Review* and elsewhere. He teaches at Rutgers University and New York University.

**Mark Gevisser** is the author, most recently, of the memoir *Lost and Found in Johannesburg*. He has completed an Open Society Fellowship, working on the Global Sexuality Frontier, and is writing a book on the subject. He lives in France and South Africa.

**Francisco Goldman** is the author of *Say Her Name, The Interior Circuit: A Mexico City Chronicle* and four other books. He lives in Mexico City and teaches one semester at Trinity College in Hartford, Connecticut, annually.

**Kent Haruf** is the author of five novels, including *Plainsong, Eventide* and *Benediction*. He lives in Colorado with his wife, Cathy.

**Michael Hofmann** is a poet and a translator. He has translated the works of Bertolt Brecht, Franz Kafka, Hans Fallada and Joseph Roth, among others. He teaches at the University of Florida in Gainesville.

**Miranda July** is a film-maker, writer and artist. Her short fiction has been published in the *New Yorker*, the *Paris Review, Harper's* and *Zoetrope*. 'Some Heat' is an extract from *The First Bad Man*, forthcoming from Scribner in the US and Canongate in the UK.

**S.J. Naudé** was born in South Africa, studied at Cambridge University and Columbia University and practised law in New York and London. 'The Alphabet of Birds' is taken from 'Van', a story in his first collection, *The Alphabet of Birds*, forthcoming from And Other Stories in 2015.

**Helen Oyeyemi** is the author of five novels, most recently *Mr Fox* and *Boy, Snow, Bird*. In 2013 she was included in *Granta*'s Best of Young British Novelists list. 'Books and Roses' is an extract from a new project. She lives in Prague.

**Cynthia Ozick** is the author of numerous works of fiction and non-fiction. She lives with her husband in Westchester County, New York.

**Barbara Ras**'s most recent book of poetry is *The Last Skin*. She lives in San Antonio, Texas, where she directs Trinity University Press.

**Joseph Roth**'s novels include *What I Saw*, *The Legend of the Holy Drinker*, *The Emperor's Tomb* and *The Radetzky March*. 'Where the World War Began' is taken from an essay collection, *The Hotel Pieces*, forthcoming from Granta Books.

**Mary Ruefle** is the author of fifteen books of poetry and prose, as well as seventy-two erasure books. Her most recent work is *Trances of the Blast*. She teaches in the MFA programme at Vermont College of Fine Arts.

**Ianthe Ruthven** is a photographer with a particular interest in landscape, architecture and interiors. 'The Atlantic Wall: Hitler's Coastal Fortress from the Arctic to the Pyrenees' was exhibited at the Royal Geographical Society in June 2014.

**Will Self** is the author of ten novels, six collections of shorter fiction and six works of non-fiction. He is the Professor of Contemporary Thought at Brunel University. He lives in south London.

**Saša Stanišić** was born in 1978 in Višegrad, Bosnia–Herzegovina, and has been living in Germany since 1992. His first novel, *How the Soldier Repairs the Gramophone*, has been translated into thirty languages. 'The Ferryman Is Dead' is an extract from *Before the Feast*, to be published by Pushkin Press in 2015.

**Andrea Stuart** grew up in the Caribbean and now lives in London. She has written three books: *Showgirls*, *The Rose of Martinique: A Life of Napoleon's Josephine* and *Sugar in the Blood: A Family's Story of Slavery and Empire*. She is currently writer in residence at Kingston University.

**Anjan Sundaram** was born in India and studied at Yale University. He has reported from Central Africa for nearly a decade for the Associated Press, the *New York Times* and several other publications. He is the author of *Stringer: A Reporter's Journey in the Congo*.

**Isabella Tree** is the author of four non-fiction books, the latest of which is *The Living Goddess: A Journey into the Heart of Kathmandu*, to be published in February 2015.

**Tim Winton** has published twenty-five books for adults and children. His most recent novel is *Eyrie*.